Psychology and Social Issues

Contemporary Psychology Series

Series Editor: Professor Raymond Cochrane
School of Psychology
The University of Birmingham
Birmingham B15 2TT
United Kingdom

This series of books on contemporary psychological issues is aimed primarily at 'A' Level students and those beginning their undergraduate degree. All of these volumes are introductory in the sense that they assume no, or very little, previous acquaintance with the subject, while aiming to take the reader through to the end of his or her first course on the topic they cover. For this reason the series will also appeal to those who encounter psychology in the course of their professional work: nurses, social workers, police and probation officers, speech therapists and medical students. Written in a clear and jargon-free style, each book generally includes a full (and in some cases annotated) bibliography and points the way explicitly to further reading on the subject covered.

Forthcoming titles:

On Being Old: The Psychology of Later Life
Graham Stokes, *Gulson Hospital, Coventry*

Health Psychology: Stress, Behaviour and Disease
Douglas Carroll, *Glasgow Polytechnic*

Families: A Context for Development
David White and Anne Woollett, *Polytechnic of East London*

Food and Drink: The Psychology of Nutrition
David Booth, *University of Birmingham*

The Psychology of Childhood
Peter Mitchell, *The University of Wales College at Swansea*

Criminal Behaviour: Explanation and Prevention
Clive Hollin, *University of Birmingham*

Contemporary Psychology Series: 1

Psychology and Social Issues:
A Tutorial Text

Edited by

Raymond Cochrane and Douglas Carroll

The Falmer Press
(A member of the Taylor & Francis Group)
London • New York • Philadelphia

UK The Falmer Press, 4 John Street, London WC1N 2ET

USA The Falmer Press, Taylor & Francis Inc., 1900 Frost Road, Suite 101, Bristol, PA 19007

First published 1991
Reprinted 1993 and 1995

British Library Cataloguing in Publication Data
Psychology and social issues: a tutorial text.
1. Social psychology
I. Cochrane, Raymond   II. Carroll, Douglas
302

ISBN 1-85000-835-3
ISBN 1-85000-836-1

Library of Congress Cataloging-in-Publication Data
Psychology and social issues: a tutorial text/edited by Raymond
  Cochrane and Douglas Carroll.
    p.   cm. (Contemporary psychology series)
  Includes index.
  ISBN 1-85000-835-3 (HC). — ISBN 1-85000-836-1 (SC)
  1. Social psychology.   2. Social problems.
  I. Cochrane, Raymond.   II. Carroll, Douglas.   III. Series:
  Contemporary psychology series (London, England)
  HM251.P834   1991
  302—dc20   90-48668
                                                                   CIP

Jacket design by Benedict Evans

Typeset in 10/11 Garamond by
Chapterhouse, The Cloisters, Formby L37 3PX

Printed in Great Britain by Burgess Science Press, Basingstoke on paper which has a specified pH value on final paper manufacture of not less than 7.5 and is therefore 'acid free'.

Contents

Preface

Douglas Carroll and Raymond Cochrane

In his novel, *Changing Places*, David Lodge presents us with an image of an English Literature tutorial seen through the eyes of Maurice Zapp, an American Professor visiting an English provincial University.

> Three students and me, for an hour at a time. We're supposed to discuss some text I've assigned. This, apparently, can be anything that comes into my head, except that the campus bookshop doesn't have anything that comes into my head. But supposing we manage to agree, me and the students, on some book of which four copies can be scratched together, one of them writes a paper and reads it out to the rest of us. After about three minutes the eyes of the other two glaze over and they begin to sag in their chairs. It's clear they have stopped listening. I'm listening like hell but can't understand a word because of the guy's limey accent. All too soon, he stops. 'Thank you,' I say, flashing him an appreciative smile. He looks at me reproachfully as he blows his nose, then carries on from where he paused, in mid-sentence. The other two students wake up briefly, exchange glances and snigger. That's the most animation they ever show. When the guy reading the paper finally winds it up, I ask for comments. Silence. They avoid my eye. I volunteer a comment myself. Silence falls again. It's so quiet you can hear the guy's beard growing. Desperately I ask one of them a direct question. 'And what did you think of the text, Miss Archer?' Miss Archer falls off her chair in a swoon.

Like much good comic invention, what is important about Maurice Zapp's account is that it offers us an outsider's view of something obvious yet unremarked, that for many students and even some tutors, tutorials are often embarrassing encounters of little educational worth. His description, while not typical of every tutorial, characterizes sufficient of them to make it all too painfully recognizable. Nor is it possible to dismiss Zapp's experience as something particular to tutorials on English Literature. He could have observed much of the same had he stepped across the Rummidge campus to the School of Psychology.

Yet we believe that the tutorial system is not fundamentally ill-conceived. On the contrary, potentially it affords one of few opportunities within higher education's otherwise formal and didactic diet of lectures, practicals and seminars for students and teachers to interact, to explore ideas, to discuss and defend interpretations, to debate and to argue. While such a facility is important to students throughout higher education, it is nowhere more so than in such relatively controversial subjects as Psychology and Social Science.

There are undoubtedly a variety of reasons why the reality of many tutorials falls short of this potential. The students' perceptions of the status and power differential between themselves and their tutors undoubtedly have a bearing as does the students' fear of making fools of themselves. Such inhibitions can be much exacerbated by tutors who strike supercilious, over-challenging and otherwise intimidatory postures. In addition, the practice, common enough, of having a student read a formal, prepared paper is unlikely to prove appropriately provocative; Zapp's account bears witness to the intellectual excitement that such an approach generates.

Zapp mentions another consideration that would seem to us central. It is the relative paucity of suitable reading material: accessible texts which are likely to stimulate rather than inhibit discussion and argument. In Psychology, students in tutorials rarely warm to the prospect of recapitulating the material currently being covered in their lecture courses. It is only close to examinations that such an exercise attracts any enthusiasm. Rather, students seem more usually fired by matters of more current social relevance. Certainly, that has been our experience, as well as those who have contributed to this text. However, few of us have the expertise, time or facilities to collect accessible material for anything but a restricted range of potentially provocative topics of this sort.

The current text was conceived to broaden that range, by bringing together contributors with diverse interests. As such it offers discussions of a wide variety of topics and issues likely to engage psychology and social science students: drug abuse, AIDS, rape, gender relations, animal experimentation, child sexual abuse to name a few. In all twenty such topics have been selected for inclusion, each constituting a separate, specially written chapter. The number chosen was not arbitrary; it corresponds approximately to the number of tutorials that students are required to attend in many higher education institutions. As such, the text has the potential to support the whole of a year's tutorial meetings, taking one topic each tutorial. In addition, the chapters have been grouped as far as possible (for example those on drugs, tobacco and alcohol) so that common themes can be explored in consecutive tutorial meetings.

Another problem faced in providing tutorial reading concerns form rather than topic. What is most readily available is often so seemingly expert that it offers little apparent scope for discussion and argument. Faced with such authoritativeness, it is perhaps hardly surprising that students tend to recount rather than argue about the contents of their reading. The current text attempts to overcome this in two ways. First of all, the brief to contributors was to write with the goal of trying to encourage rather than to stifle students' subsequent discussion of the topic, by where possible, posing questions and issues rather than advocating solutions and particular answers. Secondly, contributors were asked to append to their chapters a number of specific questions which might act as prompts for tutorial discussion. In addition, only a few textual references are included in each. Instead each contributor offers a few key readings which the student can follow up.

We believe our text will be broadly informative and of interest to all students concerned with the personal, social and cultural issues that have recently exercised psychologists and social scientists. Most of all, though, we hope it will provide a basis for lively tutorial argument and debate. As Michael Billig has so persuasively argued, the sound of argument and debate should resonate in a place of learning, 'for the simple reason that the sound of argument is the sound of thinking'.

Douglas Carroll and
Raymond Cochrane
August 1990

Chapter 1

The Psychology of Humour and Laughter

Hugh Foot

Introduction

The psychological study of humour is still greeted by some academics and professionals as a flippant exercise and as a source of amusement in itself. Traditionally behavioural scientists with a genuine interest in the subject have only confessed to dabbling with it 'on the side', and of course it is hardly the kind of subject matter which attracts much attention in the allocation of research funding.

Nevertheless there has been a remarkable upsurge of research interest in humour and laughter over the last two decades since the emergence of Goldstein and McGhee's (1972) seminal compilation of theoretical perspectives and empirical studies and spurred on by Chapman and Foot's (1976) review volume. The First International Conference on Humour and Laughter was held in Cardiff in 1976 and since then there have been seven other international conferences. From a pre-1970 publication rate of probably four to five publications per year worldwide, there are now scores of papers appearing each year and at least two journals (*International Journal of Humor Research* and the *Humor Research Newsletter* dedicated exclusively to publishing cross-disciplinary articles on humour.

Why has there been this relatively sudden explosion in interest among behavioural scientists — and not just among psychologists but also anthropologists, sociologists, linguists, communication analysts, counsellors and therapists? Two reasons spring to mind immediately, although no doubt there are others. First there has been the shedding of what Gordon Allport termed the 'tenderness tabu' in the field of human emotional experience, which referred to the disproportionate pre-occupation of researchers with negative and unpleasant emotions such as fear, anger and aggression at the expense of positive emotions like joy, happiness, love and mirth. It seems no coincidence that the pessimistic international climate of the late 1950s and early 1960s when the cold war was at its height should be associated with a research emphasis on the nature of human aggression, which was a very popular topic at that time, especially among ethologists. With the gradual improvement in international relations in the late 1960s and into the 1970s, interest shifted to more positive emotions and prosocial behaviours like altruism, cooperation, self-fulfilment, love and happiness. Perhaps inevitably then, humour was just another positive human emotion swept along in this tide of new research interest.

A second reason for this interest in humour was the growing realization of its potential importance as an area worthy of study. Psychologically it is a very 'exciting' behaviour, not just because of its prevalence in a myriad of different social contexts — serious and frivolous, comic and tragic — but also because of the light it throws upon processes of social interaction and upon cognitive change in the developing child. It is impossible in one short chapter to do justice to the many issues which humour research has addressed. I shall attempt to summarize some of the main conceptual issues, discuss the role of humour and laughter in everyday social interaction and consider some of the applications of humour as a source of social influence.

Conceptual and Theoretical Issues

Many discussions of what humour is adopt a historical approach, of which fuller accounts can be found in Chapman and Foot (1976) and McGhee (1979). A particular point of interest is the way that humour has come to be used to relate to an individual's general disposition as is nowadays assumed when we refer to people possessing or lacking a sense of humour. The Latin origin of the term 'humour' means fluid or moisture, and according to ancient, medieval and Renaissance physiology there were four basic bodily fluids or humors which played a major role in determining a person's mood or temperament. To describe someone as choleric, melancholic, sanguine or phlegmatic, therefore, was to describe both the state of their bodily fluids and, by implication, their disposition — although, of course, the latter would normally be the visible sign of their bodily state. Being in 'good humor' or 'out of humor' then was a description of the balance or imbalance between the four humors.

This relationship between dispositional and bodily states is more than just of historical interest because it relates to current thinking about, for example, the therapeutic value of humour in which the possession of humour is linked to a healthy psychological perspective. We shall return to this point later.

It is also interesting to note historically that humour and laughter have not always enjoyed their current status as desirable social assets or attributes. Since Ancient Greek or Roman times humour and laughter have been characterized as essentially perverse and degenerate, fit only for the ignorant and foolish and reflecting an unfortunate lack of self-knowledge. It was only in the seventeenth and eighteenth centuries with writers like Ben Jonson, Molière and Swift that humour lost its distinction as a socially disruptive force and gained favour as a social corrective in its use as criticism of the follies of mankind.

In terms of modern day usage our disposition or frame of mind is only one aspect of our experience of humour; we know that we are more likely to see it and appreciate it in some moods rather than in others. One of the problems is that humour is so multi-faceted: it serves as a stimulus and a response as well as a disposition, and it has been frequently acknowledged that it is simply not possible to develop a single broad theory that adequately embraces all the main qualities of humour simultaneously. As McGhee says, psychologists have developed explanations that are effective in accounting for certain aspects of humour while disregarding others:

Like the three blind men who offered varying descriptions of an elephant, depending on which part of the animal's body they came into contact with, humor theorists interested in different aspects of humor have advanced a highly diverse set of explanations of humor (McGhee, 1979: 2).

Rather than attempt to review humour theories as such, I shall outline a few of the key conceptual variables which have been the focus of attention among different theorists.

Incongruity

Much of the research on humour has occupied itself with explaining why we find jokes funny or why we are amused by certain incidents in real life. One crucial ingredient here is incongruity which in its broadest sense includes any juxtaposition of ideas or situations which is surprising, unexpected, illogical, absurd, disjointed or out of context. By many incongruity is regarded as a *necessary* condition for all humour, but clearly it is not a *sufficient* condition because many incongruous ideas or events can produce puzzlement, confusion, disgust or fear which are incompatible reactions with humour. There are several views about the way in which incongruity operates: one view is that humour can be divided into two parts: first, the 'discovery' of the incongruity, second, the 'resolution' of it. Schultz (1976) found about one half of the verbal jokes which he analyzed contained such resolution on the basis of linguistic ambiguity; this might operate at different levels. Using Chomsky's linguistic theory, for example, he differentiates levels of ambiguity as follows:

> *Surface structure ambiguity*: 'Can you tell me how long cows should be milked?' The farmer answers, 'They should be milked the same as short ones, of course'.
>
> *Deep structure ambiguity*: 'Did you know that natives like potatoes even more than missionaries?' 'Yes, but the missionaries are more nutritious.'

Both jokes require knowledge of cultural as well as linguistic factors for their humour to be appreciated. Comprehension of the joke employing deep structure ambiguity depends upon a long chain of associations involving cultural awareness and more sophisticated rules about language structure.

The evidence here is of particular interest for cognitive development because it relates to processes by which understanding is reached. The resolution of incongruity may not contribute to appreciation of humour until a child is 7 or 8 years of age. Young children's humour may depend on 'pure incongruity', that is the mere discovery that an incongruity exists. Even if information is available to resolve the incongruity, the limited cognitive capacities of the child may interfere with appreciation of it, or the information is simply not used to interpret the incongruous relationship. Schultz supplies a good example:

> *Q.* Why did the farmer name his pig 'Ink'?
> *A1.* Because it kept running out of the pen (original answer).
> or *A2.* Because it kept getting away (resolution — removed answer).

Children under the age of 7 or 8 find the second (resolution — removed) answer just as funny as the first one because they are responding to the incongruous idea of calling a pig 'Ink'. They have not grasped how the first answer makes 'Ink' an understandable name for a pig. For an older child, of course, the humour generated by the first answer depends upon the resolution of the incongruity by connecting ink with the other meaning of the word 'pen'. The second answer produces no humour reaction at all in them.

Of course, in this case, the younger children may have just had difficulty understanding the linguistic ambiguity responsible for the humour. If the humour stimuli are simplified or converted into visual incongruities, then it has been shown that even 4-or 5-year-olds are capable of appreciating the resolution of a cartoon or joke.

McGhee rightly questions whether children ever pass through a stage in which they are capable of appreciating the fact that incongruity exists or that it needs to be resolved. 'Many forms of humor can truly be called nonsense humor, in the sense that there is no resolution intended.' McGhee himself proposes a developmental-stage approach to incongruity which describes the types of incongruities understood by children across the stages of their increasing cognitive development. For example, the child first recognizes incongruity when he or she makes pretend actions with an absent object based upon an internal image of that object; then the child learns the fun associated with giving incongruous labels to objects or people: 'mummy' may be called 'daddy' or vice versa; 'horses' may be called 'cows'. Later on come more subtle forms of incongruity like endowing animals with human characteristics and learning that words and phrases may have multiple meanings.

Superiority

Another common ingredient of humour is superiority, based upon the notion that humour stems from the weakness, deformity or failures of others. Humour that disparages or humiliates, therefore, derives from the fleeting sense of superiority experienced in comparison with the belittled other. We take delight particularly in the downfall of our enemies or groups that we despise. Zillman (1983) takes a 'dispositional' view that humour appreciation varies inversely with the favourableness of the disposition towards the person or object being disparaged. Thus the less friendly disposed we are towards someone or some group, the more humorous we find jokes or stories in which that person or group is the butt or victim. Superiority, of course, lies at the core of ethnic humour and at the core of all humour that compares a reference group to which the humorist belongs with an out-group, be it religious, political, social, etc. Disparagement humour may in fact serve various purposes associated with group identity: it may reinforce the values and standards of the reference group, it may enhance one's acceptance or status as a member of that reference group in the eyes of other members, it may help to maintain or sharpen the boundaries, real or imagined, between the in-group and out-group.

Of course, this is not to argue that we do not occasionally turn aggressive humour either on those we love or indeed on ourselves. Strong relationships can endure a certain degree of resentment-based mirth as well as a large amount of mild jocular bantering. As far as self-directed disparagement is concerned many humour theorists would define a sense of humour as the capacity to laugh at one's own expense. If not carried too far such self-disparagement is often perceived by others as endearing and symptomatic of a healthy self-awareness.

Arousal

A number of theories have been proposed which suggest that the most important qualities of humour operate at a physiological level. These theories assume that the initiation of humour brings about measurable arousal changes which directly influence the experience of amusement. Humour is associated with fluctuations in arousal in two ways. First, it may serve to reduce arousal in a situation where the indiviudual is already in a relatively high state of arousal: for example, the joke or amusing incident which elicits exaggerated mirth in a dentist's waiting room as people wait in a state of mild anxiety. Such experiences in public situations are commonplace where an amusing incident readily discharges pent up negative emotional arousal. Second, the humour itself may be associated with moderate increases in arousal followed by a sudden drop. This 'arousal boost-jag' phenomenon, as it has been called, accounts for the pleasure derived from many jokes: the build-up to the joke is moderately arousing in that it attracts attention and challenges the audience to recognize and resolve the incongruity. The joke may be additionally stimulating by virtue of having a sexual, aggressive or anxiety-arousing theme, or it may be intellectually challenging. When the audience is suitably aroused and hunting for a resolution to the joke, the punch-line comes, supplying the resolution and causing a rapid dissipation of arousal frequently associated with laughter. Both the build-up and subsequent dissipation of arousal are rewarding and pleasurable, and produce the experience of amusement.

Other Conceptions

A number of other factors have been highlighted in further theoretical approaches to humour and laughter. Psychoanalytic approaches share with arousal theories the view that humour serves a physiological as well as psychological function by manipulating level of felt tension or arousal. Freud saw humour as akin to dreaming in that they both serve to regulate sexual and aggressive desires. Wit and humour are socially acceptable outlets for repressed sexual and aggressive wishes which have been pushed into the unconscious due to society's prohibition of their expression. The process of repression requires 'psychic energy' which is saved once the joke has been made and the tension associated with the repressed desire has momentarily been released. Another psychodynamic view is expressed in the writings of Bokun that

> amusement and laughter are intimately connected with the world of apprehension and fears created by the mind and its over-seriousness. Over-seriousness is not the opposite of ridicule, it is ridicule, it is the very source of amusement and laughter (Bokun, 1986: 36).

This view stresses the need for humour as a vehicle for providing us with a realistic vision of ourselves and the world around us, stripped of all our fears, frustrations and suffering. Having a sense of humour, then, implies a mature perception of reality, freedom and self-imposed fears and worries, and the ability to cope with the trials and tribulations of everyday living.

The link between humour and coping is also expressed in developmental studies on the pleasure involved in mastery. Children enjoy mastering physical, cognitive and other aspects of their interaction with the environment as evidenced by their overt merriment when they first stand up unaided, name an object correctly for the first time or ride a bicycle. Indeed it has been suggested that the initial development of a sense of humour emerges through the child feeling superiority over other children in skills that he or she has just mastered, but which others have not. Similarly amusement at absurd and nonsensical verbal humour may depend upon children's mastery of the rules and organization of ideas and language, and of the unsuccessful attempt of those absurd thoughts to undermine that mastery.

Our Social Experience of Humour and Laughter

So far we have not drawn any distinction between humour and laughter, and clearly many of the functions of laughter overlap with the functions served by encoding humour. As has already been mentioned, most of the theories of humour address the issue of why we find jokes or incidents amusing, in other words the decoding of humour, and laughter is an overt behavioural expression of a subjectively experienced affective state.

One point which ought to be made before we proceed to examining the social contexts in which humour and laughter are used relates to the relationship between laughter and smiling which have been attributed to quite different phylogenetic origins. Laughter may, of course, appear to be little more than high-intensity smiling where the teeth are bared more widely and the lips extended more broadly than in smiling and where expelled breath is sufficiently massive and rapid to precipitate an articulated sound. Sometimes laughs grow out of increasingly broad smiles, and sometimes a thin smile is the tail-end of an expansive laugh. Yet there are situations, as perhaps when disparaging another person or when highly anxious, where laughter and smiling are not interchangeable responses. Our social meanings may be conveyed by a range of other non-verbal behaviours. Believe it or not, attempts have been made to decipher different functions of laughter by its physical characteristics (e.g. amplitude, intensity) but such attempts have met with little success: there is nothing about a derisive or sarcastic laugh which reliably differentiates it from, say, a humorous laugh.

Adopting a social psychological approach I would wish to stress the essentially social and shared nature of humour. While we may decode humour in private, for example by savouring jokes and cartoons that we read or see on television, most if not all of our encoded humour is in response to a social situation and it is initiated for a specific reason. Despite the occasional experience of an apt comment or witticism just 'popping out' on the spur of the moment, most of our decisions to initiate humour are under our own conscious control.

One feature of humour rarely emphasized in the research literature on the encoding of humour is that we use it essentially as a social skill; we cultivate it just like we cultivate other conversational and non-verbal skills. Indeed there are few more useful and wide-ranging social skills than humour across the board of human experience. We find humour in death and dying, there is 'gallows humour', there is humour in chronic illness and adversity, there is humour about old age, puberty and adolescence, sex, love and marriage, aggression and war. There is hardly a subject so taboo that is escapes humour's insightful eye. And the power of humour as a source of social influence is formidable: we can use it to say what we mean, we can use it to say the opposite of what we mean. Because it is playful, we can retract our message at any time if it appears to give offence. The idea that humour can be interpreted in different ways has been empirically supported. For example, a male speaker's joke about women-libbers to a group of liberated women is interpreted entirely in terms of the audience's reaction: if they laugh, the speaker is ascribed liberated views and he is not assumed to agree with the joke's content; if they glare, he is seen as chauvinistic. Of course, the ultimate response to the affronted victim of any joke is, 'Can't you take a joke?'.

There are at least six basic ways in which we may use humour as a social skill: as a means of searching for information about others, as a means of giving information about oneself, in interpersonal control, in group control, in managing anxiety and in changing and sustaining social attitudes.

Humour as a means of seeking information

Commonly when we talk to people who are comparative strangers we endeavour to discover whether they share similar attitudes and interests with us. However we may not wish to embark upon a lengthy discussion about politics, jobs, religion or anything else which direct questioning might commit us to. By introducing a topic in a light-hearted way we can gently probe our partner's general views and hold open the option to pursue or change the topic depending on the reaction given.

In addition to probing others' social attitudes, humour may also help us find out how others respond to us: their reactions to our jokes or amusing stories may measure their acceptance of us or the warmth of their feelings towards us.

Humour as a means of giving information

Humour is a useful device for disclosing our motives and intentions to others, particularly when we wish to share feelings that we might not ordinarily wish to reveal too publicly: for example, our worries about a forthcoming operation, our anxiety about a lecture or seminar we have to present. Humour may also convey fairly explicit sexual interest in a companion but in a light-hearted and socially acceptable way, which is easily retracted or shrugged off if the 'message' is not reciprocated. Although there is no research to confirm this, I suspect that a substantial amount of what many women might regard as sexual harassment consists of persistent overtures of a 'humorous' nature (at least the perpetrator may defend his advances as meant only in jest).

Just as humour may be a way of intimating the presence of serious intent or concern, so it can serve as denial of serious intent or 'decommitment' as it has been termed. When we face failure or are about to be discovered in a lie, such use of humour enables us to back down without psychological injury. Clearly this is a self-serving device aimed at avoiding a challenge to our motives and restoring our credibility.

Using humour to keep intact our own social credibility has its obverse in its potential for unmasking the hypocrisy of others. This information-giving function of humour is when we use ridicule or sarcasm to denounce someone else's declared or apparent motivation for their actions. Political columnists and cartoonists may take delight in satirizing the professed motivation for the actions and pronouncements of cabinet ministers and prestigious political figures. In our everyday lives we may have occasion to jestingly rebuke those who project a pretentious image of themselves that we do not accept.

Humour in interpersonal control

We have already mentioned examples of humour being used to manage a certain impression of self, but we also use it to further our social relationships and intimacies. Because humour is, used judiciously, a social asset, it confers upon its encoder the animated attention and welcoming approval of others. Fundamentally then, it promotes friendship, affiliation and shared intimacy by winning and sustaining the approval of those whose friendship we value and wish to maintain. Conversely humour is a socially acceptable way of expressing personal hostility towards people whom we do not like. Derisive laughter, stemming from feelings of superiority, may be out of all proportion to the mishaps or downfalls they experience.

Humour not only regulates the affective 'temperature' of our interactions with others, but also the fluency and tempo of our daily encounters, for example, by filling pauses in conversation, smoothing the transition between conversational topics and maintaining conversational interest. It helps create a mood of conviviality and breaks the ice at awkward social encounters. A more manipulative function of humour in social interaction might be ingratiation: to win the approval of others from whom favours are sought or who hold positions of prestige or power. Humorous self-disparagement may well prove a successful tactic for expressing dependency or submissiveness in order to solicit favours or help.

Humour in group control

Humour may serve as the very cement by which a group maintains its cohesiveness and well-being. In-group jokes tend to esteem group members and solidify positive group feeling. Analyses of group process have consistently demonstrated that well-established groups have a member or members who act as emotional catalysts in channelling the affective responses of the group. These members may be 'cheer-leaders' in mobilizing emotional and comic relief, or they may be the victims or scapegoats of others' emotional outbursts. Basically, though, the group needs safe outlets by which to express its feelings, sustain its morale, and deal with internal conflict if it is to remain intact; humour plays a crucial role in these processes.

These intragroup control processes of humour are paralleled by inter-group control. Anti-out-group humour often expresses hostility towards out-group members and helps therefore to preserve distance or distinctiveness between the in-group and out-group. Anti-out-group humour may be aimed at producing dissension and disruption in the out-group, but may in fact work the opposite effect as out-group members close ranks to meet the threat to their position. Sarcastic political wit is a stock-in-trade tactic among politicians in their attempts to score points for their own party and make life difficult for the opposition.

Humour in managing anxiety

The arousal properties of humour and laughter have already been discussed. In practice humour can serve to pleasurably *stimulate* arousal during tedious activities like queuing for a bus or listening to a boring conversation. On the other hand, it can assist in *discharging* unwanted and unpleasantly high levels of anxiety and stress. It is not unknown for hysterical laughter to occur in response to the sudden release from extreme levels of stress, as when an aeroplane makes a safe landing after the threat of crashing, or when a hijacker releases his hostages. The laughter here is undoubtedly related to the immense relief derived from coming through the ordeal safely. Yet high arousal *per se* can produce laughter: the news of the death of a loved one or close relative can trigger laughter which appears totally incongruous in the circumstances and for which considerable embarrassment and guilt is subsequently experienced.

Whilst humour and laughter may be a safety-valve for excessive arousal, they also help us cope on a daily basis with mildly arousing embarrassments. Humour helps restore composure or save face on occasions where the image of ourselves we wish to convey is spoiled by some little mishap. Joking may be about the only way to save the situation, treating the event as trivial, as an accident that could happen to anyone. We may also use laughter evasively or apologetically. Evasive laughter provides an emotional cloak behind which we hide our true feelings. It may give the impression that we are sharing in the prevailing feeling of the group when we are not; it may help us stall for time when we are not quite sure what our companion's comments to us mean. Apologetic or defensive laughter may precede an action on our part, the outcome of which we are uncertain about. When we embark on a novel task we may voice our misgivings: 'I've never done this before', 'I can't guarantee what will happen'. Laughter may accompany or substitute for our utterance, but its meaning is clear: we are paving the way for possible failure and inducing our audience to believe that we are not taking the situation too seriously ourselves.

Humour in changing and sustaining social attitudes

Humour presents us with a curious paradox. On the one hand, it has tremendous emancipating power: it frees us from conventional language and thought; it allows us to escape from our moral inhibitions; it liberates us from the shackles of our mundane lives and feelings of inadequacy. All of these emancipating features of humour and laughter are lyrically described by Mindess (1971). In this sense, humour can be seen as a revolt against the structure and fabric of society and therefore as an inevitable force for social change. This is not to argue that humour *has* directly brought about much change in the world, but it may have indirectly helped change society's thinking in innumerable, immeasurable ways.

Yet the paradox is that, despite its liberating potential, humour serves to sustain and indeed reinforce narrow-minded attitudes and bigotry in society. Because it is socially acceptable, it may be the only way in which we can legitimately give expression to our prejudices and blinkered vision. How else, except through humour, do we derive our stereotyped and prejudicial views about different ethnic and religious groups, about homosexuality, about sexual and racial discrimination? It might be somewhat overstating the case, but we may grossly underestimate the power of humour in perpetrating and bolstering myths and prejudices. In an ironic way, the mere use of racial and sexual jokes sustains the idea of a tolerant society (since such humour is supposed to be a characteristic of tolerance), and yet these types of jokes teach and reinforce the very ideas from which they are striving to free us.

Applications of Humour

We can all remember influential people in our lives who injected humour into their work or dealings with us: the parish priest who gave amusing but memorable sermons, the doctor who told funny stories to put us at our ease, the teacher who used sarcastic wit to intimidate his class. Yet the professional use of humour has hardly received any research attention at all. Even in the media, studies on the creation or production of humour by, for example, comedy scriptwriters or professional comedians are extremely sparse, and one gleans from them very few psychological insights about the processes of generating humour.

The media apart, opportunities for developing humour in our professional and working relationships are probably far greater than we realize.

In some professions, such as nursing and the ambulance, fire and funeral services, there may be special reasons, indeed need, for the cultivation of humour and it would be my (untested) guess that people working in these professions more than in any others develop a much greater fund of in-group or 'in-service' humour merely in order to help them come to terms with the horror and grief which sometimes confront them in their work.

From what has been written about the applications of humour, two main themes can be detected: first, that it is healthy and, second, that it is persuasive. Let us briefly examine these themes.

Health and humour

It is common experience that those with a keen sense of humour are attributed with a well-balanced, healthy psychological outlook on life. Humorous self-disparagement, in particular, is regarded as displaying a healthy self-awareness and appreciation of how others might see us.

There have been few studies attempting to determine the impact of humour on physical illness, although Cousins (1976) gave serious consideration of a possible relationship quite a boost when he wrote of how he laughed his way to recovery from a degenerative spinal condition. Of course laughter does produce beneficial physiological results since it exercises the heart and lungs, it stimulates the circulatory system, and in the words of Cousins it is a kind of 'internal jogging': it 'oxygenates the blood' and 'massages vital organs'. In this sense it can be put on a par with deep-breathing exercises or actual jogging. Of course we don't normally laugh for quite that long! It also has to be said that there are documented cases of people laughing themselves to death, where uncontrollable laughter has brought on a massive heart attack.

More usually though, humour's impact is therapeutic: it helps relieve high anxiety and tension and is a valuable coping mechanism among both hospital patients and staff. In the past twenty years since Mindess (1971) there have been a number of books dealing substantially with humour and psychotherapy (e.g. Bokun, 1986; Robinson, 1977).

The role of humour in coping with and adjusting to the demands of everyday living seems to be the crucial point in the psychotherapeutic literature. In general terms it has been shown that people who appreciate humour have a more con-structive and creative orientation to life; conversely those who lead a more repressed and limited lifestyle are more constrained in their reactions to humour. Patients from psychiatric populations often fail to see the humour in jokes that are closely related to their own area of conflict, although they may appreciate other types of humour. Perhaps not surprisingly acutely depressed patients may exhibit complete absence of laughter and joking; they may be so bound up with their own problems and state of mind that they have lost the (sociocentric) ability of standing to one side and seeing themselves through the eyes of others. Mindess is of the view that the key to recovery in such cases is to train the patient to adopt a wider perspective of him or herself and to become more self-detached. Humour can clearly play an unobtrusive part in this: when the patient begins to see the irony, absurdity, tragicomedy of his or her predicament, then a more balanced and mature perspective is taking shape.

Persuasion and humour

The use of humour in drawing and holding our attention is considerable. Injected into a serious message, it might be expected to enhance the persuasiveness of that message. The reasons for this seem straightforward: humour favourably disposes us towards the source of the message; it increases the credibility of the source and therefore the persuasiveness of the message; it is entertaining, makes the message more interesting and therefore renders the message more memorable; it may distract us from any corrupting ideas which could undermine the persuasiveness of the message; finally it may relax us and make us more receptive to the message.

However, despite the existence of research evidence to support most of the points, there is generally remarkably *little* evidence that humour does persuade us to act in accordance with the message, at least in comparison with any other intrin-sically persuasive features of the message. It could be that there is a very fine balance between being popular but not influential on the one hand (e.g. too much of the clown), and being influential but not popular on the other (e.g. too caustic). It is certainly true that politicians who court popularity by the over-liberal use of humour may lose some political credibility.

It is in the arena of advertising and political propaganda that much of the interest in the application of humour lies and pitifully little research has been done. It is well known that verbal and visual humour is very popular among television advertisers and one has a gut feeling that it *must* be successful in helping to sell products. Certainly there were reported to be significant increases in sales of cigarettes, soft drinks, cosmetics and airline tickets in the USA when advertisers turned from straight to humorous advertising, but in the absence of rigorous field testing, we do not really know if these increases in sales were brought about purely by the introduction of humour or by changes in other features of the advertisements. At least advertisers can be assured that there is no evidence suggesting that humour detracts from the persuasiveness of a message!

Other applied contexts in which humour has an important role to play are in public speaking and in teaching. In public speaking (especially of the after-dinner variety) the whole purpose may be purely to entertain and there is ample evidence of the power of humour in holding an audience's rapt attention. There is clearly also a place for humour in the classroom: it makes learning more enjoyable. Television educational programmes often present lessons in an atmosphere of fun (e.g. *Sesame Street*), and many public information films aimed at children (e.g. not talking to strangers) are put across via animated cartoon figures. The question is, does humour help children learn? Again, one has a strong feeling that it must, BUT, again, the research evidence is equivocal. It is always possible that the humour draws the child's attention towards the joke and away from the message, but if the humour is related to and integrated directly with the information to be learned, it may assist learning.

Tutorial Discussion Questions

1 What role might humour play in interpersonal attraction?
2 Can we reconcile humour's emancipating power in liberating us from the shackles of society with its power in sustaining existing prejudices?
3 Is humour the most powerful force in society for perpetuating bigotry and discrimination in socially acceptable ways?
4 Can incongruity and superiority theories explain sex differencs in humour preferences?
5 Can the use of humour help an influential political figure gain popularity and credibility?

References

BOKUN, B. (1986) *Humour Therapy*, London, Vita Books.

CHAPMAN, A.J. and FOOT, H.C. (Eds) (1976) *Humour and Laughter: Theory, Research and Applications*, Chichester, John Wiley.

COUSINS, N. (1976) *Anatomy of an Illness*, New York, Norton.

GOLDSTEIN, J.H. and McGHEE, P.E. (1972) *The Psychology of Humor: Theoretical Perspectives and Empirical Issues*, New York, Academic Press.

McGHEE, P.E. (1979) *Humor: Its Origin and Development*, San Francisco, Freeman.

MINDESS, H. (1971) *Laughter and Liberation*, Los Angeles, Nash Publishing.

ROBINSON, V.M. (1977) *Humor and the Health Profession*, Thorofare, NJ, Slack.

SCHULTZ, T.R. (1976) 'A cognitive developmental analysis of humour', in CHAPMAN, A.J. and FOOT, H.C. (Eds) *Humour and Laughter: Theory, Research and Applications*. Chichester, John Wiley, pp. 11–36.

ZILLMANN, D. (1983) 'Disparagement humor', in McGHEE, P.E. and GOLDSTEIN, J.H. (Eds) *Handbook of Humor Research, Vol. 1: Basic Issues*. New York, Springer-Verlag.

Further Reading

CHAPMAN, A. J. and FOOT, H. C. (1977) *It's a Funny Thing, Humour*. Oxford, Pergamon.

FOOT, H. C. (1986) 'Humour and laughter', in HARGIE, O. (Ed.) *A Handbook of Communication Skills*. London, Croom Helm.

MULKAY, M. (1988) *On Humour: Its Nature and Its Place in Modern Society*. Cambridge, Polity Press.

Chapter 2

Do Babies Need Mothers?

Gill Harris

The immediate answer to this question would seem to be that babies certainly do need mothers. Babies are helpless, they need a mother to feed them, care for them, perhaps even teach them all they need to know to function in their society. But is a mother the only person who could adequately fulfil all of these requirements? In considering this question we need firstly to define what we mean when we use the word 'mother'. We might define a mother as the female biological parent. We might also define a mother as the central figure in providing consistent care for the infant, and with whom the infant will form a primary attachment. Therefore, when we ask our question, 'Do babies need mothers?', we must also ask whether all of these aspects of our definition are necessary to the infant, or just some of them. That is, does the infant need to be cared for by the biological parent; does the infant need to be cared for by a female parent; and, perhaps the most important question of all, does the infant need a primary attachment figure — one essential other who is consistently in charge of the infant's care. Could the infant have a variety of caregivers, or is consistency of care important, or even perhaps essential for the infant's well-being?

We can elaborate on our three main questions a little further. If we feel that consistency of care is important then we are suggesting that a one-to-one relationship between caregiver and infant is somehow significant. But is it important from the caregiver's point of view, or from the infant's point of view. If it is important from the infant's point of view then the infant must be aware that caregiving is consistent. So at what age does consistency of care start to become important? Is it, perhaps, necessary for the infant to have a consistent caregiver from birth? This implies that the infant is able to recognize the caregiver at birth. If the infant is not capable of such recognition then at what age might knowledge or recognition of the caregiver develop? Once we accept that an infant can recognize and form an attachment to one person, then we must also ask what the effect might be on the infant of having more than one caregiver. What then might be the effect of separation from the caregiver, or what length of period of separation from the caregiver might the infant be able to tolerate? And, when and how might these effects of separation or deprivation manifest themselves? These are all questions we must ask when we consider whether or not an infant needs the continued presence of the biological female parent for optimal psychosocial development.

It has often been suggested that there is something about the birth process itself, or about the period immediately after birth, that makes it a particularly salient time in the formation of the relationship between infant and caregiver. If a necessary 'bond' is formed at the time of birth then it would seem to indicate that only the female biological parent can be the primary caregiver, and that rearing by adoptive parents or other blood relatives would put the child at some sort of disadvantage. If there is no necessary 'bond' formed at birth, then anyone might be able to fill the role of primary caregiver, regardless of age or gender. Unless, of course, we assume that only women are suited to child-care.

How Might the Infant Need a Mother?

Let us reconsider our original question, which we have already divided into three, more explicit, questions. Does the infant need a single consistent primary caregiver, and if so, does the primary caregiver need to be the biological parent? If the primary caregiver does not need to be the biological parent, does the caregiver need to be female, or even adult? However, before we can begin to address these questions, we also have to consider what we mean by 'need'. How might the infant 'need' a mother?

Human babies are born relatively helpless and therefore obviously need physical care and protection from a competent other. It is also clear that if the infant's needs were confined only to physical aspects of care then it would not much matter who provided them. Someone may point out, however, that the biological mother is best equipped to feed the baby. This point is indisputably true. A newborn infant must be fed suitable milk from a sterile container. The most suitable milk for a human child is breast-milk, the most sterile of containers is the breast. It does not, however, have to be the breast, or the breast-milk of the biological mother, Any breast will do. Unfortunately the only women who lactate are those who have recently given birth, or those who have maintained their breast-milk supply by continued feeding. So if we are to say that an infant needs breast-milk in order to survive then we must say that babies need, not necessarily the biological mother, but a lactating female, who will, of necessity be of child-bearing age.

But how necessary is breast-milk to the infant? Does it have special qualities? It is certainly more fit for the infant's digestive system than other commercially available milk, and in transmitting the mother's antibodies to the child, also provides immunity against infection. But despite this slight advantage, over half of the infants in the UK are satisfactorily reared on commercially available infant milks. And although some of those who wish to promote breast-feeding claim that there is a psychological advantage to the child in being breast-fed, no advantage has been conclusively demonstrated by research findings. So, in affluent societies where adult literacy is high, that is where adults are able to afford commercially available milks and prepare them correctly, breast-milk is not a necessity for the infant. This means that child-care, from a nutritional perspective at least, need not be confined to women of child-bearing age. In undeveloped countries, however, artificial feeding is linked with high infant mortality rates, and prolonged and adequate breast-feeding is the infant's best chance of survival.

Perhaps we can assume that the infant might not necessarily be at any physical risk if not reared by the biological mother, but we have also to consider other areas of risk. The idea that the child's subsequent socio-emotional well-being might be affected by disruption in the pattern of early infant care was first suggested by John Bowlby (1951). Although, of course, the idea that early childhood events might affect adult mental health appeared much earlier with the advent of the psychoanalytic movement. But, until Bowlby's work became widely known, all child-care manuals advocated regimes which were based on the maintenance of the infant's physical health, or on training the child's personality to one which would suit the prevailing social climate. Even as late as the nineteenth century, infants of the upper classes were sent away to be wet-nursed, or were cared for by a succession of servants. During the Second World War children were evacuated away from their parents, and still, as late as the 1960s, when children were hospitalized their parents were prevented from seeing them for long periods. It did not seem relevant to the child's well-being that a single continued attachment to a parent should be established and maintained.

Bowlby, however, noticed that many adolescents whose behaviour was perceived to be deviant had had disruptions in the pattern of care given to them in their childhood. In some cases, because children had been in institutional care, they had had no single stable attachment figure at all in their early lives. As a consequence of these observations Bowlby suggested that, in order to attain optimal socio-emotional health in adult life, each child must be able to establish an attachment in infancy which would be continued into adolescence. That is, the infant must have a single caregiver, and the relationship with that caregiver must not be disrupted. The person most fit for the role of caregiver would, of course, in the 1950s be the mother. Bowlby's ideas changed the nature of institutional care for children, eventually changed hosptial-visiting policies, and also added a potential element of guilt to the life of the child-rearing mother. Any mother who was remiss enough to absent herself from her infant for even a short period of time would cause her child to become at least neurotic, at worst socially deviant.

This theory, that an attachment must be formed between infant and mother for socio-emotional functioning to be normal in adult life, was supported further by Harlow's (1959) work with monkeys. One of his first, and possibly the most widely known study, was of a stressed infant rhesus monkey's choice between a wire 'mother' incorporating a feeding bottle, and a terry-towelling 'mother' without feeding bottle. The infant rhesus monkey clung to the soft 'mother' from whom it could gain only comfort, rather than to the wire 'mother' from whom it gained food. The role of the mother, even for a monkey, would seem to be greater than just that of the provision of food, or even just of physical care. Harlow continued his work to study the effect of isolation, or separation from the mother on the monkey's subsequent functioning in adult life. Any monkey reared from birth in isolation became a socially deviant adult: aggressive, unable to play, unwilling to mate. Female monkeys reared in isolation, who later became mothers, were unable to care for their offspring, although it was not clear whether this was due to the absence of the mother, or to isolation from any social stimulation.

The Bonding Hypothesis

The evidence from the work of Bowlby and Harlow does seem to support the idea that an infant must have a stable attachment figure in early life. And this was seen to be a role appropriate to the mother. But does this role have to be taken by the biological female parent? Does it even have to be taken by a woman? To answer the first question we must consider the contentious issue of 'bonding'. As with many issues in child-care this cannot be separated from its political or economic expediency. In societies where women are needed in the labour force, perhaps especially in times of war, then infants are not considered to suffer if they are reared in the partial absence of their mothers. However, in times of high unemployment it seems to become expedient to promote research which emphasizes the infant's need for its biological mother, and therefore to move mothers out of the workforce and back into the home. After the end of the Second World War, in the 1950s, Bowlby's theory of the importance to the infant's psychological well-being of a continued attachment to the biological mother was timely in encouraging mothers who had, of necessity, been in full-time employment to return to full-time child-care. The women's jobs were needed for men returning from the war.

This concept, of the absolute necessity to the infant of the biological mother, returned in the 1970s, under a new guise. Following in the footsteps of work carried out on imprinting in birds, it was hypothesized that there might be a similar period of instant and critical recognition between human infant and mother. It was thought that this period of bonding might be linked to the hormonal surge found in the mother after the birth, and dependent upon the period of alertness observed in most infants shortly after normal delivery. This process of bonding was thought to be instantaneous, automatic and irreversible; and on it depended the subsequent strength of attachment between mother and child. Bonding had to occur for optimal social and emotional functioning in the infant's later life. Where bonding has occurred, so mothering was enhanced. The concept was linked to incidences of child abuse; for it was known that abuse was more common against children of premature births, who would have been taken from their mothers immediately after delivery. The concept of bonding meant therefore that the biological mother would have to be the best person to care for a child.

Many research studies were carried out in an attempt to support the concept of bonding (Sluckin, Herbert and Sluckin, 1983), and many early studies appeared to do so. But few of them were well designed, and there were problems when interpreting the data. It was not clear how long the period of early contact between mother and infant had to be. Mothers who were included in studies looking at the effects of increased early contact knew that they were part of a special research programme. There were problems over working definitions of 'good' or 'enhanced' mothering. Such definitions differ from culture to culture, age to age. Some studies looked at large numbers of measures and, not surprisingly, found differences between experimental and control groups in a few of them. Other studies found differences between extended contact and normal contact groups in the early months, but the differences had disappeared in follow-up studies. The only reliable effect that was found to be due to extended contact time between mother and infant in the hours after birth was that on the mothering abilities of young single girls — an effect which might have more to do with increases in motivation and perceived responsibility, than to do with chemical 'glueing'.

The bonding debate does therefore seem to have lost momentum. We know that newborn infants will orient towards their mothers' voice and smell, but that this seems to have little to do with the subsequent strength of attachment between mother and child. We also know that infants may have some rudimentary skills in face recognition. However, whatever function early recognition between mother and child might once have had in primitive mankind, like many of the innate reflexes found in the neonate, it now seems to have lost its former importance. Indeed, to have a lifelong attachment which was dependent upon a few hours' contact after an extremely arduous and risky process such as giving birth seems too tenuous a system on which to base the continuation of a very robust species.

The Importance of the Primary Attachment Figure

So when does attachment to any one caregiver begin? The process is a gradual one of learned recognition and recall, of learned patterns of interaction with the significant other. Certainly by the age of 7 or 8 months the infant will start to show separation anxiety when parted from the primary caregiver. So we might say that by this age an attachment has formed. But this also means that an attachment does not necessarily have to be formed with the biological mother. The first minutes are not critical; in fact the first months are not critical. There are no studies which show that children who are adopted early are more likely to have emotional problems in later life than children who remain with the biological mother. In fact if we look at a review of the literature on maternal deprivation (Rutter, 1972), we find that continuation of early care with one caregiver is less important than Bowlby first thought. Children can withstand considerable disruption in care if other stressors are kept to a minimum; they may show distress at the time, but long-term consequences are unlikely. They can certainly cope with short-term separations, such as being left with another carer while the mother goes out to work. Even an occasional traumatic separation, such as the mother going into hospital, is unlikely to have any long-term effects.

The total loss of a primary attachment figure may cause greater problems, perhaps leading to depression or suicide in some children. However, most at risk is the child who is unable to form an attachment with any one central figure. This inability is more likely to cause some form of psychopathology by the time the child has reached adolescence. It is also important to remember, however, while making such sweeping statements about the incidence of gross psychopathology within populations, that individual differences in parenting patterns, which are perpetuated throughout childhood, will always affect the development of the child in some way. For example, aberrant patterns of parenting are likely to be repeated as the child comes to adulthood; and abused children are most likely to become child abusers in their turn.

Therefore, we can probably accept that enabling a long-term attachment between a child and at least one caregiver is necessary for subsequent emotional stability. We can also accept that the attachment figure does not have to be the biological mother. Does the primary caregiver, however, have to be a mother-type figure? Is the primary attachment between the infant and mother qualitatively different from that experienced with others within the family? Schaffer and Emerson (1964), in a large study of parenting patterns in Glasgow, found that infants' primary attachments were frequently not to the mother, even when she was present in the family. Primary attachment figures could be fathers, grandparents or even older siblings. They also found that these attachment figures need not necessarily participate in the infant's day-to-day physical care. So not only may the primary caregiver not have to be the biological mother, it may not even have to be a woman.

Research is only now beginning to be carried out on the effect on the child, or on the family, if the infant is reared in a two-parent family but with the father as the primary caregiver. The long-term outcome is as yet unknown, but it is unlikely to be poor. Most differences between men and women are socialized. If it becomes appropriate for men to perform primary care duties for infants then the appropriate caring behaviour should be attainable by them. Women do not inherit the ability to care for infants, the skills are learned. There is no sex-linked nappy-changing gene present in women, but absent in men. Even so-called 'motherese', the special language and repertoire of behaviours used specifically with infants, is adopted both by male and female children and by male and female adults, especially where they have experience of interacting with infants.

An attachment figure can, therefore, be any adult. In fact it could be more than one adult. We have hitherto worked on the assumption that one attachment figure is necessary for the emotional stability of the child. However, if we reconsider the possible detrimental effects of separation from one primary attachment figure we find that the effects are lessened by the presence of other, strong, attachment figures. So the effect on the child of, say, the mother going into hospital is less traumatic if the child stays at home with a father and siblings. A father, mother and, perhaps even, nanny can tall take turns in caring for a child with no adverse effect on its later emotional development. In these situations there may be one attachment figure who is more strongly responded to in times of stress; it has even been suggested that most infants have a hierarchy of attachment figures, and each attachment figure would have a style of interaction specific to the relationship with the infant. This arrangement, of having multiple attachment figures, would seem to be the most sensible for the infant's optimal integration into society, and would seem to ensure the greatest emotional security. A wide range of learning experiences are made available to the child, and if one attachment figure is absent than another can take over.

Attachment to Siblings and Peers

We can see from the Schaffer and Emerson study that siblings were quite frequently cited as being among infants' attachment figures. What might happen, however, if a sibling were to be the only or primary attachment figure? Would such an attachment figure be sufficient to outweigh the possible effects of parental deprivation? Harlow and Harlow (1962), when looking at the effect of social deprivation in rhesus monkeys, observed some groups of motherless infants who had been raised only with experience of each other. At the age of 1 year the monkeys were normal in social and sexual development; they showed no signs of maternal deprivation. However, in early infancy the monkeys had shown a very characteristic style of interaction, they would stay together and move together in a group, each animal clinging to the back of another animal. Such groups of motherless monkeys were called 'together-together' groups. Similar patterns of interaction have been observed between groups of children raised together in concentration camps without adult attachment figures. Such children were fiercely resistent to separation on their subsequent release.

Hinde (1974), in another study carried out with monkeys, showed that one role of the mother was to foster independence in the infant. As the infant monkey matured, so the mother would increasingly resist the infant's attempts to cling to her. It was not only that the infant gradually moved away from her to explore, but also that she pushed the infant away, ensuring the establishment of independence. Perhaps one of the effects of raising children together, where their primary attachment figures are other children, is a diminution of autonomy. Part of the role of an adult caregiver is to establish, in the child, independence of the attachment figure.

A source of information about what happens if children are raised primarily with their peers, and with less opportunity to form strong attachments to adults, is the kibbutz system. In these Israeli communes children are placed away from their mothers, when only a few days old, in communal child-houses. Here they are reared with a group of age-mates. They are primarily cared for by a metapalet, who does not perceive it as her role to form an emotional bond with the children. The infants' contact with their parents would be, at most, a few hours a day, and nights are spent in the communal nurseries.

Bettelheim (1972) studied the effect that kibbutzim life had on the social and emotional development of its members. He found a very strong group cohesion between age-mates, but also an emotional 'flatness'. He described an inability to show any deep personal emotion and linked this to the fact that in the kibbutz all things are shared. He found the kibbutzniks were unable to have a personal opinion that differed from that of the group, and described age-mates as having a group ego. He also found less resistant autonomy, that is, less of a desire to have one's own way, but a greater tendency to think and behave as a group. There was a tendency to behave for the good of the group rather than the good of oneself. Some of the founding mothers did miss the opportunity to form an intimate attachment with their children. The second generation members, those who were raised in the children's houses, were, however, more ready to accept their emotional separation from their children. Children raised in the kibbutz do therefore seem to be less individualistic than those raised in a traditional family structure. They rely less on one-to-one attachments, and invest less in personal opinion and private emotion. However, this is not to condemn the kibbutzim system, for children so raised also benefit in that they are unlikely to suffer the negative aspects of the family system such as poverty, neglect or abuse.

Forming a primary attachment to an age-mate or sibling is, it seems, unlikely to cause any gross psychopathology in the child. However, a child reared in this way may be less autonomous, but would still be able to function well in most societies. We might therefore conclude that although an infant may need the presence of consistent attachment figures for subsequent optimal emotional health, such an attachment figure does not have to be the biological female parent. Neither does the attachment figure need to be female, nor does it have to be adult. However, it should be remembered that this interpretation of the available data is being made by a woman, and one who is herself a biological female parent. Might I not be interpreting the data to fit with my own feminist ideology?

Perhaps we should also look at child-rearing styles from a wider perspective. We can perhaps state quite clearly that a child raised without any stable attachment figures is at risk, and likely to show grossly deviant behaviour in adulthood. We may, however, be a little unsure about the time-scales involved here, and about whether the effect is reversible. We can also begin to suspect that different child-rearing stratagems may produce children best fit for different societies. Does an emphasis on autonomy produce children for a capitalist society, and an emphasis on communal living produce children for a socialist, egalitarian society? If so can we ever say that there is a correct, or even optimal, way in which to raise children. Can we only say that certain child-rearing styles will best fit certain societies? Perhaps new societies, new ideologies, arise because of changes in child-care, such as the change from the extended to the nuclear family. So we might ask instead, for what sort of a society do babies need mothers?

One of the outcomes of the kibbutzim experience was that women in the communes began to express a wish to care for their own children. This fact has been used in arguments against the equality of the sexes, that women are tied to their biological destiny. Perhaps they just wished for the opportunity to form one-to-one attachments. Does this fact raise yet another question: do mothers need babies?

Tutorial Discussion Questions

1 Do babies need mothers?
2 How important is early social experience to the subsequent emotional development of the child?
3 Why might premature babies more frequently be victims of physical abuse?
4 Are popular theories of child-care based on political expediency?
5 How are fathers likely to fare as primary caregivers?
6 Do we get the children we deserve?
7 Are children formed by a society to be fit only for that society?
8 Do mothers need babies?

References

BETTELHEIM, B. (1972) *The Children of the Dream*, London, Paladin.
BOWLBY, J. (1951) *Maternal Care and Mental Health*, Geneva, World Health Organization.
HARLOW, H. F. (1959), 'Love in infant monkeys', *Scientific American*, **200**, 6, pp. 68–74.
HARLOW, H. F. and HARLOW, M. K. (1962) 'Social deprivation in monkeys', *Scientific American*, **252**, 5, pp.136–46.
HINDE, R. A. (1974) *The Biological Basis of Social Behaviour*, New York, McGraw Hill.
RUTTER, M. (1972) *Maternal Deprivation Reassessed*, Harmondsworth, Penguin.
SCHAFFER, H. R. and EMERSON, P. E. (1964) 'The development of social attachments in infancy' *Monographs of Social Research in Child Development*, **29**, p. 94.
SLUCKIN, W., HERBERT, M. and SLUCKIN, A. (1983) *Maternal Bonding*, Oxford, Blackwell.

Further Reading

RUTTER, M. (1972) *Maternal Deprivation Reassessed*, Harmondsworth, Penguin.
SLUCKIN, W., HERBERT, M. and SLUCKIN, A. (1983) *Maternal Bonding*, Oxford, Blackwell.

Chapter 3

The Social Context of Eating Disorders

Vivien J. Lewis and Alan Blair

Introduction

A large and apparently increasing number of people in Western cultures evidence sets of behaviour, attitudes and feelings which can be classified as eating-disordered. Such an experience is not equally spread across social groups, however. Rather it is predominantly, although not exclusively, a female experience. This epidemiological pattern requires an explanation which involves reference to the cultural and historical conditions in which eating disorders have emerged and proliferated. This chapter seeks to identify the conditions which comprise such a social context for eating disorders, viewing such behaviour as frequently the vehicle through which women have tried to resolve internalized contradictions and express emotional distress (cf. Brumberg, 1988).

'Eating Disorders' and Problems Associated With Food and Body Image

What exactly constitutes an eating disorder? A variety of hypotheses have been formulated with regard to their nature, cause and cure, but there remains little consensus about their definition. Anorexia nervosa and bulimia are perhaps the best known and most broadly agreed upon eating disorders, although by no means the commonest if other food-related syndromes are included in this category, such as compulsive eating. Nevertheless, it was anorexia nervosa that came most prominently to public and professional attention in the 1960s and 1970s, although cases had been cited at least 100 years previously by E. C. Laseque in 1873 and W. W. Gull in 1888 who are often credited with 'discovering' the disorder. This is perhaps because Sir William Gull originally coined the phrase 'anorexia nervosa'. However, even earlier in 1689, Dr Richard Morton, describing what he called 'nervous consumption', presented the case of an 18-year-old female starving herself and looking like a 'skeleton only clad with skin'. Some recent authors have argued that, while historically such behaviour had ascetic motivations, more recently the primary motivation has become a concern with body weight.

The most prominent characteristics of an individual suffering from anorexia nervosa are that there will have been extreme weight loss often (but not always) resulting in an emaciated appearance, that they have a dread of becoming fat and often (in association) fear and guilt around consuming food, and that they frequently may have a distorted conception of their body size. Diagnostic criteria differ in detail (as with bulimia), but the general features are fairly consistent across authors. Nevertheless, with distortions in body image, for example, some authors argue that this is a perceptual disturbance, whereas the evidence now both clinically and from research suggests that individuals *feel* that they are fat and can in fact be enabled to perceive their dimensions as accurately as normal-weight or obese individuals.

Bulimia has a more recent history, although again reports of feasts prolonged by intermittent vomiting (and hence partial emptying of the stomach's contents) date back to Roman times. However, while binge-eating is essential for diagnosis of bulimia, self-induced vomiting is not (although it does occur in the majority of cases). More central to the disorder is the feeling that eating is out of the individual's control, accompanied by self-deprecating thoughts and depression following a binge.

These disorders have been seen to overlap, or one to follow from the other. Indeed, partial or combined syndromes have led to various other classifications arising in the literature, such as 'dietary chaos' and 'bulimarexia'. Furthermore, although it does not have a psychiatric classification, compulsive eating is commonly recognized as highly prevalent in the general population. In this case, individuals may experience episodes of over-eating prompted (or compelled) by emotional rather than physiological stimuli.

Prevalence of Eating Disorders

Estimates for the prevalence of eating problems in the general population are dependent upon various factors, including the classification selected and the population being sampled. If one considers the broadest category of dissatisfaction with body shape and/or eating pattern, then most authors would agree that this occurs among well in excess of 50 per cent of the female adult (and adolescent) population in Western cultures. If, however, only the frank eating disorders are considered, then for anorexia nervosa prevalence estimates vary between about 1 in 10,000 females to as many as 1 in 20 females. The higher figures are, however, from samples of modelling and dance students and likely to be skewed. The best estimate is that, currently, 1 female in every 100 in the UK will experience anorexia nervosa at some time in their lives. Bulimia is far more common, with as many as 5 or more females in every 100 fulfilling diagnostic criteria.

The above figures are estimates of the prevalence of eating disorders for the late 1980s. However, 20 or 30 years ago prevalence rates would have been less than a quarter of the current figures. Although some authors have argued that this dramatic increase in incidence has arisen through the greater awareness and more frequent presentation of such disorders to clinicians, the consistency of changes across the UK, continental Europe and North America suggest that at least some of the observed rise reflects a real increase in prevalence. Furthermore, while the frank eating disorders were presumed to occur predominantly in 'higher' socio-economic groups among high-achieving families, there is evidence now that these disorders are also being diagnosed more frequently among those in the manual social class groups. Significantly although eating disorders do occur in males, this is a small proportion of the total incidence. For example, fewer than 1 in 20 diagnosed cases of anorexia nervosa are males.

Aetiology of Eating Disorders

There is common agreement that eating disorders are, at least to an extent, culturally based, with a marked preponderance of such experiences being among females within Western cultures. However, accounts of this observation vary markedly and such accounts frequently have implications for the types of therapeutic strategies which have been developed.

Hilde Bruch (e.g. 1973, 1985) has been a pioneer in this area since the 1950s. When she began her work, she viewed anorexia nervosa psychoanalytically, focusing on the 'oral' component: 'a form of conversion hysteria that symbolically expressed repudiation of sexuality, specifically of oral impregnation fantasies'. However, more recently, Bruch has moved towards acknowledging the influence of the Western cultural emphasis on increasing slenderness in women, while continuing to stress the psychological complexity of the experience of eating disorders. She and others assert the importance of the recent changes in status of and expectations for women this century, which has given rise to a wide body of feminist literature concerning the area of disorders of eating.

Other authors, such as Crisp (1980), espouse an aetiology for eating disorders (in particular anorexia nervosa) based on the concept that the disorder develops as an adaptive approach to the resolution of conflicts experienced in adolescence, most notably relating to emerging sexuality. Such a view is an attractive one, especially in the light of the regression to a pre-pubertal body shape (and function) found in anorexia nervosa. It fails to account fully, however, for the vastly greater prevalence amongst females and for onset later in life. Moreover, it does not provide an adequate explanation for other disorders of eating such as bulimia nervosa. In these other disorders sexual behaviour is often not affected and, indeed, it is sometimes the case that within an individual bulimia will follow on from anorexia nervosa.

Few clinicians or researchers now support a wholly physiological explanation for eating disorders, although most would agree (albeit to differing extents) that there may be a genetic contribution to a predisposition for obesity. There has been little speculation or research regarding the possibility of physical precursors to bulimia. However, it has sometimes been suggested that hormonal dysfunctions in centres concerned with sexual motivation in the anterior and posterior hypothalamus and in lateral hypothalamic feeding centres are responsible for the onset of anorexia nervosa. These speculations are based on weak findings of alimentary malfunction and the few cases where amenorrhoea has preceded weight loss. Consequently, by far the greatest majority of theories relating to disorders of eating are psychosocial in nature and conceptualize of such disorders as multi-determined.

One such approach to the aetiology of anorexia nervosa and bulimia nervosa put forward by Peter Slade (1982) attempts to reduce these disorders to what are effectively mathematical equations. Slade proposes 'antecedent events' which combine to produce the 'behaviour' (e.g. in anorexia nervosa 'hypothalamic dysfunction', 'cessation of menstruation', 'initial dieting and weight loss') which in turn leads to certain 'consequences' which 'determine maintenance, exacerbation and change over time'. In Slade's 'functional analyses', he pays scant attention to the undeniable fact that eating disorders are overwhelmingly the domain of females and, thus, being female *per se* is not considered as an 'antecedent' or 'setting condition'. One might speculate that such an omission, by no means uncommon in this field, can frequently be linked to the author's gender. It is noteworthy that female authors generally have considered much more explicitly the reasons why females are predominantly the victims of problems associated with food and body weight. While various cognitions, psychodynamic or family process factors may be necessary for eating disorders to occur within an individual, we require also to consider what it is about being female in contemporary Western society which makes such an experience more likely. Thus, the prevailing sociocultural context provides the 'ground' onto which the 'figure' of eating disorders can be located.

The Historical Context

To understand fully the social epidemiology of eating disorders, the experience of women needs to be located in a cultural and historical context. As Susie Orbach (1986) stated, analysis of the disorder (anorexia nervosa) and treatment approaches 'must take into account the psychological construction of femininity and the vicissitudes of the passage from girlhood to womanhood in contemporary society'. Thus, given the dramatic rise in the incidence of eating disorders in the past forty years or so, we need to consider this phenomenon in the context of recent history.

How far has Western society moved on from the days (in the not-so-distant past) when women were men's property in law? Only this century were women accorded the right to vote, but that equality in the electoral system was not paralleled by equality in other domains. During the course of the Second World War in the UK, for example, the working male population gradually diminished as men were involved in active combat. This led to a shortage of workers essential for wartime production and, consequently, to a recruitment of women for occupations previously undertaken predominantly by men. Thus, women were taken out of the domestic environment and placed in positions of responsibility and decision-making which ranged beyond the immediate family. However, post-war, when males returning from combat re-entered the labour force, women, who formed a 'reserve army of labour', were pressurized to give up their positions of paid employment and relative independence. Indeed, an overt campaign was organized which encouraged women to return to the 'kitchens', that is, the site of their traditional role in food preparation and nurturing. The campaign re-emphasized women's household roles, including mothering and the purchase, preparation and provision of food. Moreover, within the arena of the family, women's relationship with food came to symbolize a vehicle for the transmission of emotional nurturance and love.

Females' socialization includes a variety of implicit gender-specific rules. Within the family, one message is that they must take second place, deny themselves for the sake of males and defer to males. Another message is that females should be able to anticipate and meet the needs of other people, in particular males. A further message is that females should find a full sense of selfindentity only through association with a male. Thus, women are encouraged to suppress their own needs and to repeat their mother's pattern by attachment to a male (in marriage) and identification and self-value through him.

Since the Second World War and its aftermath, however, females have entered increasingly into previously male-dominated sectors of work, and women now have more opportunities to become independent and autonomous. Notably, this move began among the higher socio-economic strata and in higher-achieving families, and particularly in those families that had been upwardly-mobile through improved education, initiative or enterprise. Among the new messages which have been transmitted to females is the importance for social approval of achieving in educational arenas and the workplace. However, this message has not replaced the more traditional concepts of women's roles. Rather it has been added to them and it can be argued that females today receive contradictory messages focused, on the one hand, on creating, raising and caring for a family and, on the other hand, developing and maintaining a career. In our society, such contradictions are manifested in a variety of ways. Within the workplace, women continue to enter into stereotypically 'female' occupations, serving others, such as nurse, secretary and shop assistant. Within the family, women who work and have children often express guilt at not raising their children full-time themselves, whereas those who stay at home to rear their families express both guilt at not contributing independent income towards the family budget and also frustration at not achieving self-fulfilment through their unpaid labour.

From this perspective, we can see that young girls are brought up with a variety of conflicting messages and pressures and, moreover, the social changes that have taken place during and after the Second World War and since may have created increased contradictions and confusion for women. Indeed, anorexia nervosa can be viewed as a reactive attempt by females to impose control over a crucial area of their lives, particularly when other aspects of their lives feel out of their control. Bulimia, contrastingly, can be seen as a mirror for the conflicts that are going on within the individual.

The Family Context

In the development of eating disorders, the relationship between mother and daughter has been viewed as crucial. It might be argued that mothers have taught their daughters in what they believe to be gender-appropriate ways, but they themselves have been aware at some level of unsatisfied needs from their own youth. Because of the mother's possible bias towards attending to the needs of male children over female children and demonstrating that her own needs are secondary or 'unimportant', daughters may not receive sufficient gratification of their own early dependency needs. Thus, such daughters grow up feeling less worthwhile and less entitled and their desires for autonomy are suppressed. Hence, problems may begin to arise during the developmental process of separation-individuation for both daughter and mother who each lack a sufficient sense of identity. The daughter may find herself in conflict between a wish for detachment and a wish for protection and this adolescent struggle to find an identity separate from the family can lead, paradoxically, to a strong desire to conform.

The social group with which such adolescents are most likely to conform is the peer group. While, within the relationship between mother and daughter, there may be excessive concern on the mother's part with her daughter's food-related behaviours and body shape (especially during puberty), the daughter seeks self-affirmation and understanding outside the immediate family context. For females, value and affirmation is typically conferred by society with reference to appearance, most obviously in the constantly changing aesthetic ideal for the female body shape. Here, then, is a vehicle through which females can express their conflicts and confusions and, through their body shapes and dress, females can choose to conform or reject contemporary ideals of femininity.

The 'Aesthetic' Context

That women have been valued in terms of their physical appearance can be identified through evaluation and interpretation of historical and contemporary discourse. For example, in Western art, unlike men, women have typically been portrayed and given value with reference to prevailing culture-based notions of beauty. This has perhaps in part reflected an ideology which has represented women as the property of men, passed on from father to husband. Given the use of property to represent wealth and status, it is not surprising that the aesthetic ideal for women historically has been a rounder body shape. Large bodies for females were seen as more desirable since, if food was scarcer, then the larger body became a statement that the man was sufficiently wealthy to be able to provide food plentifully for his woman. Research has demonstrated that, in present times in other cultures where food is scarce, larger body shapes for women are still seen to be the ideal. This also continues to occur in some poorer sections of affluent cultures, for example among certain ethnic groups in the US. Concomitantly, the incidence of anorexia nervosa in economic and cultural conditions in which food is relatively scarce is extremely low.

Given the role of patriarchy and the changing socio-economic conditions, it is noteworthy that considerable control has been exerted over the female body shape through time, from the Rubenesque figures of 400 years ago in Europe to the relatively emaciated figure of Twiggy in the 1960s. Earlier this century the Duchess of Windsor, Wallace Simpson, said that a woman could never be 'too rich or too thin' and, indeed, studies have shown that the measurements of women's figures in magazines and beauty contests have diminished steadily over the past few decades. Currently, food in this country is, if not always nutritious, relatively plentiful. Thus 'roundness', because it is so easily attainable and sustainable, can no longer be a symbol of wealth. In fact, low-energy high-protein foods are frequently more expensive, so that (ironically) increasing slenderness has perhaps become a better representation of wealth and status.

The Biological Context

Some authors have argued that this prescription for how a woman should shape her body has arisen out of a fear of the power that women have biologically, namely the power to reproduce. In this arena, it can again be conceptualized that women have been subjugated in Western cultures, medically and psychologically. Indeed, men have used women's biological function of reproduction to impose and maintain women's central role as the nurturance and rearing of children. They have also made recourse through a biological discourse to the argument that women were too irrational and emotional (because of their erratic hormone function) to be able to maintain a career. Such patriarchal discourses continue, to some extent, in present times, with men holding the majority of positions of power, women continuing to be poorly paid, prejudice against women in employment over possible or actual pregnancy, and so on. Indeed, women too have been socialized (by their mothers, as well as by society at large) to maintain this system. Contrastingly, there are also powerful economic and social pressures for females to engage in paid employment, increasing feelings of confusion and instability. This is not to argue that men do not also feel certain contradictions with regard to their positions and roles, but for women this is particularly intense.

The Consequences of Sociocultural Influences

Such social pressures have an important link with eating disorders. Increased knowledge has led to a growing awareness of the ways in which women's needs have been ignored or suppressed. At the same time, vastly raised demands have been placed on women, largely by themselves in an attempt to seek autonomy and their own independent identity. Because of both women's idiosyncratic relationship with food and with feeding and also the conflicts they experience about conformity with a societally prescribed ideal for their body shape, what better arena for the struggle within themselves to take place?

So the individual with anorexia nervosa almost religiously starves herself, in apparently supreme conformity to the prescribed ideal. She finds control in the area of food, where the rest of her life seems to be out of her control. She may enthusiastically feed the rest of her family with elaborate meals while eating virtually nothing herself (exhibiting much self-denial) and feeling extreme guilt about the little she does eat. Anorexia nervosa becomes for her the only escape from a game which she feels she cannot play. To become a 'successful woman' she internalizes the pressures to achieve (often academically), to value herself in terms of body shape, to be sexual, to esteem herself through success in finding a male partner for whom to make a home, and to give up her own identity for the sake of becoming a 'good mother'. Resolution is sought for such pressures and contradictions through a withdrawal into her pre-pubescent body shape, in a sense both conforming to and resisting internalized social pressures simultaneously.

In bulimia similar conflicts may be experienced, but the processes by which the individual attempts to deal with or resolve such conflicts may differ. To the outside world the individual appears to be in complete control of her eating, with female-appropriate self-denial. In secret, she may hoard sometimes large quantities of the food she deprives herself of publicly and, through binge-eating, may attempt to numb temporarily her feelings of distress while eating. Nevertheless, the individual with bulimia frequently experiences feelings of guilt after binge-eating, in part through a realization that she feels out of control and that she has failed to be the 'successful woman' which others perceive her to be.

Many of the other problems for women associated with food and body shape, including compulsive and emotional eating, 'dietary chaos', overweight and obesity, also have a grounding in the sociocultural context, including the psychosocial development of 'femininity'. Women may comfort themselves in private with that which they are told to deprive themselves of publicly. In this way, the attempt to conform with the current aesthetic ideal for their body shape (by dieting and, perhaps, excessive exercise) is opposed by either an often anger-driven wish to rebel against the prescribed norms or by feelings of deprivation and neediness. Indeed, a vicious circle may ensue with the guilt at feelings of failure prompting further eating which, in turn, alternates with drastic attempts to meet a standard for 'perfect womanhood'.

Such are some of the internalized cultural pressures experienced by many women, pressures which are reflected and reinforced by a variety of social mechanisms. Industries involved in the production and marketing of clothing, hairstyles, dieting products, perfumes, deodorants and so on all benefit from and seek to encourage females to value themselves in terms of their body. The media, for example, is effective in disseminating messages designed to ridicule female ugliness, smelliness and fatness and in encouraging the use of a variety of slimming products or the adoption of some dietary regimen. Unfortunately, research has shown that dieting, particularly if engaging in severe caloric restriction, can prove not only ineffective but also counter-productive in the long-term with regard to achieving weight reduction or shape change. Also, as has already been suggested, such encouragement towards a preoccupation with weight loss and body shape can increase the likelihood of becoming eating disordered.

Furthermore, the interventions of clinicians can sometimes serve to maintain or exacerbate the problem, rather than alleviate it. Diets are prescribed for overweight and obese women, regardless of the research demonstrating that weight loss seldom occurs safely and enduringly. Often, when the women fail to achieve and maintain a weight loss, they may be described as lacking in 'will-power' without anyone addressing the question of whether there might be underlying reasons for the apparent failure to 'undereat'. Indeed, perhaps the 'will-power' is there, but there is also another 'will' which does not wish to conform with the 'ideal'. Too often clinicians 'treat' the disorder without considering the individual. Behavioural approaches may disempower the individual and, for those that already feel disempowered, such interventions may serve only to decrease an already fragile sense of self-worth and self-esteem.

Similarly, it would be folly to involve an individual of 4 stones suffering from anorexia nervosa in psychoanalysis and yet, for women with problems related to food and body shape, interventions need to take into account the person as a whole. Cognitive therapy, like behaviour therapy, aims to change aspects of the disorder including to turn negative thoughts into positive ones. But again this may serve to disempower the individual and at the same time, by focusing on cognitive distortions, may invalidate much of the individual's valid experience of their eating disorder. For that individual, what she thinks and does may be a logical response to what she perceives society demands from her. On the contrary, women need to be enabled to seek alternative solutions for themselves, to be educated and informed and to be made aware of how their position in their family and society has arisen and how they can choose to change it.

To summarize, therefore, the socio-economic and cultural conditions which currently exist within Western societies have set the backdrop against which the experience of eating disorders in their present form has emerged. One powerful

Vivien J. Lewis and Alan Blair

theme underlying this phenomenon is the emphasis placed by a patriarchal society on the valuation of women in terms of physical appearance, in particular their body shape. Combined with other sociocultural messages which place contradicting pressures on females, eating-disordered behaviour can be seen as a rational, if self-damaging, response. The incidence of eating disorders is, thus, unlikely to decrease substantially without marked changes in the pattern of gender relations within society.

Tutorial Discussion Questions

1 In what way might sociocultural factors account for eating disorders occuring in males?
2 What reasons might there be for the increase in incidence of eating disorders over the past forty years or so?
3 Eating disorders have occurred predominantly in 'higher' socio-economic groups among high-achieving families. How might this be explained, and what reasons might there be for the increasing prevalence currently in the manual social class groups?
4 What factors serve to maintain the 'aesthetic ideal' for female body shape in modern Western society, and why?
5 How might the percepts, attitudes, emotions and behaviour of both mothers and fathers contribute to the likelihood of a female child developing an eating disorder?
6 What differences might there be between anorexia nervosa, bulimia and compulsive/emotional overeating in terms of the ways in which they represent responses to sociocultural pressures?

References

BRUCH, H. (1973) *Eating Disorders*, New York, Basic Books.
BRUCH, H. (1985) 'Four decades of eating disorders', In GARNER, D. M. and GARFINKEL, P. E. (Eds) *Handbook of Psychotherapy for Anorexia Nervosa and Bulimia*, New York, Guilford, pp. 7–18.
BRUMBERG, J. J. (1988) *Fasting Girls: The Emergence of Anorexia Nervosa as a Modern Disease*, Cambridge, Harvard University Press.
CRISP, A. H. (1980) *Anorexia Nervosa: Let Me Be*, London, Academic Press.
ORBACH, S. (1978) *Fat is a Feminist Issue: How to Lose Weight Permanently without Dieting*, London, Paddington Press.
ORBACH, S. (1986) *Hunger Strike*, London, Faber and Faber.
SLADE, P. (1982) 'Towards a functional analysis of anorexia nervosa and bulimia nervosa', *British Journal of Clinical Psychology*, 21, pp. 167–79.

Further Reading

CHERNIN, K. (1985) *The Hungry Self: Women, Eating and Identity*, London, Virago.
LAWRENCE, M. (Ed.) (1987) *Fed Up and Hungry: Women, Oppression and Food*, London, The Women's Press.

Chapter 4

Child Sexual Abuse

Glyn Thomas

Recent research suggests that many children are sexually abused, but are too frightened to tell anyone about it. Some people disbelieve the evidence, and argue that the problem is exaggerated. Others are so convinced child sexual abuse is a serious problem that their attempts to protect abused children have split up innocent families where abuse was wrongly suspected. In this chapter I try to present enough of the arguments and evidence for you to form your own judgment of the seriousness of the problem.

What Is Sexual Abuse of Children?

By definition, child sexual abuse is any sexual encounter between a child and an older person: at least 5 years older for children under the age of 13 years and at least 10 years older for children aged 13 to 16 (Finkelhor, 1984). In defining abuse it is important to exclude the normal physical intimacies (such as cuddling) which frequently occur between children and parents. A father touching his little daughter's genitals while bathing her, for example, should not necessarily be considered as sexually abusing her. To meet this problem, many authorities have suggested that to count as sexual abuse an activity must bring sexual gratification to the perpetrator. Thus, innocent bathing of baby daughters would not be considered as abuse. Conversely, a superficially innocuous activity, such as a grandfather bouncing his young granddaughter on his knee, could count as abuse if the grandfather gained some sexual gratification from it. Note that this definition means that a child could be abused without being aware of it.

How Common Is Sexual Abuse?

The private nature of most sexual encounters makes it difficult to determine the precise incidence of the sexual abuse of children. There are two main sources of information, and these yield dramatically different estimates of the numbers of victims. Firstly, studies of children referred to the police, social services or doctors because of suspected sexual abuse suggest a very low rate, as few as three children in every thousand, for example. On the other hand, surveys of the general adult population, who have been asked about their childhood experiences, suggest that up to 40 per cent of women and approximately 10 per cent of men (in the UK and USA) may have been sexually abused as children.

The low rates of professional referrals undoubtedly underestimate the true scale of abuse; many children must be too frightened, ashamed or confused to tell anyone of their plight, and many professionals may be insensitive to indications that children have been abused.

The interpretation of surveys also requires care because some people declined to answer the very personal questions. Consequently, we cannot be sure that those who did reply were representative of the general population. Furthermore, other research suggests that recollections about long past and emotionally sensitive events are often inaccurate.

These difficulties notwithstanding, it seems undeniable that sexual abuse of children is relatively common. Furthermore, there has been a recent dramatic increase in the frequency with which sexual abuse is reported. The number of cases of sexual abuse registered with the National Society for the Prevention of Cruelty to Children, for example, has increased twelvefold between 1983 and 1988. It is difficult to tell, however, whether this increase in reporting reflects only greater public awareness and thus better detection of abuse, or whether there really has been an increase in the number of incidents.

To put these alarming figures into perspective, we should remember that for most victims sexual abuse occurs on only one occasion. For as many as 25 per cent of victims, however, the abuse is repeated and prolonged. The most common type of sexual activity reported is fondling (including genital fondling). Cases of actual intercourse are infrequent, perhaps 5 to 10 per cent of all incidents. Oral sex occurs in as many as 30 per cent of cases involving boys, and in approximately 5 per cent of cases involving girls. Incidents of abuse in which there was no physical contact (such as indecent exposure) are usually found to account for 20 to 30 per cent of the total number of cases.

Who Abuses Whom?

Surveys have generally found that the majority of abuse victims are girls. Although boys may be less willing to report abuse than girls, it still seems most likely that at least twice as many girls than boys are victims of sexual abuse by an older person. Most abusers are men; fewer than 5 per cent of abusers are women when the victims are girls, and fewer than 20 per cent are women when the victims are boys.

Children aged between 8 and 14 years seem to be at the greatest risk of sexual abuse, although even infants have become victims. It is possible, however, that younger children suffer as much abuse as older ones, but are less willing to disclose it or are less likely to be believed.

There is relatively little information on class or cultural variations in the incidence of abuse. Overall, sexual abuse is found most often in poorer families, but it also occurs in middle- and upper-class families. Because sexual abuse is such a secret activity it is possible that it is equally common in all social classes, just better detected in poorer families who may have less privacy. There is no clear evidence that the incidence of sexual abuse varies across ethnic groupings.

Some parental characteristics which are linked with the likelihood of sexual abuse include mental illness, alcoholism, criminality and a history of previous physical or sexual abuse. Men who were themselves victims of sexual abuse when children seem particularly likely to become offenders. Family disturbance also increases the likelihood of sexual abuse, in part because it often introduces a variety of adult males (stepfathers, mother's boyfriends) who may be likely to commit abuse (see below).

In popular mythology the typical sexual abuser of children is a stranger in a dirty raincoat. In reality, most victims are abused by someone already known to them. In one British study (Russell, 1983), for example, only 11 per cent of abusers were total strangers to their victims. This same study found that in 29 per cent of cases the abuser and victim were relatives, leaving 60 per cent of victims who were abused by someone known to them, but who was not a relative.

Fathers are responsible for a significant number of cases of abuse, Russell found that 1 in every 40 girls had been abused by her biological father. Stepfathers seem to pose a particularly severe threat: 1 in 6 women with a stepfather had been sexually abused by him when she was a child. Parker and Parker (1986) concluded that the absence of a father (or stepfather) in the earliest years of a daughter's life was the most significant factor placing that girl at risk of sexual abuse by him. They hypothesized that involvement in caring for his baby daughter creates powerful prohibitions in a man against subsequently sexually abusing her in any way.

Finkelhor (1984) also found that there are some particular features of mothers that place their daughters at risk of sexual abuse. In his survey, women who reported that their mothers were ill or unaffectionate were more likely to have been victims of abuse. Girls brought up without mothers (but not girls with working mothers) were also more likely to have been abuse victims.

Some children are sexually abused when recruited into child sex rings, operating for money. Wild (1986) found that out of a sample of 30 cases of sexual abuse referred to paediatricians in Leeds, 7 cases involved girls who had become involved in sex rings. In a survey of 200 prostitutes in California, Silbert and Pines (1981) found that 78 per cent reported that they had started prostitution when still legally a juvenile. These data suggest that commercial sexual exploitation of children is a significant social problem. On the other hand, the kidnapping of children for sexual abuse and satanic rituals, although horrifying and widely publicized, probably account for at most a tiny percentage of all cases of abuse.

Who Is to Blame?

Sexual abuse is commonly blamed on the men who commit the abuse, the victims themselves, their mothers or society.

Blaming the Men

This theory attributes abuse to paedophiles — men who are sexually attracted to children rather than to adults. The evidence suggests, however, that many abusers are sexually active with adult partners as well as children. Furthermore, there appear to be no personality characteristics which are especially associated with a propensity to abuse children. Given that abuse is widespread, and that much abuse occurs within families it seems quite unlikely that sexually deviant men are responsible for more than a small proportion of incidents.

Blaming the Victims

We are here invited to believe that children solicit sexual interactions with adults. The idea of children as sexual provocateurs is propagated in many forms of pornography, and even in 'respectable' art. The name of Lolita has come to mean a sexually precocious nymphet. (In Nabokov's novel of that name, Lolita was actually entrapped by her adult seducer, who then systematically bullied and abused her sexually. It is a popular distortion of the story to exaggerate the sexuality of the girl). In cold reality, the notion of a grown man being corrupted by a little child seems very unconvincing.

Nevertheless, children *do* have interests and desires which are definitely sensual, if not sexual. Freud's theories of child sexuality dispelled sentimental Victorian notions about the 'innocence' of children. Children do enjoy physical contact and intimacy with adults, and may solicit adult attention for that purpose. Such contacts are considered essential for normal development, but should not be considered as sexual initiatives in the adult sense. It is also possible that children may learn to welcome sexual interactions if these have been the only form of affection they have received from adults. Even if a child does appear to invite a sexual contact, surely it is the adult's responsibility to gently refuse it?

Blaming the Mothers

Mothers are often blamed in cases of incest. An absent, ill or unaffectionate wife fails to satisfy the natural sexual desires of her husband, who then resorts to his daughters instead. Some experts have suggested that mothers in these cases actually collude in the abuse, by refusing to believe their daughters' complaints, or doing nothing to prevent the abuse from occurring.

Even if these claims of collusion are true, it seems to me that we must distinguish between the responsibilities of a woman who may have created conditions which make abuse more likely, and the responsibilities of a man who actually commits the abuse itself. To blame only the mother is like blaming an understrength police force for the activities of burglars. Furthermore, this account fails to explain why a frustrated husband should resort to children for sexual gratification, rather than embarking on an affair with another woman.

Blaming Society

This perspective on abuse suggests that it is a consequence of the particular gender roles fostered by our Western culture. This view is sometimes linked with the feminist movement, but it is an important psychological theory as well as a political argument. Sexual abuse of children, this theory suggests, is a by-product of the social construction of men as powerful and active, and of women (and children) as passive and dependent. In the terms of feminist theory, all men are potential abusers because they are socially conditioned to think of their sexuality as active and demanding, and that of women as passive and yielding. Given this construction of the gender roles, it is hardly surprising that some men will exploit and abuse children, who like women are seen as passive and dependent. Indeed, for this theory it is a problem to explain why so many men do *not* sexually abuse children, given the social conditioning of their sexuality.

Consistent with this theory, the overwhelming majority of abusers are men, and most of their victims are girls. In Finkelhor's (1984) survey, women who reported that their fathers held conservative values and showed limited physical affection were more likely than other women to have been abused in childhood, though not necessarily by their fathers. Other American studies have found that authoritarian, traditionally religious, and patriarchal men (perhaps those most strongly conditioned by the stereotype of male power and female dependence) may be more likely than other fathers to physically abuse their wives, and sexually abuse their daughters (Haugaard and Reppucci, 1988).

It is a mistake to think that there is one single cause for sexual abuse of children. Finkelhor (1984) suggested that four preconditions have to be met before sexual abuse of a child can occur. Firstly, a potential offender must have some initial motivation for sexual contact with a child. In terms of our earlier discussion this could be deviant sexual arousal, arrested emotional development, or perhaps lack of more suitable partners. Secondly, the potential offender must overcome internal inhibitions to molest children. Thus, alcohol, which lowers inhibitions, it known to be a factor in many incidents of abuse. Thirdly, the potential offender must overcome external impediments to abuse. Thus, children who lack the protection of their mother or who live in socially isolated families are particularly at risk. Finally, the potential offender must overcome, by persuasion or force, any resistance that the child may offer. With regard to this final factor, it is clear that children who are emotionally insecure or deprived, for example, may be more vulnerable than others. Children with learning difficulties are often particularly vulnerable to sexual abuse, perhaps because they can be physically and sexually mature, but lack understanding of sexual activities and may therefore be particularly susceptible to persuasion by selfish adults.

Consequences of Abuse

A minority of victims contract veneral diseases or suffer physical injuries. Most incidents of sexual abuse, however, produce no physical signs. Much of the damage is emotional and psychological.

Accurate assessment of possible psychological consequences of abuse is not always easy. It is not enough, for example, to show that abused children are more emotionally disturbed than non-abused children. Quite possibly the factors which increased the risk of abuse (an unaffectionate or absent mother, for example) might also be responsible for the emotional disturbance. Nevertheless, it is possible to identify some likely consequences of abuse.

Guilt seems to be one of the most frequent miseries suffered by abuse victims. This finding should come as no surprise, because many children are made to feel guilty about even normal and healthy sexual acts, let alone illicit ones. Feelings of guilt are reported to be more common in children who have experienced repeated abuse, perhaps because the mere fact of its repetition raises questions about the child's acquiescence. Older children may also suffer more guilt, perhaps because they may be more likely to believe that they could have stopped the abuse had they *really* wanted to. Children who found aspects of the sexual activity pleasurable may be particularly vulnerable to feelings of guilt, at enjoying something they believe to be bad.

An important source of guilt is the victim's often irrational feeling of personal responsibility for what has happened. Even when totally passive during the encounter a child may still feel responsible for having been selected by the abuser as a sexual partner.

Clinicians report that an abused child may suffer from feelings of powerlessness, because she was unable to prevent the forced invasion of her body. Other victims experience feelings of helplessness at the hands of officials, who may separate children from their families regardless of the victim's own wishes. Removal of an abused child from her home can also seem to her like a punishment and thus confirm her belief that she really is to blame.

There may also be consequences of abuse that only become apparent over a long period. Some studies have found that women who were abused as children are more likely than other women to experience sexual difficulties, suffer from low self-esteem, become alcoholics or drug abusers, seek psychotherapy or suffer from serious mental illness. Similarly, early sexual abuse may leave children more vulnerable to subsequent sexual exploitation as prostitutes.

There can be no doubt, therefore, that some sexually abused children suffer severe and lasting harm. That said, there are many incidents of sexual abuse that may not damge the victim significantly. Children for whom the abuse was an isolated incident, and were reassured convincingly that the abuse was not their fault seem particularly likely to emerge unscathed from the experience.

Some children have actually been more harmed by events and official actions taken following disclosure of abuse, than by the abuse itself. I am reminded of the schoolgirl who revealed to her teacher that her father had fondled her genitals on only two occasions several years previously. The occasion of the disclosure had been a school programme on the prevention of sexual abuse; the girl revealed the abuse because the programme indicated that she should do so, and not because she had been previously worried about it. The ensuing arrest of the father and subsequent official investigations proved far more traumatic for the child and her family than the original sexual encounters appear to have been (Haugaard and Reppucci, 1988).

We perhaps should note here an alternative view that, in a more sexually liberated society, a sexual encounter between a child and a sensitive and caring adult could actually be a positive experience for the child. The possibilities of selfish adult exploitation of dependent children seem so great, however, that most people consider this view to be dangerous.

The Detection of Abuse: Witch-Hunt or Crusade?

What should our response be to the discovery from retrospective surveys that many children suffer sexual abuse, but do not tell anyone about it at the time? There are several issues to be disentangled here. First, we need to consider why children are reluctant to disclose that abuse has occurred. Then we need to assess the accuracy with which undisclosed abuse can be detected by other means. Finally, we need to think about the possible courses of action that can be taken where abuse is suspected.

Children's reluctance to disclose abuse becomes understandable once we consider the conflicting feelings and pressures many abused children have to endure. Many adults have difficulty discussing sexual matters with children, and children quickly detect this embarrassment. There is likely, therefore, to be a general reluctance to report sexual encounters. This reluctance will be reinforced if the child perceives that there is any chance that she will be held partly responsible for what has happened to her, or that she will not be believed. Note that one particularly pernicious consequence of Freud's theories is that children's reports that they have been abused have often been dismissed as wish-fulfilling fantasy.

If, as is often the case, the abuser is known to the child or is a relative, then the child's feelings are likely to be thoroughly confused. Distaste for the abuse will conflict with the respect with which most children regard adults. If the abuser is emotionally and materially important (a father or stepfather, for example), then the conflicts become extreme.

Additional inhibitions against disclosure may be created if the abuser requests or demands secrecy. In one notorious case in California, alleged abusers were said to have killed pet animals in front of the children in order to frighten them into silence. Even if threats are not explicit, children may feel that disclosure will have bad consequences for themselves or their abuser, and so be prevented from talking.

Although may people feel very strongly about rescuing children from abusers, the truth is that suspicions of sexual abuse are not easy to substantiate. Most sexual abuse produces no physical signs. Furthermore, some alleged signs of abuse can be the result of other factors. In the well-known Cleveland controversy, for example, doctors relied heavily on a physical sign (anal dilatation) which can be a consequence of sexual abuse by anal penetration. It turns out, however, that anal dilatation can be produced by factors other than sexual abuse, and can occur in non-abused children. It is likely that these doctors did discover some genuine cases of abuse, but they almost certainly incorrectly identified some non-abused children as victims of anal abuse. It is worth noting that the sheer numbers of 'abused' children 'identified' by the anal dilatation test implies an incidence of abuse by anal penetration which is many times higher than the rate of such abuse suggested by retrospective surveys (Bell, 1988).

There are also some behavioural signs that seem likely to result from abuse. Inappropriate sexual knowledge or behaviour, for example, would be regarded as suspicious. Children who become depressed and withdrawn without apparent reason may also be abuse victims. It is often difficult, however, to substantiate suspicions of abuse when both abuser and victim persist in denying that anything untoward has occurred.

Some social workers and others have considered that is is justifiable in these circumstances to apply pressure to disclose in order to counteract the pressure for secrecy that an abuser may have applied. The great danger here, of course, is that, under such pressure, suggestible children will 'report' incidents which did not in fact occur. Recent research suggest that children's testimony can be reliable, but only if non-leading questions are asked in a non-challenging manner in an appropriate setting (see Dent, 1988).

It scarcely needs to be said that interventions based on a mistaken diagnosis of abuse can have utterly devastating consequences for innocent parents and their children. The Cleveland controversy was fuelled in part by the widespread conviction that overconfident professionals were removing children from their families on the basis of flawed or inadequate evidence.

Treatment of Abuse

Children who have been severely damaged by sexual abuse deserve careful and sensitive treatment. For this reason alone, a 'gung-ho' approach in which children are dramatically 'rescued' from their abuser and lodged in a 'place of safety' is to be deplored. Sexual abuse, particularly that involving family members, is often embedded in a complex of emotional and personal problems in which all participants are enmeshed. Consequently, the discovery or disclosure of sexual abuse can be very stressful by threatening what little emotional/personal security the participants have managed to achieve. To illustrate the dangers, O'Hagen (1989) reports that in Leeds (and the surrounding area) between 1982 and 1986 there were no fewer than 7 fatalities (3 suicides and 4 murders) ensuing from the disclosure of abuse. The handling of disclosure and its consequences clearly demands skill and sensitivity from all professionals involved.

There are three main aims of interventions in sexual abuse. The first is to stop the abuse, either by removing the child to a place of safety (often a foster home) or by removing the perpetrator from the child's environment. In North America the latter has sometimes been achieved by requiring that an abusing father, for example, live apart from his family and contact them only under carefully regulated conditions.

The second aim of treatment is to try to correct the damage that the abuse has produced in the victim. Many therapists agree that counteracting unwarranted feelings of responsibility and guilt must be a priority here. Restoration of self-confidence and assertiveness training are also frequently attempted.

The third aim concerns the treatment of the perpetrator. There are two possible courses of action — they can be punished as criminals, or they can be treated as patients in need of help and therapy. There is no evidence that punishment is effective as a deterrent, especially in cases of abuse within families. Indeed, the choice of therapy, rather than punishment, seems particularly appropriate when the abuser is (still) a potentially important figure in his victim's life. While prevention of recurrence of abuse is clearly a major aim, an important additional aim of treatment may be the reconciliation of abuser and victim (daughter and father, for example). A thorough discussion of treatment issues is provided by Haugaard and Reppucci (1988) and by O'Hagen (1989).

Prevention

If sexual abuse of children is so widespread, so hard to detect and potentially has such serious consequences, it is natural that attempts should be made to prevent its occurrence. Much effort has recently been spent on educational programmes for children, designed to help them avoid being sexually abused. 'Kidscape' is one well-known example. Most of these programmes attempt:

1 To increase children's understanding of sexual behaviour (teaching the difference between good and bad touching, for example).
2 To teach them that they have a right to say 'No' to adults who offer unwanted sexual encounters.
3 To stress the importance of telling trusted adults about any incidents of sexual abuse.

Reppucci and Haugaard (1989) have critically reviewed the available evidence on the value of such programmes, and counsel caution.

Some programmes, for example, try to teach complex concepts and distinctions — such as the difference between 'good' and 'bad' touching, or when to say 'No' to adults — which very young children may not be capable of comprehending. It is also apparent that some programme presenters (teachers, parents, religious workers) are uncomfortable telling children that their family friends and relatives may pose a sexual threat. In consequence, many preventative programmes give children the incorrect impression that they are in greatest danger of sexual abuse from strangers, whereas people they already know pose the greatest threat in reality. Misguided preventative programmes could also inhibit children's sexual activities with their age peers, or their normal and healthy physical intimacies with their family.

Some cases of sexual abuse are truly horrific, and prevention is a logical and highly desirable aim. It is important, however, to evaluate programmes to ensure that they are effective. Many cases of sexual abuse involve isolated incidents, which may not harm the victims as much as a misconceived and badly presented preventative programme might.

An alternative strategy for prevention without the potential problems of child-centred programmes would be to address some of the other factors which make abuse more likely. Attempts to change traditional stereotypes of male supremacy and sexual dominance, for example, should in the long run reduce the tendency of men to abuse both women and children. Similarly, encouraging men into greater involvement in the care of their baby children could also reduce the likelihood of subsequent sexual abuse (see p. 35) as well as undermining traditional gender-role stereotypes. It may be, too that restrictions on child pornography might be helpful in reducing sexual abuse of children, although many believe that any form of censorship brings other dangers which could outweigh the benfits.

Difficult Choices

Most people consider that society has a responsibilty to protect children from sexual abuse. Stopping abuse is naturally a highly desirable aim. If the abuse is serious and the abuser is the child's father (or stepfather), then there is likely to be an outcry that officials should have acted to protect the child by removing her from danger. On the other hand, there have been cases when officials have taken children from their families to protect them from suspected abuse, and the suspicions of abuse have turned out to be unfounded. Again, there is likely to be a public outcry, this time about meddlesome professionals.

There are some difficult issues to be faced here, concerning the rights of parents and children to be with each other in families, and a public responsibility to protect children at risk. These interests come into conflict because it is not always possible to make accurate and reliable assessments of the risk of abuse. The urgent need to protect children from abuse has to be balanced against the equally serious consequences of misdiagnosis and the wrongful removal of children from their families.

We should not expect our public servants (such as social workers) to achieve the impossible. Realistically, it is likely that some children will continue to suffer from undetected sexual abuse because the steps needed to protect them would involve official monitoring of family life on a scale that would be politically and economically impossible.

Acknowledgments. I wish to thank Delia Cushway and Helen Dent for their comments on an earlier draft of this chapter.

Tutorial Discussion Questions

1 Can a child be sexually abused without being aware of it?
2 Has the problem of sexual abuse been exaggerated?
3 Are all men potential abusers?
4 Why do victims so often blame themselves for the abuse?
5 Can sex between an adult and a child ever be acceptable?
6 Should a child ever be removed from her family against her wishes?
7 Should some kinds of pornography be banned?

References

BELL, S. (1988) *When Salem Came to the Boro: The True Story of the Cleveland Child Abuse Crisis*, London, Pan Books.

DENT, H. R. (1988) 'Children's eyewitness evidence: A brief review' in GRUNEBERG, M. *et al.* (Eds) *Practical Aspects of Memory: Current Research and Issues*, Chichester, John Wiley. pp. 101–06.

FINKELHOR, D. (1984) *Child Sexual Abuse*, New York, Free Press.

HAUGAARD, J. J. and REPPUCCI, N. D. (1988) *The Sexual Abuse of Children*, London, Jossey-Bass.

O'HAGEN, K. (1989) *Working with Child Sexual Abuse*, Milton Keynes, Open University Press.

PARKER, H. and PARKER, S. (1986) 'Father-daughter sexual abuse: An emerging perspective', *American Journal of Orthopsychiatry*, 56, 4, pp. 531–48.

REPPUCCI, N. D. and HAUGAARD, J. J. (1989) 'Prevention of child sexual abuse', *American Psychologist*, 44, 10, pp. 1266–75.

RUSSELL, D. (1983) 'The incidence and prevalence of intrafamilial sexual abuse of female children', *Child Abuse and Neglect*, 7, pp. 133–46.

SILBERT, M. H. and PINES, A. M. (1981) 'Sexual abuse as an antecedent to prostitution', *Child Abuse and Neglect*, 5, pp. 407–11.

WILD, N. J. (1986) 'Sexual abuse of children in Leeds', *British Medical Journal*, 292, pp. 1113–16.

Further Reading

FINKELHOR, D. (1984) *Child Sexual Abuse*, New York, Free Press.

GLASER, D. and FROSH, S. (1988) *Child Sexual Abuse*, London, Macmillan.

HAUGAARD, J. J. and REPPUCCI, N. D. (1988) *The Sexual Abuse of Children*, London, Jossey-Bass.

RUSH, F. (1980) *The Best Kept Secret: Sexual Abuse of Children*, New York, Prentice-Hall.

Chapter 5

Sex Differences and Gender Relations:
Yes, But Who Does the Washing Up?

Christine Griffin

There has been a considerable increase in psychological research on sex and gender since the mid-1970s, mainly due to the impact of feminism and the increasing number of women entering higher education. Gender relations is one aspect of human social behaviour with which we all have considerable experience. Most contemporary cultures make some degree of distinction between those activities which are seen as 'women's work' and those which are deemed to be 'men's work'. The organization of sex and gender varies considerably across different cultures and in different historical periods. In India it is considered acceptable for women to work as rubble carriers on building sites, for example, while in Britain very few women have managed to gain access to what is still an almost exclusively 'male' occupation. In the Indian context, the job of rubble carrier is poorly paid and of low status, and it is considered an appropriate job for women of low caste groups. In Britain, women are even less welcome on the building site. It is not unknown for employers to demand that female applicants be willing to strip to the waist in order to be considered for building site work.

It is sometimes argued that women's lesser physcial strength compared to men justifies the relatively low proportion of women working in construction, engineering and so on. We only have to compare the physiques of Fatima Whitbread, the javelin thrower and Colin Moynihan a former British Minister for Sport, to realize that this is a gross generalization. There are plenty of strong women and weedy men, although it is certainly more acceptable for men to be strong and muscular. Boys and men are more likely to be encouraged to build their physical strength compared to their female peers: muscles are still seen as relatively unfeminine. In practice, many manual jobs do not actually require extremes of physical effort, as a female engineering apprentice told me during a study of young women's entry to the Birmingham job market:

> Everybody thinks that because it's a man's job that you are throwing lumps of metal about, you've about two ton in weight, just pigging 'em around for an encore, and it's just not true. Now I can show you places where men are lifting half a ton, a ton, and I can do it, 'cos all you need to do is go on a slinging course. You've got radio-operated cranes and crane drivers, nobody lifts anything in this day and age. Well they do, but not

all the time. It's rubbish anyway, some men are small and weedy, and couldn't lift a feather, and some girls are dead strong.

It is seldom acknowledged, but much of the effort involved in domestic work and childcare can be extremely strenuous. I remember watching a woman with two small children squeezing along the gangway of a crowded bus. One child was perched on her hip, while the other clutched her free hand, which held a full shopping bag. This woman was about seven months pregnant, and the picture did not match the common sense assumption that women are weak, fragile creatures who are incapable of heavy physical work, especially when they are pregnant.

In contemporary Britain, women have had the right to vote for over 50 years; we have been able to study for degrees for around 50 years (although Cambridge University only began to award degrees to women in the late 1940s); and single women working in teaching and the civil service need no longer leave their jobs if they get married. Women have entered many occupations and areas of higher education which were previously the exclusive preserve of men, especially women from more affluent White and middle-class groups. While much has changed in education and employment over the past 50 years, most women to not actually work alongside men at the same jobs, and major areas of inequality remain. However, the one area which has seen far less change in the distribution of women's and men's work has been the domestic sphere. This chapter is concerned with the ways in which psychology has looked at distinctions between 'women's work' and 'men's work' and their effects on our everyday lives, especially in relation to domestic work and family life. Home and family life is still seen as a private space, as a cosy refuge from the harsh pressures of the public domain, and as a place where differential sex roles are assumed to be naturally ordained.

In the majority of British households, there is a marked sex and age distinction in distribution of domestic jobs. Older women (usually mothers) tend to do most of the cleaning, cooking, shopping, washing and childcare, regardless of whether they are employed in a job outside the home. Younger women (usually daughters) tend to 'help out' with some of these tasks, perhaps cooking the tea or washing up each day. Older men (usually fathers) most often do car maintenance (or at least take the car to a garage) and do some of the gardening and decorating jobs. If paid workers are employed to do some of these tasks, they are usually women, their wages are low, and the money often comes out of the mother's pay packet. Boys and men are the least likely to do housework or childcare on a regular basis, unless perhaps it is paid work.

Psychological Theories of Sex Differences and Gender Relations

Psychology has put forward several explanations for gender-based divisions of labour, such as those between 'women's jobs' and 'men's jobs' in the home. The first rests on *biological determinism*, and argues that males and females differ in their psychological and social aptitudes and abilities as a result of fundamental variations in biological or physiological characteristics. These theories point to inbuilt genetic or physiological variations, or different hormonal patterns between the sexes as the prime causes of any apparent sex differences in behaviour. So we have Jerre Levy, an American psychologist, arguing in 1972 that women are not suited to work in engineering or the business world because of the different lateralization of their brain hemispheres compared to men. These ideas have been reasserted in recent years by the British geneticist Ann Moir, and by some British and North American psychologists.

There is another element which is often treated as part of these biological determinist ideas: evolutionary theories which have drawn on versions of Charles Darwin's work. This approach argues that contemporary sex roles in which men are breadwinners and women the primary caregivers and domestic workers in the home are a result of evolutionary developments from the so-called 'hunter-gatherer' societies. Some contemporary researchers argue that differential sex roles stem from a biological imperative which is now reflected in the inherited characteristics of all women and men, rather than being a product of specific social, environmental, economic and political conditions. There is considerable debate about whether such distinctions between 'man the hunter' and 'woman the nurturer and gatherer' ever did have a universal relevance. Biological determinism argues that inherent sex differences are immutable, natural and universal. Biological determinist theories usually ally themselves with the status quo, and any attempts to change patterns of behaviour are then assumed to be 'going against nature'. These assumptions are not supported by available research evidence.

According to these various biological determinist theories, women are assumed to be more 'naturally' suited to housework (and child-care): more patient, nurturant, caring and capable of self-sacrifice than men. There are several problems with this assumption. Firstly, psychological research on sex differences, of which there is a great deal, indicates that there are hardly any consistent or universal variations between women and men in behaviour, aptitudes, abilities or personality characteristics. Even where sex differences do seem to exist, closer examination reveals a greater degree of variation *within* each sex than *between* them. That is, there is greater variability between individual women and between individual men than there is between women as a group and men as a group.

Patterns of behaviour and social expectations about appropriate female and male attributes vary considerably in different cultures. Any sex differences which have been identified appear to be highly situation-specific, or dependent on the precise social context. There is no clear evidence of a consistent genetic, hormonal or physiological differences between women and men which would imply that women are more 'naturally' suited to do the vacuuming, cleaning or the shopping, and men to work in engineering or construction, or to be waited on hand and foot in the home. There is no physiological evidence for the 'maternal instinct', or for children's need to have a primary caregiver who is their biological mother. Infants do appear to thrive with one consistent, affectionate primary caregiver, but that person does not have to be female, or even their biological parent. As yet, geneticists have found no evidence of a gene for cleaning up babies' sick. There is no solely biological, physiological or evolutionary justification for the marked sex differences in the distribution of women's and men's jobs in the home, or in the labour market.

Of course, significant biological and physiological differences between women and men *do* exist, and they can have a major impact on our lives. Most women are capable of bearing children, while men are not, and most women menstruate for a major portion of their lives, which men do not. Yet even here, we can never separate such biological variations from their social context. Women who are malnourished due to poverty (or anorexia nervosa) will be less likely to menstruate and may lose the capacity to conceive children — at least on a temporary basis.

The other major explanation which psychologists have put forward to explain apparent sex differences in behaviour or attitudes are usually referred to as *social constructionsim*. This argues that all societies operate with powerful and pervasive ideologies about appropriate behaviour for women and men, which encourage us to adopt suitably feminine and masculine attributes and abilities according to our biological sex. The process by which such ideas are transmitted is known as *socialization*, and when this is used with specific reference to sex and gender it is usually termed *sex-role socialization*.

One of the key means of transmitting messages about dominant sex and gender expectations is through gender (or sex-role) *stereotyping*. Stereotypes can be defined as perceptions of people or social groups based on relatively rigid, oversimplified and overgeneralized beliefs or assumptions. When people perceive in terms of stereotypes they tend to exaggerate differences between social categories, and to minimize differences within social categories, or to disregard individual differences. So we tend to focus on differences between women as a group and men as a group, and ignore variations between individual women and individual men. Gender stereotypes are among the most commonly held of all stereotypes, and they have proved extremely difficult to change, particularly among men. Stereotyped beliefs may, or may not, have any objective basis, or the basis on which they were originally founded may have changed long ago. According to such gender stereotypes women are expected to conform to dominant ideas about feminity and men to dominant ideas about masculinity.

We are all expected to fit within the gender stereotypes and sex roles of our society, which are cross-cut by age, race, class and culture. These have varied considerably in different historical periods. The dominant feminine stereotype includes the image of the weak and fragile woman who is supposedly incapable of strenuous mental or physical effort. This wilting figure emerged during the last century in Western industrial societies, at a time when most women of the upper classes were encased in restrictive and damaging corsets and hampered by long skirts, as well as the narrow-minded ideas of Victorian patriarchs. The image of the weak female was used to undermine women's attempts to attain equal access to the education provided for their male peers. Although weakness was supposed to be an inherently feminine characteristic, such fragility was not expected of poorer working-class and Black women. As Sojourner Truth, an ex-slave, pointed out in 1851 at the First National Convention on Women's Rights held in the USA:

> I have ploughed, and planted, and gathered into barns and no man could head me! And ain't I a woman? I could work as much and eat as much as a man — when I could get it — and bear the lash as well! And ain't I a woman? I have borne thirteen children and seen them most all sold off to slavery, and when I cried out with my mother's grief, none but Jesus heard me! And ain't I a woman?

The roles of wife and mother (for which all women are assumed to be destined) are associated with characteristics of nurturance, caring, always being at the service of the rest of the family, and doing most of the housework and child-care. The roles of husband and father are associated with being the breadwinner and financial provider, the authority figure whose place is at the head of the household, and the one who is not generally expected to clean the bathroom.

According to the social constructionist argument, women do most of the domestic work not because of a 'natural' propensity to do the dusting, but because girls are taught from an early age that housework is an integral part of the female role, and boys are taught that it is definitely *not* part of the male role. Nurturance, tolerance for boring unpaid work and making sacrifices for others are seen as appropriately feminine characteristics, while competitiveness, aggression and independence are viewed as desirable masculine characteristics, at least in Western industralized societies. In addition, many people are surrounded by appropriate sex role models. Most of our own mothers will probably have done much of the housework and child-care, with fathers (and other male household members) doing far less. Allied to this we have a set of common ideas which present such an inequitable distribution of domestic work as 'natural', despite research evidence to the contrary.

Even today the media continue to portray women and men quite differently. Women are usually presented as mother figures and skivvies, dumb blondes, helpless victims (usually in a white dress and high-heeled shoes) or evil temptresses (frequently portrayed with dark hair). Men appear as more active characters, the centres of attention, glamorous lovers who ride off into the sunset, or aggressive murderers and macho heroes. In the Western media, most characters are still White and European, with working-class and Black characters usually portrayed as deviants, criminals or humourous figures. Some feature films and commercials are beginning to go against this trend, but they are still exceptions to the general rule. The main change in recent years has been the increased portrayal of women as competent (or at least as existing) in the workplace in more prestigious white collar jobs. In the kitchen very little has changed in the media as in everyday life.

Most contemporary psychologists prefer to adopt an *interactive* approach to the debate about Nature versus Nurture, viewing biological and physiological factors as parallel influences which operate alongside social and cultural forces. Most recent psychological research has attributed apparent sex differences to socialization, stereotyping and the role of ideological and cultural pressures. Explanations for gender imbalances in the distribution of housework and child-care lie in the organization of our social lives, rather than our genetic make-up, hormonal cycles, physiology or human evolution. The argument that man is the 'natural' breadwinner and woman must be the sole caregiver and guardian of hearth and home wears rather thin when in 1981, only 5 per cent of British households fitted the ideal nuclear family pattern of father in full-time waged work, mother as a full-time housewife and 2 or 3 children. Although contemporary Western societies present the nuclear family as a universal ideal and the heart of civilized society, it is actually a fairly recent historical development which is most common among White European middle-class groups.

If most psychological research refutes the notion of consistent and universal sex differences, why do women still do most of the housework, even in households with women in waged work and unemployed males, which became increasingly common during the 1980s? Why do ideas about women's and men's 'natural' roles continue to exert such a powerful influence? The answer may lie partly in the treatment of gender relations and domestic work in the mass media and in some sectors of the research literature, which has until recently mirrored dominant ideas about housework and child-care being 'women's jobs'. For example, Stanley Parker, an early theorist in the sociology of leisure, referred to housewives in 1971 as having 'nothing but free time'. Any woman (or man) who has actually undertaken primary responsibility for unpaid domestic work, with or without paid employment, will appreciate the fallacy of this notion. Unlike paid work, housework is never-ending, a continual battle against grime, fluff and clutter. It is usually only noticed when it is *not* done, and there are no agreed criteria of cleanliness.

Stanley Parker took men in full-time paid work as the norm for his analysis of work and leisure in contemporary British society. No doubt he had never undertaken domestic work on a full-time basis, nor even listened to the experiences of full-time housewives, or he would have hesitated before including the latter alongside 'prisoners, the unemployed and the idle rich' as one of those groups with 'nothing but leisure'. This tendency to treat work as synonymous with waged work, and the pattern of unbroken full-time employment as the norm is fairly common in research studies and in the popular press. Unpaid domestic work and employment which has been interrupted by child-care commitments, are both presented as different from this norm, and then treated as problems which must be solved. Such assumptions overlook an alternative approach, which would see men's relative lack of responsibility for domestic work and child-care as the real problem.

Yet Stanley Parker's ideas are also reflected in some of the 'excuses' made for men's tendency to avoid domestic work. Housework is not treated as 'real work', partly because it is usually unpaid, and partly because women do most of it. This connection between status and gender also operates in waged work. Occupations which have predominantly male workforce tend to have higher status, better pay and prospects than those with a mainly female workforce. In the USA, medicine is a predominantly male occupation and is highly valued, while in the Soviet Union, it is a mostly female occupation and has a relatively lower status. When particular jobs shift from having a predominantly male workforce to a majority of female employees, they tend to lose status, such as clerical work and teaching in the early part of the twentieth century, and the British newsprint industry in more recent years.

Social psychology research tells us that our everyday experiences play a crucial role in shaping our psychological appreciation of the world. Someone who has been a face worker in a coalmine for the past thirty years will probably associate a markedly different set of meanings with the notion of 'work' than the Chairman of the National Coal Board, a bank manager or a teacher. Someone who has spent the past twenty years shopping and cooking meals for a family of four will no doubt understand the notion of 'housework' rather differently compared to those who have sat at the table each day to find a meal placed before them — and washed up after they have finished. Since women do almost all of the domestic work, we can expect women to have different experiences of and attitudes towards housework and child-care compared to men. So while Stanley Parker might have had few qualms in describing full-time housewives as having 'nothing but leisure', his mother might have disagreed.

Yet people do not necessarily experience their surroundings in a straightforward way. We all operate in relation to extremely complex sets of ideas, representations, images and assumptions which form part of the dominant ideologies in a given culture. These ideologies are not neutral: certain ideas and images appear as taken-for-granted, part of the popular 'common sense', while others are presented as dangerous, unreasonable or foolish. Such dominant 'common sense' ideas can be extremely difficult to challenge, and they often reflect or justify the perspectives of those who occupy the most powerful positions in society. So the ideas of the Coal Board Chairman (can you imagine a Chair*woman* of British Coal?) would be more likely to be taken seriously than those of the face worker in a coalmine. Similarly, Stanley Parker's ideas about housework and leisure would be given more credence than the perspective of women who actually do the work, due to his status as an authoritative male academic.

While women who are full-time housewives and mothers may be unlikely to describe their work as 'easy' or to feel that they have 'nothing but free time', they may well refer to their status as 'only a housewife', reflecting back this 'common sense' devaluation of themselves and their work. We live in a society in which the vital work involved in bringing up a family is valued far below the work of a merchant banker or a nuclear physicist, at least in economic terms.

Every time a woman — or a man — obviously does not conform to prevalent ideas about what is 'natural' for their sex, this challenges the common sense idea that sex, gender and sexualities are biologically determined, universal and immutable. As pop star Boy George put it when responding to questions about his appearance:

> What I'm doing, whether I say anything or not, is making people accept effeminate men. I'm making people accept it into their homes and kitchens ... it's in your head. You don't have to be a man. Men weren't born to drink beer ... When people accept Boy George they're accepting ... that men can act in a different way from how they're expected to behave.

Sometimes such contradictions are explained away by viewing the deviant as an exception that proves the rule. An example here is provided by reactions to the female engineering apprentices in Birmingham, as Mary's supervisor, Mr Wright, put it:

> The problem is not the girls, the problem is the male chauvinists' ideas ... There's got to be a certain breed of girl who will stand the rigours of a factory like this, 'cos it's pretty heavy and dirty. They have to be pretty special.

And sometimes such 'deviants' are simply ignored, as in the mysterious disappearance of Fatima Whitbread's reaction to her record-breaking javelin throw of 77 metres at the 1986 European Games. In the live television coverage immediately following this throw, Fatima Whitbread told the ITV commentator that she was most thrilled because her performance would have given her eighth place in the men's competition. This comment was broadcast only once: it was edited out of all subsequent television coverage.

The television coverage of major athletic events provides ample evidence of the massive variety in female and male physiologies and the social construction of desirable feminine and masculine attributes and abilities. We now know that women can play tennis, run marathons and do sprint cycling without keeling over in a dead faint. It is only since 1884 (first women's Wimbledon title; played in tight corsets and long skirts), 1984 (first women's Olympic marathon) and 1990 (first women's sprint cycling competition at the Commonwealth Games) respectively that women have been able to participate in each of these sports in major competitions.

In most events the gaps between female and male performances have been narrowing at a rapid rate. These games are organized along rigidly sex-segregated lines, such that women and men hardly ever compete with each other in mixed events. In some events, such as sailing, mixed competitions ended as soon as women's performance improved to such an extent that they posed a potential threat to the men. Could it be that the only reason for separate sex competition is to prevent a woman beating a man? Might this explain the mysterious disappearance of Fatima Whitbread's comment about coming eighth in the men's javelin competition? Some events are only ever entered by women or men, and these usually fit well within the image of dominant gender stereotypes. We have the new Olympic sports of rhythmic gymnastics and synchronized swimming (in full face make-up) for women, and the suitably macho weightlifting for men. Note the words and phrases used by commentators when presenting such sporting events. Can you identify any differences between the treatment of male and female athletes, or is the commentary gender-neutral?

As we enter the 1990s, there is a common assumption that 'it's all different now' and that 'women have equality'. During a discussion of domestic responsibilities as part of the study of Birmingham school-leavers, there was some dispute about this new era of equality:

> *Vanessa*: It's always us girls that have to do the cleaning and cooking, boys never do any.
>
> *Terry (male)*: But it's not like you say really. Middle-class men are different. Things have changed now, it's more equal. What you say sounds very old-fashioned. When most married women go out to work, fathers help out in the house more now.
>
> *Vanessa, Jacinta and Penny* (shouting): No! Rubbish: When did men ever do anything? It's helping out that's all, not cleaning up sick. Men never clean the toilets.

Despite these debates about whether the age of women's liberation has really arrived, major areas of inequality remain. As a United Nations report for the Decade of Women stated in 1980:

> Women constitute half the World's population, perform nearly two-thirds of its work hours, receive one-tenth of the World's income and own less than one-hundredth of the World's property.

So we still have a long way to go. Why has the age of the mythical New Man not produced a more equal disbribution of domestic tasks? How might the relatively uneven distribution of domestic work be changed, and the continuing, if somewhat diminished, separation between 'women's jobs' and 'men's jobs' be removed? To end on a positive note, there are some households which do not fit the traditional pattern. When actress Pauline Collins was receiving an award for her part in the feature film *Shirley Valentine*, her husband John Alderton made the following comment in a television interview:

> When Pauline was working on the film, lots of people said to me, 'Oh

ow wonderful of you to look after the kids while she's working'. But no one ever said to Pauline, 'Oh how amazing, you're looking after the kids while *he*'s away'. No one ever noticed. But to me we're a partnership, so we support each other.

Tutorial Discussion Questions

1 List all the individual members of your current household, noting their age and sex. This may be a family group, or a student house. If you live alone in a flat or a room in a hall of residence, think of your family home. Now list the distribution of household jobs which are *regularly* carried out by each household member. Simply washing up every other week is not enough: these must be jobs which each person does on a regular basis, and for which they take responsibility. Include as many of the following jobs as you can:

> Washing up
> Cooking
> Shopping
> Cleaning, e.g. vacuuming, dusting, cleaning the bathroom
> Child-care (if relevant)
> Car maintenance (if relevant)
> Gardening (if relevant)
> Washing clothes, bedlinen, towels
> Painting and decorating: indoors and out (if relevant)
> Any other major tasks you can think of.

As you work through this list, try to note down whether some household members do washing, cleaning or cooking for themselves as well as other people, while others do only their own chores. In some cases, people from outside the household may be paid to do particular jobs: a daily cleaner or a child-minder. Make a note of whether anyone gets paid for these jobs, their sex and how much money they receive. When you have finished, look through your list and note whether there are any systematic variations in the distribution of domestic work in your household by age or by sex.

If you are doing this exercise in a tutorial group, make sure the tutor participates as well, and then compare notes across the whole group. Your group may well include a diverse range of household structures, some of which may be more sharply differentiated by age and sex than others. Some households may be more egalitarian in the distribution of domestic tasks, using rota systems, or have complete role reversals, with older males doing most of the child-care or cleaning, and women carrying out car maintenance and heavy gardening work.

2 Think about those household members, if there are any in your group, who do less than their share of domestic jobs. What reasons do they, or other household members, give for this? If your household is remotely similar to those sampled in recent British research, some of the following comments might strike a familiar chord:

> 'He's fairly enlightened, he just hates housework.'

50

'I could probably do it better than her, but she won't let me help.'

'He make so much mess when he *does* do it that it's easier to do it myself.'

'It's easy, but I couldn't do it.'

'I'd get bored doing it, but she's got more patience than me. I think women have more patience than men.'

'Perhaps I'm old-fashioned, but I do think this equality thing has gone too far the other way now. So we all keep to our own jobs.'

'She does most of the housework, but then it's not really work is it? Women have an easy life really.'

There are two things to point out about these 'excuses'. Firstly some of them include generalized assumptions about women as a group and men as a group ('Women have more patience than men.'). Secondly both females and males can make such comments, but the last two in the list are specific to men. You may be able to think of other points for discussion, and your group may have come across other 'excuses'.

3 Make a list of feature films or television series which include a 'career woman' character, and discuss the ways in which such characters are portrayed. Can you identify any common themes, or persistent dilemmas which 'career women' characters often face? Are they presented in a sympathetic manner, or as potentially dangerous and evil figures? What might the male version of this role look like: a 'family man', or the mythical 'new man'? Alternatively, you could examine a sample of television commercials and note how often female and male characters are presented doing housework and childcare. Can you identify any consistent patterns which are gender-specific?

4 If most psychological research refutes the notion of consistent and universal sex differences, why do women still do most the housework, even in households with women in waged work and unemployed males, which became increasingly common during the 1980s? Why do ideas about women's and men's 'natural' roles continue to exert such a powerful influence?

5 Why has the age of the mythical New Man not produced a more equal distribution of domestic tasks? How might the relatively uneven distribution of domestic work be changed, and the continuing, if somewhat diminished, separation between 'women's jobs' and 'men's jobs' be removed?

Further Reading

BLUE, A. (1987) *Grace under Pressure: The Emergence of Women in Sport*, London, Sidgwick and Jackson.

DAVIS, A. (1982) *Women, Race and Class*, London, The Women's Press.

GRIFFIN, C. (1985) *Typical Girls? Young Women from School to the Job Market*, London, Routledge and Kegan Paul.

HARGREAVES, D. and COLLEY, A. (Eds) (1986) *The Psychology of Sex Roles*, London, Harper and Row.

SAYERS, J. (1983) *Biological Politics: Feminist and Anti-Feminist Perspectives*, London, Tavistock.

SHARPE, S. (1984) *Double Identity: The Lives of Working Mothers*, Harmondsworth, Penguin.

WILKINSON, S. (1986) *Feminist Social Psychology: Developing Theory and Practice*, Milton Keynes, Open University Press.

Chapter 6

The Myths and Realities of Rape

Patti Mazelan

The Historical Context

Rape is treated by the law as the most serious of sexual offences carrying for the convicted offender a maximum penalty of life imprisonment. Unfortunately, the unambiguous definition of what rape actually is and whether or not the female has consented to have sex has generated a great deal of argument both inside and out of the courtroom.

In Great Britain, rape has been recognized as a criminal offence since Anglo-Saxon times when King Alfred deemed that the severity of punishment for rape should depend upon the social status of both the offender and the victim. If a lowly slave was the offender, he could be castrated or killed whereas a wealthy lord might be required to merely pay compensation to the father or husband of the victim. The economic status or 'bride price' of the woman remained crucial in determining the appropriate punishment for any rapist until about 1066, when the law was extended to encompass the high value then placed upon the 'virtues' of virginity and chastity. Consequently, the punishment for rape now also depended on whether the victim was a virgin or sexually experienced. In this feudal era, the legal and religious sanctity of marriage was so venerated that the custom of 'stealing an heiress' by forcible abduction and marriage became a routine method of acquiring property by adventurous, upwardly mobile knights. Gothic literature romantically imbued heiress stealing with midnight assignations, loyal maidservants and knights in shining white armour. In reality, the motives of these knights were the desire for land not love. In this period 'rape' meant to steal, to seize or to carry away (from the Latin word *rapere*), but in 1275 a statute of Westminster erased the distinction between virgin and non-virgin rape and within ten years rape had come to be identified with the modern concept of penetration of the penis.

Since these early times the rape legislation has been changed in a number of significant ways: in 1487 abduction was defined as a felony in its own right, and in 1597 the death penalty for rape was introduced. By the time of Elizabeth I, rape was viewed as a purely sexual offence independent of economic considerations. In 1736 Sir Matthew Hale, deeply concerned about 'false' accusations of rape, introduced the cautionary instruction given to the jury in rape trials and which is still in use today:

It must be remembered, that rape is an accusation easily to be made and

Patti Mazelan

hard to be proved, and harder to be defended by the party accused, tho'
never so innocent.

Hale's negative attitudes toward women were widely evident in his conduct at rape
and witchcraft trials alike, and his emphasis on the credibility of the complainant
was further reinforced in 1812 when 'past moral character' of the complainant was
made legally admissible as evidence and remained on the statutes until 1976.
Women could now be questioned on 'want of chastity', prostitution and any prior
relationship with the offender. In practice this meant that it was accepted that the
defence could name a women's sexual partners in court, could ask whether she was
a common prostitute, and even probe whether the victim was 'morally fit' to accuse
the man of the offence. In addition to Hale's cautionary instruction, the media
often gave the impression that complainants were frequently lying. Widespread
discontent resulted in the campaign for reform of the Sexual Offences Act (1956),
and public concern was heightened by the outcry at the Law Lords ruling of one
particular case which proved to be a watershed in changing the law.

The case involved a Captain in the British Army. Captain Morgan had invited
three men to have forcible intercourse with his wife, having given them the false
impression that she was extremely willing although he had warned them to expect
that she would strongly resist their advances. Even though the assailants were
initially convicted at their trial and their sentence upheld on appeal, a further
appeal to the House of Lords reversed the original guilty verdict. This judgment
highlighted a fundamental legal principle: an assailant must not only have
committed the illegal act (*actus reus*) but also should have intended to commit it
(*mens rea*).

This decision provoked a fierce controversy with many people now of the
opinion that the balance of the law had swung too far in favour of those accused of
rape. This public concern culminated in the formation of the Heilbron Committee
in 1975 which gave urgent consideration to the law of rape and recommended
changes in both the law and its practice. Following this recommendation the Sexual
Offences (Amendment) Act was passed by the House of Commons in December
1976 and this forms the basis for much of the current rape law.

Under the current law, evidence relating to the past moral character of the
victim is no longer admissable except under the judge's discretion, although in
most trials judges still allow 'moral' evidence. Other areas of the law are still
unacceptable to many: notably a man cannot rape his wife, and a 14-year-old boy is
deemed incapable of sexual intercourse and therefore cannot be convicted of rape.
However the main areas of current dissatisfaction centre on what is meant by
offender intent and victim consent. The issues touch upon a range of legal,
cultural, psychological and social factors. The changes in rape legislation reflect
prevailing social attitudes, and although current legislation attempts to protect the
victim in her own right rather than her chastity or her guardian's property, many
believe that there are still fundamental problems in inferring intent and defining
consent.

Intent and Consent

In order that a charge of rape is successfully brought to court we have seen that it is
necessary not only to prove that the act was committed but also that the assailant

intended to commit the crime. Despite the recent changes in the rape law the onus of responsibility still rests with the victim to prove that she did not precipitate the crime. Many criminologists and psychologists believe that rape victims intentionally or unintentionally trigger their own victimization, and labels such as 'collaborative', 'non-objecting', 'participatory', 'seductive', 'negligent', 'lacked discretion' and 'had some complicity' have been frequently used in describing rape victims. Some early studies even suggested that child victims of sexual offences precipitated abuse because they had behaved in an appealing, submissive and seductive manner.

From this perspective adult rape victims are seen to precipitate sexual attacks upon themselves because of their desire for aggressive sexual treatment, with the offender's use of force conveniently serving to diminish guilt feelings which normally would inhibit such willing participation. The concept of victim precipitation was first used in the context of Amercian homicide. Marvin E. Wolfgang, an American sociologist investigating a large sample of homicides in Philadelphia, was struck by the fact that many of the victims were themselves responsible for initiating a series of events which ultimately led to their own demise. For example, an aggressive individual often prompted even more severe retaliation and their own weapons could be used against them to lethal effect.

Sometimes, the victim's behaviour prior to the homicidal attack was causally implicated in the crime and this concept of 'victim precipitation' was enthusiastically transferred to the rape context by one of Wolfgang's students, Menachem Amir. In his seminal book, 'Patterns in Forcible Rape', Amir (1971) systematically documented the demographic details surrounding a large sample of rapes in the Philadelphia area. Amir adopted a very broad definition of victim precipitation and included any victim behaviour which may be interpreted by the assailant to signify that the victim was sexually available. This definition includes normal socializing and clearly favours the viewpoint of the assailant. Since almost any form of behaviour on the part of the victim could be interpreted to signify willingness to have sex, the status of victim precipitation in the rape context is suspect. In fact there appears to be only an extremely small proportion of victims of this type, although many psychodynamically oriented descriptions persist in attempting to identify these women who consciously or unconsciously precipitate their own rape.

In interpreting those approaches it must be borne in mind that there is a distinction between victim precipitation and victim vulnerability. Although both concepts are broad in scope and ill-defined, a range of factors which may predispose an individual to becoming a victim has been suggested. In one early typology, Von Hentig listed a variety of commonly conceived victim types. This list included the young, the old, mental defectives, immigrants, females, the depressed and the lonely among others. The purpose of the exercise was a naive attempt to distinguish 'born' victims from 'society-made' victims. In this view, since a woman is born a female she is a 'born' victim, whereas the 'wanton' (another Von Hentig descriptor) is a victim made by society, since her character is 'obscured and dimmed by the rough generalization' of laws and social convention. In a later typological exercise, Mendleson attempted to distinguish between the guilt of the criminal and the guilt of the victim in an attempt to evaluate their relative degree of guilty contribution to a crime.

All of these supposedly scientific offerings effectively shift the blame for a personal crime from the offender to the victim, and although the quaint language of some of the early typologies makes them an easy target for ridicule, it is apparent that the later descriptions of victim precipitation contain within them an implicit and often illogical belief that victims are responsible for the crimes committed against them. In fact there is no consistent picture of the typical victim type and many researchers have clearly demonstrated that any female can get raped. This is not to deny that there are many patterns of rape and often victims are similar to offenders in terms of age and socio-economic status. Young working-class women are more likely to get raped, although young college-educated women are more likely to attempt to resist rape. Clearly there are patterns in the incidence of rape which are discernible, but to link these patterns to the notion of victim precipitation is a contentious issue confounded by the often overlooked distinction between personal crime in general and rape in particular.

Unlike murder laws, the rape law does not include any category whereby an assailant can be charged if it has been shown that he had no intention to commit the act. In other words, there is not an equivalent to manslaughter within the rape law. Whether such a category is desirable is debatable and many have argued that the legal insistence on *mens rea* shifts the balance in the assailant's favour. The legal processing of rape cases always involves tackling the issue of determining the assailant's assumptions about the victim's willingness to consent, and this activity inevitably results in assessing the degree of responsibility or precipitation that the victim has engendered. In other words, the operation of the rape law recognizes the interplay between assailant and victim and consequently needs to deal with the perennial and sticky question of motive. Inferring covert motives from retrospective evidence is an activity fraught with difficulty. These motives cannot easily be determined and often the assailant or victim may themselves not be fully aware of their own motives in the events surrounding the crime. For example, a man apprehended for rape may not have specifically intended to commit a rape, but may have intended to shift the probability of certain events in a desired direction through his conscious and planned actions and interventions. His intention may have been to engineer a female into a situation where she was vulnerable to his sexual advances. Having achieved this he may have forcibly pressed his attentions upon his partner, assuming that her own actions had suggested consent. In an instance such as this the law requires that the motives of both parties be disentangled. In practice, this is not an easy matter.

The problem of inferring covert motives from overt behaviour is as much a psychological issue as a legal one, and Gagnon and Simon (1974) have provided a useful insight into this issue by viewing the concept of motive within the framework of 'sexual scripts'. Scripts have been defined as the 'coherent sequence of events expected by an individual, involving him as either a participant or an observer'. In other words, scripts are an internal mental representation of events in the real world, and since they are future directed, they are in a sense anticipated 'slots' into which ongoing events are encoded and understood. In this way scripts are generalizable to new situations, and social behaviour depends upon a participant selecting a particular script from his or her repertoire to represent the given social situation.

This is a critical insight into how actions may be selected on the basis of what might be called for in certain circumstances. Stevie Jackson (1978) has suggested that different sexual scripts are an important source of misunderstanding between the sexes. Many rapists claim to have genuinely misunderstood the sexual signals prior to the offence, and this may be due to the activation of their inappropriate sexual scripts which lead them to under- or overestimate certain aspects of situations.

Levine and Koenig (1983) have suggested that rapists may have a fine dividing line between fantasy and reality and this may imply that the sexual scripts of rapists are more easily activated than the sexual scripts of non-rapists. However, most studies have not found clear differences between rapsits and non-rapists despite a wide variety of measures being employed. These studies have typically used 'static' measures of intelligence, aptitudes or dispositions and the failure to detect differences may be due to the inability of these measures to tap much of relevance to the process of rape. In the context of the dynamic sequence of events which characterize such a crime, more sensitive and cognitively based measures may yet reveal critical differences between the mental structures and processes of rapists compared to the 'normal' male population. Alternatively, the feminist contention that 'all men rape' or would do so given the opportunity (for example, in conditions of war) may prove to be broadly true.

The Social Context of Rape

It is apparent that the common perceptions of what constitutes rape are influenced not only by the sexual and aggressive acts which occur but also by prevailing cultural views on what constitutes male and female sexuality. The feminist movement has significantly altered the societal view of rape. The feminists stress the systematic oppression of women by men and assume that rape is a conscious or unconscious weapon used by men to keep women dependent on men's protection:

> Man's discovery that his genitalia could serve as a weapon to generate fear must rank as one of the most important discoveries of prehistoric times, along with the use of fire and the first crude stone axe. From prehistoric times to the present, I believe, rape has played a critical function. It is nothing more or less than a conscious process of intimidation by which all men keep all women in a state of fear (Brownmiller, 1975).

> Rape is the assault of a man on a woman but it is also the symbolic enactment of social and cultural attitudes; on one level, perhaps unconscious it is a gross and extreme form of social regulation by which a woman is brutally stripped of her humanity and confronted with her definition as a non-person, a function (Metzger, 1976).

Many feminists see rape as essentially an act of violence in which the sexual aspects are less meaningful than the aggressive aspects of the attack. The focus of much feminist debate on rape has been to bring into sharp focus the symbolic nature of women's role in society. Central to the feminist understanding of rape is the complex of factors which can be called the 'cultural' component. For example, it has been argued that 'rape is the logical and psychological extension of a dominant-submissive, competitive, sex-role stereotyped culture'. In this view, sexuality is intrinsically entwined with power and aggression in some cultures. In different cultural contexts this is not the case and rape is less likely or impossible. Consequently, feminist definitions of rape tend to emphasize the aggressive component of the offence and examine it in its cultural context. This aggression against women is not always explicit but implicitly colours all those situations where men can exercise power over women. The sexual nature of rape has been emphasized in much humour, pornography and newspaper reporting so that the aggressive or violent nature of the act is frequently ignored or devalued.

The feminist emphasis on what feminists consider to be the real nature of rape highlights the numerous ways in which the offence is defined. Victims' own definitions of rape are frequently at variance with legal definitions. Women who define themselves as rape victims were typically those who had suffered acts in which the assailant's penis was involved (e.g. rape, sodomy, fellatio, masturbation by the victim). In contrast those who had been assaulted but who defined themselves as 'rape avoiders' tended to be those who suffered 'vaginal events' (e.g. cunnilingus, digital penetration of vagina or anus, kissing and fondling the woman). Legally, at least in England, rape is identified with vaginal intercourse, whereas in some American states the definition of rape includes forced anal or oral sex or vaginal penetration by foreign objects. Many feminists consider the legal definition of rape should cover more acts than are outlined in the current legislation and these should include unconsented sexual intercourse by a husband and cases of male or homosexual 'rape'.

Feminists have emphasized the fact that our society tolerates interpersonal violence, and this coupled with prevailing negative attitudes towards women result in what they have described as a 'rape culture'. This emphasis on the oppression of women by men has been valuable in reshaping people's attitudes towards the crime, although ironically the emphasis on a rape culture could be argued to diminish assailants' personal responsibility. Further, the confusion with which many people view the crime has not been diminished by definitions of rape which many feminists find acceptable. For example, the London Rape Crisis Centre defines rape as follows:

> Rape is not confined to forcible penetration of a woman's vagina by a man's penis. It is all the sexual assaults, verbal and physical, that we all suffer in our daily contact with men. These range from being 'touched-up' to being brutally sexually assaulted with objects . . . we use the word 'rape' to describe any kind of sexual assault.

Attitudes to Rape — Attributions of Responsibility

Many empirical studies have indicated that men and women have different perceptions of rape and rape victims. Typically, not only are men more sensitive to the possibility of false accusation, but they also tend to regard victim precipitation as a more important factor than do women. Some men even believe that rape would do some women good. These male perceptions of the crime are not confined to lay male sections of the society. Male physicians are often accused of displaying moralistic and judgmental attitudes toward rape victims and it has been suggested that they tend to dismiss the psychologically damaging aftermath of the crime. In a similar way, policemen and male jurors have themselves been accused of displaying negative attitudes towards rape victims and it seems that the victim must be prepared to face accusations of lying, coupled with an excessive amount of scorn and scepticism about their behaviour and lifestyle.

However it would be misleading to suggest that these negative attitudes are a male prerogative. Women also have been shown to view rape victims in a very negative light and this raises the important question of why victims are so often treated in this derogatory way. One explanation comes from the area of attribution theory, and with respect to rape research, one approach has been called the 'just world hypothesis'. This contends that people need to believe that their environment is a just and orderly place where people usually get what they deserve. In other words, people tend to blame rape victims in order to maintain a stable, predictable and controllable view of the world. Despite the intuitive appeal of attribution theory, it is less of a theory and more of an explanatory framework into which almost any result can be interpreted to fit within its domain.

The Consequences of Rape

It is useful to distinguish between the intrinsic and the extrinsic consequences of rape. Intrinsic consequences are those concerned with the short- and long-term reactions of the victims to the offence. Extrinsic consequences of rape include attitudes to the victim and the activation of the legal process. These will be discussed briefly in turn.

A large number of *rape-induced symptoms* have been identified and these have included fears and phobias (e.g. of men, sex, feeling unsafe, pregnancy, veneral disease), obsessive thoughts, somatic symptoms, quality and quantity of sleep, emotional symptoms (e.g. anger, revenge, guilt, shame) and even suicide. Most rape victims initially react to the assault with shock and disbelief and in this stunned state may be unable to think clearly or react effectively. Often during the assault itself, self-preservation and fear of injury or death are the prevailing reactions. Even in this state of shock it seems that victims try to cope by using a number of mental strategies, such as methods to keep the victim's mind off the event, memorizing details for the purposes of subsequent reporting, and recalling previous violent experiences in order to think of a means of escape.

These strategies probably serve as a means of the victim disassociating from the event in order to cope with the attack. These coping strategies appear to extend beyond the time-scale of the attack itself and the term 'rape trauma syndrome' has been coined to describe both the short-term and the long-term pattern of victim reactions. Often victims experience an acute phase of disorientation which lasts from a few days up to several weeks after the rape. In addition, a longer-term process of reorganization occurs which typically starts some 2 to 3 weeks after the attack. One consistently reported reaction is that rape victims feel a loss of control following the attack. This loss of control is similar to the reaction experienced following any highly stressful or traumatic event and takes the form of emotional insecurity characterized by a perceived inability to control the environment. In extreme cases victims become unable to care for themselves.

Rape Crisis Centres have evolved out of the concern expressed by the Women's Movement in the USA and Britain. These groups believe that rape victims have special needs and require special treatment, since negative attitudes toward victims are perpetuated in part by cultural myths which surround the crime. The apparent durability of these myths is thought to stem from the view that rape symbolizes basic divisions in a patriarchal society. In this way feminist groups view rape as much a political as a legal issue.

Rape crisis centres first appeared in the USA in the late 1960s and their initial aim was to offer sympathetic support to the victim. Practically the objective was to help the victim medically, legally and emotionally. Often it seems that all the victims required was a counsellor who was warm, calm, empathetic, firm and consistent. The first rape crisis centre appeared in this country in London in 1976 and by 1984 twenty-five or so had sprung up in the major British cities. Registered as charities and utilizing voluntary workers, they provide 24-hour telephone crisis lines, advice and information. Increasingly they have taken on the role of a pressure group, and the routine handling of rape complaints by the police has been a consistent target for severe criticism.

The *extrinsic consequences of rape* are initiated by the reporting of the offence. Of course not all offences are reported and estimates of reporting rates of rape are low compared to the reporting rates of other personal crimes such as physical assault. Following reporting, making a statement and providing forensic evidence, the subsequent stages become the responsibility of the police. Theoretically the victim need do nothing more until the offender is charged and brought to trial.

However most rape investigations generate little detection work on behalf of the police. In the bulk of those offences where the assailant is apprehended it is typically the victim who provides evidence that quickly guides the police to the suspect. It has been suggested that it is precisely those cases where the suspect knew the complainant and denies the offence which receive the least amount of police investigation. Further it appears that cases of this type the victim is less likely to see her attacker punished.

The Toronto police in Canada dichotomize rape cases as 'founded' and 'unfounded', and Clark and Lewis (1977) recategorized their rape files using their own interpretation of these terms. 'Founded' refers to those cases where the police believed the complainant and consequently initiated further police action. 'Unfounded' refers to those cases in which the police do not perceive the complaint as serious or genuine and consequently do not initiate any further police action. The authors erected a third 'founded/unfounded' category which included instances which could not be unambiguously allocated to the 'founded' or 'unfounded' categories. Clark and Lewis report that many more cases were 'founded' under their interpretation of the categories than under the police interpretation of the categories. In addition, certain victim characteristics were significantly associated with whether or not a case was categorized as 'founded' or 'unfounded' by the police. Where victims were 'idle', on welfare, cohabiting, divorced or prostitutes, it was more likely that their complaints were categorized as 'unfounded' by the police. Other studies have also demonstrated that some victims are taken less seriously than others with little justification: just as muggers can be mugged, so prostitutes can be raped.

The police are not always impartial in determining the manner in which rape victims and cases are treated within the legal system. The police can decide whether a victim is believed, whether a case is sufficiently investigated, and whether the quality of the courtroom presentation is adequate to ensure a reasonable possibility of conviction. The breadth of police power is such that the victim who does not receive full police cooperation for any reason is less likely to see her case brought to a successful outcome.

My own research has tackled the question of whether prevailing attitudes to rape and rape victims have been institutionalized into the legal and judicial system. It appears that prejudicial beliefs are part of the culture and are institutionalized in the legal system to some extent. However these do not operate in the blanket fashion suggested by many researchers in this area. Specifically, rape suspects are dealt with in four consecutive stages by the legal process, namely, apprehending, charging, appearing in court and sentencing. For a variety of reasons, not all suspects are processed through all four stages and at each stage some suspects may leave the system. Of those suspects who are apprehended, some are not charged, some do not make a court appearance, and some are not subsequently found guilty and sentenced. At each stage of the process there is a wide range of factors influencing the number of suspects who enter and leave the system. By comparing the suspect 'dropout' rates at any particular stage and relating these to key descriptive factors about the offence, it is possible to systematically examine the association between these factors and the routine management of rape cases.

A common misconception is that unless the victim resists to her utmost she is unlikely to be believed by the police or treated seriously by the courts. However my results suggest that suspects received no differential treatment by the system on the basis of the victim's resistance and reactions.

Conversely, many researchers have suggested that victims who were virgins prior to the assault are most likely to be treated seriously by the policy and courts and this was borne out by differences in suspect dropout rates. Those accused of raping a virgin were more likely to be processed further through the judicial system.

Tutorial Discussion Questions

1 Murder differs from manslaughter in that murder involves intent to kill whereas manslaughter does not. Do you think there could be any value in an equivalent unintentional rape crime and how could this be defined?
2 Few academic studies have shown many reliable psychological differences between rapists and non-rapists. Why do you think this is the case?
3 Feminists see rape as a means by which men oppress women. Do you think this is a useful way of looking at the problem of rape?
4 Do you think that rape of a virgin should be treated more seriously than rape of a prostitute?

References

AMIR, M. (1971) *Patterns in Forcible Rape*, Chicago, University of Chicago Press.
BROWNMILLER, S. (1975) *Against Our Will: Men, Women and Rape*, Harmondsworth, Penguin.
CLARK, L. and LEWIS, D. (1977) *Rape: The Price of Coercive Sexuality*, Toronto, Women's Press.
GAGNON, J. H. and SIMON, W. (1974) *Sexual Conduct*, London, Hutchinson.
LEVINE, J. and KOENIG, S. (1983) *Why Men Rape*, London, W. H. Allen.

METZGER, D. (1976) 'Is it always the woman who is raped', *American Journal of Psychiatry*, **133**, 4, pp. 405-408.

RUSSELL, D. (1975) *The Politics of Rape: The Victim's Perspective*, New York, Stein and Day.

Further Reading

HOOPER, C. A., MANNING, B. and PECK, J. (1984) *Sexual Violence: The Reality of Women*, London, The Women's Press.

KATZ, S. and MAZUR, M. A. (1979) *Understanding the Rape Victim: A Synthesis of Research Findings*, New York, Wiley.

MCNICKLE, R. V. (1977) 'Rape as a social problem. A byproduct of the feminist movement', *Social Problems*, **25**, pp. 75-89.

Chapter 7

Bereavement

Barbara Dodd

And what is the greatest marvel?
Each day death strikes and we live as though we were immortal,
This is the greatest marvel.

Mahabharata

Introduction

In contemporary society, death and bereavement present difficulties which were not experienced in the same way earlier this century. People used to signal their bereaved state by wearing black, removing themselves from society for a given length of time, and by attending death watches and wakes. This process was disturbed by the advent of the First World War. Although most people were bereaved of a family member or a friend in the resulting high death toll, the efficient continuation of the war effort required that minimal disruption was caused to the productive capacity of society. Black arm bands were introduced as the only concession within a war-stricken society. Following the end of the war the previous rites and rituals, designed to facilitate and recognize the mourning process, were not reinstated.

Added to this we have currently a much lower infant mortality rate and people live longer. In contrast Victorian families were better acquainted with death. Not only was there a higher perinatal mortality rate, but also adults died young with such diseases as tuberculosis; average life expectancy was little over 50 years. Today the majority of us die over the age of 65 and in an institution of some sort. The combination of these factors has contributed to death and the process of mourning becoming a forbidden area, ignored and even ostracized. Today bereaved people are not expected to show grief, or not for very long, and they are expected to cope without much support.

Yet people need to feel sad and to feel the pain of mourning and grief so that they can accept the reality of their loss, adjust to the environment in which the deceased person is missing, and then withdraw their emotional energy and reinvest it in another relationship (Worden, 1983). We first learn to do this as children, feeling sad at very small losses, such as when we cannot have our own way. Then we do it more directly as we learn to separate from our mother or mother-figure and she leaves us for increasing lengths of time. A degree of sadness and distress is healthy for children; if the mother is over-protective she will prevent the child from experiencing separation, sadness and loss, and as an adult that person will be very disadvantaged when trying to cope with bereavement. The opposite of this, where the mother or mother-figure leaves the child through death or desertion, can also be devastating and continue to affect the individual throughout their adult life.

While the mourning experience is unique to each individual, some commonly occurring factors can be identified. The particular constellation of these factors and their intensity, frequency and duration will depend on, for example, how close the bereaved person was to the person who died, their previous experiences of death and loss, and the nature of the death. This chapter will outline the normal bereavement process for adults and children, and it will also suggest some simple strategies to facilitate acceptance of death, aid the grieving process, and address societal taboos.

Bereaved Adults

Bereavement is a process, not a state; it is constantly changing, not a static feeling. It is characterized by a number of reactions, not all of which occur for all individuals, nor necessarily in the order to be outlined. Parkes defines four phases of mourning: numbness, pining, mitigations, and recovery.

Numbness

The initial reaction on hearing of the death of someone close is normally shock. The individual may feel bewildered, numb, lost or even mildly concussed (Parkes, 1975). This initial delay of distress can be useful if the individual needs to organize the funeral arrangements and inform other people. There is also a danger that this postponement of feeling may not be reversed, with the mourning process delayed indefinitely.

Pining

The second phase is one of yearning or pining, when the dead person is intensely missed. Along with persistent and intrusive thoughts of the person who has died may come feelings of being pushed into an unsafe, unreal and unfamiliar world. The degree of stress which the individual feels will depend on a number of factors. These include how close he or she was to the dead person, their previous experiences of death or other losses, and their ability to cope with stress and anxiety in general. Others factors include whether the death was natural, accidental, suicidal or homicidal; whether the death occurred geographically close or far away; and whether it was unexpected or there was advance warning.

Sometimes there is uncertainty about whether someone is alive or dead, particularly in wartime. If a soldier is reported missing, is he or she dead or alive? Sometimes prisoners of war are reported dead, relatives grieve and complete the mourning process, and then the prisoner returns at the end of the war. Some losses are socially unspeakable, such as suicide; others are socially negated, such as abortion; and some losses occur in the absence of a social support network. Any sort of isolation is likely to impede the mourning process, but the presence or absence of all these factors will influence the intensity, frequency and duration of distress reactions.

Grief is usually episodic pangs of severe anxiety and psychological pain, rather than prolonged depressed feelings. Physical sensations include a deep sighing respiration, dry mouth, tightness in the throat and/or chest, and a lack of energy. There may also be feelings of restlessness, aimless hyperactivity or difficulty in concentrating. Accompanying this may be an urge to search for the lost person, a behaviour common to many species of social animal; the greylag goose, for example, restlessly searches for a lost mate, uttering penetrating cries over a long period in order to locate a bird who may be in danger. When experienced by a human during the bereavement process, the individual usually wants to search through photographs, or go to places or seek objects that had a shared meaning.

During this second phase feelings of protest, anger and/or guilt may occur. These may be appropriate but they are often inappropriate as people reproach themselves for human imperfections. These feelings may be expressed as irritability or bitterness and may be misunderstood by companions as being directed against them personally.

Mitigations

The third phase is one of mitigations, where bereaved people employ various means to relieve the anxiety and tension while adjusting to their new circumstances. This is a time of cognitive restructuring as the individual creates a new mental map of their life which excludes the dead person. Even if managed successfully this can be a difficult time, when the individual goes to great lengths to 'bring back' the dead person.

One of these ways is by experiencing hallucinations. While this is often a psychiatric symptom, it is a normal and not unusual experience following the death of someone close. Auditory hallucinations include 'hearing' a key in a latch at the time of the day the person who died would previously have been expected home. Visual hallucinations include 'seeing' the person among a crowd. Similarly illusions occur when the bereaved person acts 'as if' the person is not dead, and lays a place at the table. Depersonalization may be experienced when the bereaved person feels as if they are not in their own body. This is a limbo state while he or she restructures their reality. Another aspect of this third phase is 'worry work' which is a painful repetitive recollection of the loss experience. For many people this is a necessary part of the grieving process which gradually allows them to restructure their lives.

All or any of these experiences may be expected during bereavement and they are all normal if they are short-lived and not severe. Some may not occur at all, or not in the order that has been given, or they may be unexpectedly re-experienced, as people differ in the way they react. Similarly the timing of the phases varies from one person to another, but this is not a process which is completed in a few short weeks. Even if the individual has started to enter the fourth phase of recovery within twelve months it is likely that the anniversary of the death will trigger a recurrence of some of the thoughts and feelings of an earlier phase.

Recovery

The recovery phase is when the bereaved person starts the process of gaining a new identity. After pining there is often a period of uncertainty and apathy with feelings of depression. Eventually the individual habituates and can then start learning and putting into practice new solutions to the difficulties posed by the death of someone close.

Helping Bereaved Adults

There are four basic tasks to be addressed if the mourning process is to be completed satisfactorily. The first is to accept the reality of the death; the second is to identify and express the associated feelings; the third is to find alternative solutions to the problems posed by the death of someone close; and the fourth is to withdraw the emotional energy from, and say a final goodbye to, the person who has died so that the energy can be reinvested in other relationships.

These four tasks can be applied to the counselling steps necessary for facilitating uncomplicated grief or to intervening therapeutically in the case of pathological grief. However the structure of these tasks is also useful in providing guidance for social interaction with people who have been recently bereaved, and this will be outlined here. It can sometimes be difficult for people who have never experienced bereavement to know what to do to help and it can be equally difficult for bereaved people to ask for the help they need.

The initial shock and numbness will probably make the immediate acceptance of the death unlikely. Instead the bereaved individual may need help with even the simplest decisions, and value company and support during the final visit, the journey home, while informing other people, making funeral arrangements and just getting on with daily tasks. Seeing the body either at the hospital or in an open casket at the undertakers can initiate the process of acceptance. Attending the funeral will further help to register the death and can help to draw the family closer and provide social support. If there are exceptional circumstances preventing attendance at the funeral, such as severe psychological trauma because of the nature of the death or physical injuries sustained in an accident, a memorial service arranged for a later date can fulfil much the same purpose.

Acceptance usually comes gradually and often over many weeks, and can continue while tasks two and three are being addressed. The provision of a quiet supportive atmosphere will often be sufficient for an individual to feel secure enough to express their feelings. People mostly need an opportunity to talk, to start the process of 'worry work'. This can give them permission to mention emotional reactions too, especially if the listener can accept whatever is expressed without probing or avoiding the grief. The feelings may include anger, guilt, fearfulness or helplessness. Listening, accepting the feelings and sharing the tears and sadness without being ashamed or destroyed by them is probably the most useful and valuable activity that can be offered at this stage. Some protection from intruders, but without possessiveness, may also be welcome early in the process (Parkes, 1975).

Religious institutions can also provide enormous support for some people, whether they are normally religious or not. However some people experience a temporary loss of faith, so a sensitive approach is crucial. Organizations such as CRUSE, Compassionate Friends, and Samaritans are also prepared to offer time, support and a listening ear. CRUSE was initially organized to support widows, but has more recently widened its brief to support anyone who requests help. Compassionate Friends is an organization of bereaved parents prepared to support other bereaved parents. Samaritans is a telephone helpline open to anyone who feels depressed, without hope, or suicidal.

Bereaved people sometimes find that their intake of alcohol is higher than normal or that they are smoking more than they usually do. Similarly medication may be requested because of difficulty in sleeping. Grieving can be very debilitating early in the process and sleeplessness can contribute further cumulative distress. There is however a danger that these mitigating procedures can be used as a substitute for grieving and block the process. They need give no cause for concern in the short term, as long as they are used circumspectly, and they are relinquished early in order to allow the grieving process to take its natural course.

Sometimes people need to be reassured that they are not going mad. Vivid nightmares, distractibility, hallucinations and unusually strong emotions can be frightening. Similarly the need to weep does not mean that a person is on the edge of a nervous breakdown. All the symptoms and experiences outlined above can be expected during grieving, and they are all normal, particularly if they are short-lived. On the other hand the mortality rate of widows and widowers is considerably increased over normal expectations in the six months following the death of a spouse. Signs that the individual may need professional help include an absence of grief when it is expected, lasting physical symptoms, excessive guilt or anger, and a persistent intense grieving or thoughts of suicide.

The third task of finding alternative solutions to the problems posed by the death of someone close can be illustrated by a young widow with children living at home and lacking a supportive network of relatives living near. Her difficulties may be compounded if, for example, her husband managed the household finances, or she has a history of depressive illness, or she comes from a family background that did not encourage the expression of feelings. Parkes comments that

> in any bereavement it is seldom clear exactly what is lost. A loss of a husband, for instance, may or may not mean the loss of a sexual partner, companion, accountant, gardener, baby minder, audience, bed warmer, and so on, depending on the particular roles normally performed by this husband.

While initially a young widow is likely to be understandably overwhelmed by an amorphous grief, very gradually she will become aware of the problems posed by the absence of her husband. Once these have been identified she is in a position to evaluate the various solutions. For example, she may want to learn very quickly how to manage the household finances if this had previously been her husband's responsibility. This can be particularly crucial if her husband's death caused a change in the family's income. In general recently bereaved people should avoid making any further major life changes if possible, such as moving house, changing job or career, or forming a new sexual relationship. At one level it may appear that such changes could facilitate the move towards a new identity, but if this is done too quickly the grieving process will not be completed. The resulting delayed grief may be expressed in physical or psychiatric symptoms which are only relieved by grieving intensely later when it can be more difficult for the person to go back and work through the pain he or she has been avoiding.

The difficulties involved in decision-making following the death of someone close need to be acknowledged. Previously these decisions may have been shared, and if we stay with the example of a young widow, her need to make them alone can result in a feeling of desolating isolation. This is particularly true when decisions over children need to be made. Some widows find enormous comfort in their children. The danger then is that the children may be called upon to support their mother when they need supporting themselves. Conversely the mother may find her children an added burden, yet feel guilty that she is being a poor mother, and is not making alternative arrangements for them. Gentle suggestions to call upon the social network available will avoid an unhealthy insularity of the family, provide alternative solutions to problems, help the mother to develop any necessary skills, and ultimately increase her self-esteem.

This will help her to deal with the fourth task when this is timely, and to say a final goodbye to her husband and reinvest her emotional energy in another lifestyle. This recovery process may begin with going on holiday, a move which can be particularly significant if holidays were previously always shared. A widow may also need overt permission to stop mourning with reassurances that she is not being disloyal to her deceased husband. This can be particularly apposite if she wishes to enlarge her social activities to meet new men and women. It is important though that she establishes her autonomy and independence with a new identity before she commits herself to a new sexual relationship, which may be expected to take about two years.

Bereaved Children

The process of bereavement for children is not essentially different from that for adults, but it is not so easy to discern and it is expressed differently according to the age of the child. Children bereaved of either parent or of a sibling are a rarity in our society, so they are likely to be unique within their social and school environments, which may compound their mourning difficulties.

The child's reaction will depend on a number of factors, including his or her age, how close their relationship was with the person who died, and the presence or absence of immediate substitutes. Also important is the child's previous experience of loss and the family's attitude towards death. However the most important factor is the child's relationship with the person who has died; the most traumatic bereavement experience is the death of the mother or mother-figure.

Reactions vary with the child's age, and these will be outlined in more detail below, but they are likely to be more intense if there is evasion or lying, or if the child is excluded from the family's grief and mourning. Even if the child remains at home with a loving father and mother-substitute, is told the truth and participates in the family mourning, some disturbed behaviour may be expected. The child may regress to earlier patterns of behaviour or evidence fears of the dark, illness, dying or punishment. Other symptoms include sleeping difficulties, the possibility of nightmares, eating disturbances, breathing difficulties at night, fear of ghosts and anger over feeling abandoned.

From Birth to Six Months Old

In the case of a child less than 6 months old, Winnacott (1958) stated that 'there is no such thing as a baby'. He wanted to emphasize the inseparability of infant and caretaker, and that an infant cannot survive and grow without an intimate, individual relationship with an adult who is usually his or her mother. So the unit is not the 'baby' but the 'mother and baby'. If the mother dies suddenly the baby should be cared for, if possible, by someone who knows him or her, in the child's own home, but the most important factor is that the person should be able to give him or herself up fully to the child.

It can be hard for a grief-stricken father to do this when he also needs to give himself time and space to mourn his own loss. Another member of the family, not so affected by grief, may be more appropriate, but no more than three people at the most should be closely involved. Babies can pine when they lose someone to whom they are closely attached. They show it by not eating or sleeping, by crying and irritability, and by frequent illnesses. Most babies will recover quickly if they can form an attachment with another care-taker (Black).

Six Months to Two Years Old

From 6 months to 2 years of age a child is increasingly able to hold the concept of a person in their absence. He or she is also increasingly attached to the mother as a separate and specific person, and will search for her in her absence. So how old does a child need to be to understand 'dead'? It helps if the child has had some concrete experience with death and can name something as dead, such as a goldfish, a bird or an insect. The child will not understand in the abstract, but can understand that it will not live again.

It can be confusing for a child if bodily death and the hereafter are not kept separate. Explanations such as 'gone to heaven' or 'gone to be with Jesus' may be intended to shield the child (as well as help the adult avoid their own pain). Unfortunately for the child who thinks concretely, this may mean that the parent has gone away somewhere and is refusing to come back.

Even at this young age, the bereavement process is one of shock, followed by protest with loud screams and obvious anger, despair, pining and longing. The child withdraws and is uninterested in toys, food or activities. If this separation response continues the infant will become detached from his or her mother and from other people. The child needs a constant caring person to take over, and this may not be easy. It is with infants of this age that parents' and other adults' denial of childhood bereavement begins. This is possibly because the child's distress makes their own distress unbearable. At first the infant may be inconsolable for its mother. Initially no one can replace her or remove the anguish. It seems that no amount of comforting eases the pain but the comforting must continue because only that way will the pain eventually be eased.

Barbara Dodd

Two to Five Years Old

Two-year-olds may approach death not with horror but with fascination. There may be a matter-of-fact curiosity about death, but their understanding is complicated by the attempts of adults to protect them. The permanence of death may be difficult to grasp and the child may really expect that the dead person will return. Or they may have fears of sleep if they are told 'death is like going to sleep'. Their thinking is very concrete, so they may translate 'gone to heaven' as being a star. They are also very egocentric, so may think that they have caused the death.

For children with little opportunity for accurate information, magical thinking can surround death. What the child is told at the time of death can be crucially important and can increase either comprehension or magical conceptions. If the child is 'protected' then the mystery plus the family's distress are likely to foster fantasies yet Furman (1974) found that children from 2 to 8 years old can mourn appropriately. When children do not seem to understand fully and ask seemingly inappropriate questions, parents erroneously perceive their children as being little affected. Behavioural changes may not appear for several weeks, but children's concerns are revealed in their play and children can be affected by the distress of the bereavement for many months and sometimes for years afterwards.

Five to Eight Years Old

By 8 years of age, the child's conceptualization would seem to be very similar to that of an adult. Death is understood as a natural process, it is irreversible and it can happen to anyone — including the child. With the development of a conscience there is also a sense of guilt. The child may believe, even more so than in younger years, that the death was the result of their own actions or inactions, or of their secret wishes.

The child is now less dependent on actions for expression and is more verbal, and may use denial as a defence. He or she is particularly likely at this age to act as if nothing had happened and even appear as uncaring, unaffected and unloving. If this is misunderstood and the child is not comforted their need to mourn may be ignored. This may be compounded if the child hides tears because of a fear of loss of control, exposure or infantile dependency. He or she may also fear that the other parent is vulnerable, or that they will be expected to replace the dead person, or that they could have, or should have, prevented the death in some way. In addition they may also idealize the lost parent and create a fantasy bearing little relationship to the actual parent.

Eight to Twelve Years Old

The child's understanding of death is now equivalent to that of an adult, although abstract concepts such as heaven may still be difficult. The child is increasingly aware of the possibility of its own death with the associated fear. Some children experience these fears directly, some displace or project them, and others deny them. Many children fear sleep or darkness and search their bodies for symptoms of disease. They may be frightened by what they think they find, yet seek no help.

Children of this age (and older adolescents and adults, too) may revert to egocentric and magical thinking.

Helping Bereaved Children

Furman (1974) emphasizes the importance of coping well with the experience of the first few stressful days following the death of someone close to a child, because it sets the stage for all aspects of mourning. If it is a parent who has died the child will need the surviving parent's physical presence and emotional closeness. If the parent is overwhelmed, or is not as available as he or she would like to be, a significant other person can play a complementary role. Similar support will also be necessary in the event of the death of a sibling.

The child will need to be told the news of the death clearly and unequivocally, in an age-appropriate manner by someone who is close to and trusted by the child. It is important that he or she is told the truth and helped to accept the finality and irreversibility of the death: 'Your mummy has died. That means she will never return'. This is a difficult task which may need to be repeated as the child is unlikely to take everything in immediately.

The child should be encouraged to participate in the funeral or burial rites and in the mourning rituals of the family and the community, otherwise the person may be perceived as having inexplicably 'vanished'. The adults around a child will need to strike a balance between offering sympathy and giving clear permission for the child to mourn his or her loss in overt and intense grief until time heals. They can also talk about their sadness and share with the child their regret that the person is no longer able to share ordinary everyday pleasures. This may help to bring to light any problems such as guilt. Similarly enquiries about what the child really knows of the causes of death can help to undo any magic or mystery. Use can be made of play with the child, particularly of playing house with a bereaved family.

Idealization by the child can be avoided by not emphasizing the parent's attractive side, and isolation can be avoided by encouraging the child to seek consolation outside the broken nuclear family. As the child moves towards the recovery phase, the adults will need to address the balance between security and adventure and gently encourage the child to be appropriately adventurous physically, socially, mentally and emotionally.

Tutorial Discussion Questions

The bereavement process is about loss, not just about death, and can be related to other loss experiences such as divorce/separation, the effects of the emigration of a young family on an older generation, redundancy, amputation of a body part, HIV/AIDS, national disasters, rape and so on.

1   What differences or similarities would you expect for each of these?
2   What difficulties do you think are involved in defining an abnormal grieving reaction, e.g. getting 'stuck' in the bereavement process; having a higher than expected intensity, frequency or duration of reactions; or experiencing a complete absence of reactions when they might be expected?

3 If an abnormal grieving reaction is defined, how would the four tasks described on pages 70–72 be applied to help resolve the difficulties?

4 Would you expect preparation or advanced warning to ameliorate bereavement effects for you? The research on this is equivocal.

5 Finally, sadness is an inevitable part of loss but regrets can be minimized if the death taboo is addressed. With this in mind what would you like to say now to the important people in your life?

References

BLACK, D. *The Motherless Child — A Few Words for Widowed Fathers*, A CRUSE publication leaflet.

FURMAN, E. (1974) *A Child's Parent Dies: Studies in Childhood Bereavement*, New Haven, CT, Yale University Press.

PARKES, C. M. (1975) *Bereavement: Studies of Grief in Adult Life*, Harmondsworth, Penguin.

WINNACOTT, D. W. (1958) *Collected Papers: Through Paediatrics to Psychoanalysis*, London, Tavistock.

Further Reading

BOWLBY, J. (1980) *Attachment and Loss: Loss, Sadness and Depression, Vol. III*, New York, Basic Books.

RAPHAEL, B. (1983) *The Anatomy of Bereavement*, New York, Basic Books.

WORDEN, J. W. (1983) *Grief Counselling and Grief Therapy*, London, Tavistock.

Chapter 8

AIDS: Psychological, Social and Political Reactions to a Modern Epidemic

Keith Phillips and David White

It is barely credible that nine years ago Acquired Immune Deficiency Syndrome (AIDS) was unknown. In the brief time since, AIDS has become a major medical and social issue. It has provoked varied reactions from nations, institutions and individuals and spawned fierce debate of matters rarely researched previously, including individuals' sexual practices. The statistics upon AIDS and the manner in which they have been presented have generated much fear and given rise to myths surrounding the disease. Persons with AIDS have been stigmatized and victimized. Important moral, ethical and legal questions have been raised concerning individuals' rights to conduct their behaviour in private and society's need to protect the public health.

The medical facts of AIDS are well established. It is caused by the human immunodeficiency virus (HIV) which attacks one type of the body's white blood cells, the T-helper lymphocytes, reducing the competence of the immune system and rendering the body vulnerable to opportunistic attack by malignancies and infections. Infection with HIV is not the same as AIDS. HIV infection may be entirely asymptomatic, or accompanied by a range of symptoms including swollen glands, weight loss, diarrhoea, fever and fatigue. The presence of these symptoms is referred to as AIDS-related complex (ARC). The diagnosis of AIDS requires additional identification of an opportunistic infection or malignancy that otherwise does not occur in humans with an intact immune system. Most AIDS fatalities are caused by a particular variety of pneumonia (*Pneumocystis carinii*), a rare cancer of the skin called Kaposi's sarcoma, or tumours of the lymphatic system.

A vaccine against the virus has not been developed and in the absence of an effective medical treatment the only viable strategy against AIDS is primary prevention by limiting the spread of HIV infection in the population. That can only be achieved by persuading individuals voluntarily to adopt behaviours that are likely to minimize the spread of the virus. Modifying behaviour in this regard is a major challenge for psychologists since evidence indicates that health behaviours (e.g. smoking, alcohol abuse) are not easily changed. This chapter evaluates steps so far taken to encourage behavioural change to prevent AIDS and questions whether psychological principles indicate that alternative approaches should be adopted.

Behavioural Transmission of HIV

Mere exposure to HIV does not inevitably result in infection since the virus is poorly transmitted. Despite this the spread of AIDS worldwide has been rapid. The first four cases were reported in 1981 in the USA. By August 1989 that American figure had increased to over 100,000 and it is estimated that there are now 1.5 million Americans infected with HIV. Worldwide, 186,803 cases of AIDS have been reported from 152 different countries, although owing to under-reporting the true figure is estimated by the World Health Organization to be 500,000. In the UK the number of confirmed cases of AIDS in November 1989 was 2,717 of which 1,465 had resulted in death, and at least 10,000 individuals are estimated to be infected by HIV.

Statistics show that AIDS first spread within epicentres of HIV infection such as San Francisco, New York and Los Angeles and was associated with individuals with histories of homosexuality or bisexuality. Subsequently cases were reported amongst haemophiliacs and injecting drug users (idus) who had been infected by contaminated blood products. The initial prevalence of HIV/AIDS among these groups encouraged the erroneous social representation of AIDS as a disease confined to deviant or marginal groups. This myth has led to social injustices and the victimization of persons with HIV or AIDS. It also has acted as an obstacle to the adoption of behaviours to limit the spread of HIV by encouraging notions of invulnerability in persons who do not see themselves as belonging to 'risk groups'. Individuals outside those groups do not regard AIDS as something to concern them. Metaphors used by the media reinforce the myths about AIDS and the language used by even well-informed individuals suggests that they have internalized these. For example, language that refers to 'innocent victims' confirm the suspicion that perceptions of innocence and therefore guilt exist. The moral judgments implied have significant implications for intentions to modify one's own behaviour. Strategies against AIDS must eliminate the myth that AIDS is spread by particular groups such as gay men, rather than by behaviours that allow transfer of body fluids from an infected person to someone non-infected.

Although the statistics show that in Western countries HIV infection has been particularly associated with homosexual or bisexual males and with idus, it is not confined to these groups. Heterosexual transmission is increasing in the USA and UK, as too is prenatal and perinatal transmission from mother to infant. The patterns of transmission vary in different parts of the world. In Central Africa AIDS is a heterosexual disease with approximately equal numbers of women and men infected with HIV. Transmission here occurs through heterosexual intercourse and non-sterile medical procedures.

Transmission of HIV can occur by several routes but primarily by the exchange from an infected to a non-infected individual of sexual fluids (male-to-male, male-to-female, female-to-male) or the exchange of blood products that have not been screened for HIV (haemophiliacs, blood transfusions, injection with non-sterile needles, perinatal exchange from mother to child). Particular behaviours that have been identified as potential risks are: unprotected intercourse (without the use of condom), either vaginal or anal, with a partner who is HIV infected; exchanging blood with an infected person via non-sterile needles and syringes as may occur by the sharing of 'works' between injecting drug users. Engaging in these behaviours with many different partners further increases an individual's personal risk of encountering HIV. These risk behaviours account for the vast majority of cases of AIDS in the USA and UK. Although HIV has been detected in many body fluids including blood, semen, saliva and tears, no cases of transmission have been reported from either saliva or tears and there is no evidence that the virus is transmitted through casual contacts such as kissing, touching or sharing cutlery.

Reactions of Governments

Evidence that the rate of spread of AIDS was doubling each year, that no cure was available, and that it would spread rapidly within entire populations on a worldwide basis forced governments to respond to the challenge. Different governments have responded in different ways. These various reactions reflect something of the political and economic structures of those various countries. An approach widely considered is screening and testing for antibodies which signify HIV infection. This approach is one that appeals also to many members of the public. Secondly, the introduction of mass education campaigns designed to alert the public to the existence of HIV infection and to encourage changes in behaviour has been widely employed. The following two sections consider the value of these two measures as precautions against AIDS.

Screening for HIV

A number of countries (e.g. Cuba, Bulgaria) have expressed a wish for mandatory screening for HIV of their entire population. Others require testing of citizens returning from abroad (Iraq), of foreign visitors (USSR), or immigrants (USA). Many more have introduced legislation that allows mandatory testing of selected individuals such as prostitutes, idus, or in some instances individuals suspected of these activities. In all of these instances the authorities have ignored the danger inherent in such measures, namely that the problem is not eliminated but simply driven underground causing the emergence of marginal groups outside the reach of health services and beyond the scope of educational programmes. Appeals for mass screening also ignore the prohibitive financial cost involved, as to be effective screening would need to be repeated at regular intervals. Long-term reliance upon screening to prevent AIDS is a recipe for the increasing prevalence of HIV infection.

Anonymous HIV testing has been a contentious issue in the UK. There has been considerable debate among doctors and politicians as to whether blood taken from a patient for other tests should be tested anonymously for HIV. Anonymous testing would allow statistics to be gathered to show the true incidence of HIV infection in the population, something that is otherwise difficult to establish. That statistic is necessary for accurate forecasting of future health needs for AIDS patients and their likely costs. Critics argue that anonymous testing is an abuse of individual rights that offers no advantage to the individual since donors could be neither informed of the outcome of the test nor advised of their health status. Even though it might establish the prevalence of HIV, anonymous testing would be of limited value for policies of prevention since it provides no information at all about the way in which the virus is being transmitted within a population. This information is critical for planning interventions that might be effective against further transmission in that population. Preventive measures must take account of different patterns of transmission in different populations and different countries.

In September 1989 the UK government revealed plans to introduce anonymous testing of half a million people for HIV from routine blood samples taken from newborn babies tested for treatable disorders, attenders at clinics for sexually transmitted diseases, hospital in-patients and pregnant women. The patients could not benefit from the tests as the samples would not be identified by individual simply by origin. Despite objections that such tests taken without specific consent of the patient are unethical, the proposals are supported by the British Medical Association and many AIDS experts because of the need to gather accurate statistics to allow planning and policies about AIDS.

Voluntary tests for HIV are offered by health services in several countries and may be regarded as a compassionate measure that should be available on demand to individuals who see themselves at risk. Even in this instance, however, there may be costs for the individual. Someone whose test is negative on one occasion may continue to engage in behaviours that place them at risk for the future. There must be guarantees of confidentiality if discrimination against individuals is to be avoided and counselling must be provided for all clients, not only after their test results are known but also before, to explore the meaning of the test and the possible social, health and employment consequences for someone taking the test. In some instances of course, voluntary testing may be of considerable value. For example, pregnant women may wish to know their HIV status if they consider themselves at risk and would wish to consider therapeutic abortion if they found themselves to be infected. Similarly women injecting drugs may wish to know their HIV status in consideration of contraception or planned pregnancies.

An undesirable consequence of screening is that individuals may see this as an effective protection against AIDS. Studies in the UK and France have shown that well-educated and knowledgeable adults and young people identify vetting of individual partners or screening the population for HIV as effective precautions against AIDS. They deny or fail to recognize the obvious shortcoming of personal vetting, that those potential partners with most to deny might be least forthcoming about their past behaviours, and the economic impracticality of mass screening programmes. It must be recognized that a negative test result can only be taken to mean that a person did not carry antibodies to HIV at that moment. It is not a lifetime guarantee of immunity.

Public Education Campaigns

National AIDS campaigns have provided public education by means of messages distributed via delivery of leaflets to individual homes, television, radio and print media. The assumption underlying these mass education campaigns has been that knowledge about AIDS will cause people's attitudes to change which in turn will lead to changes in behaviour. Unfortunately, there is no compelling evidence that mass education campaigns have been altogether effective in achieving the first step in this chain, namely communicating accurate information and increasing knowledge about HIV and AIDS. The majority report that television is their major source of information about AIDS. Unfortunately, although television is an effective medium for conveying simple facts and raising awareness of an issue, it is not the best medium for conveying complex health messages. Evaluations of these campaigns in the UK, USA and Sweden clearly show that they have been highly effective in increasing awareness of AIDS among the general population, but of itself this does not lead to behaviour change. Knowledge of HIV/AIDS has increased over the years. Early studies reported only moderate levels of knowledge about AIDS among adolescents, students and other adults. Recent studies show higher levels, although some gaps in knowledge still exist. Despite these gains in knowledge there is little evidence of intentions to alter behaviours.

One difficulty is that the public are not passive receivers of information. They have 'lay beliefs' that influence their attention to, and their willingness to accept or reject, the 'truth' of those messages. Individuals' lay beliefs may be determined by information from other sources including media metaphors that distort the facts or confirm myths and stereotypes associated with AIDS or persons with AIDS. Furthermore they do not share equal amounts of knowledge about AIDS, and public messages that contain no new information for some may be beyond the comprehension of others. This is a particular problem when trying to present material that is appropriate for young people who may, for example, have limited personal experience of sexual practices. Lay beliefs may further interfere with accurate perceptions of risk and provide obstacles to the adoption of preventive behaviours. Education based upon personalized learning experiences is beyond the scope of mass campaigns, but may be necessary to bring about changes in behaviour. This theme is considered later.

To increase knowledge is difficult, but to alter attitudes has proved yet more problematic. Several surveys in different countries have examined people's knowledge and attitudes towards AIDS, before and after particular education campaigns, or as trends over time following cumulative exposure to public education campaigns about AIDS. They find that although the general level of knowledge has increased in recent years attitudes have changed much less.

Many studies have shown that individuals and particularly heterosexuals are not adopting effective preventive measures and do not intend to alter their sexual behaviours. A study of adolescents found that although 70 per cent reported themselves as sexually active only 15 per cent had changed their behaviour as a result of AIDS. Questionnaire surveys of students' knowledge, worry and moral perceptions of AIDS conducted before and after the UK national AIDS campaign in 1987 found little evidence of change. A significant reduction in 'worry about AIDS' had occurred. However there was not change in students' moral attitudes towards AIDS, and though more knowledgeable there was little evidence that these students believed that behaviours to reduce the risk of HIV infection would change. Similarly another survey of sexual intentions and practices of students found little evidence of behavioural change, or appreciation of individual risk even for those engaging in high-risk activities.

There is little evidence that mass campaigns have been successful in bringing about changes in behaviour that effectively protect against AIDS. This is not surprising when one considers the psychological processes that underlie behaviour change. This simple idea of a sequential process where knowledge leads to a rational decision to alter behaviours in favour of prevention without any regard to the costs that may result is clearly inadequate. It fails to take account of both the complex interactions of variables that determine people's behaviours and the fact that behaviours do not exist in isolation; change in one behaviour has implications for other aspects of an individual's life that may be unacceptable. Further interventions are required to bring out the desired modifications of behaviour.

Psychology and AIDS Prevention

What might psychology contribute to persuasive campaigns encouraging preventive behaviours? These should be based upon models that identify the determinants of behaviour change. Unfortunately modelling preventive health behaviour has proved to be an enormously difficult task, largely because individuals regard their behaviour as private and personal, and they do not perceive them as a threat to either their own health or that of others. Of the several models for preventive health two have been particularly influential: the health belief model and the theory of reasoned action.

The health belief model attempts to explain health behaviours by identifying the factors that influence individuals' decisions about the perceived utility of their actions. According to this model the significant variables that determine behaviour in relation to a health threat are perceived vulnerability to the particular health threat, its perceived severity, and the cost-benefit payoff associated with adopting preventive behaviours. An additional factor that may be added to this model is cues to action. Health education campaigns may play a valuable role in this regard by reminding individuals of the need for risk reduction.

Consideration of these variables in relation to AIDS indicates the difficulties faced by health educators. Research shows that individuals perceive HIV / AIDS as a severe disease, more severe than any other, and one that they would wish to avoid. However, despite that, they do not see the need to change their own behaviours. A significant obstacle to change is that individuals are unrealistically optimistic about their own health and see themselves as being at less risk than others in a similar situation. This 'illusion of invulnerability' prevents people from making realistic estimates of personal risk which in turn acts against the adoption of preventive behaviours. This is a fundamental problem for preventive health programmes and though not unique to AIDS its impact can be seen in studies of sexual behaviours and contraceptive use. A recent study of Oxford University undergraduates found that these students estimated their own personal risk of AIDS to be less than that for others of their age and sex. This was true even for individuals who were engaging in activities associated with greater risk for AIDS such as unprotected intercourse with bisexual partners, idus and prostitutes.

Despite public education campaigns there is little evidence that the bulk of the population see themselves as personally vulnerable to HIV infection. It must be remembered that preventive measures are directed to individuals who are currently well and who may not perceive much risk to themselves. Decisions to adopt healthy behaviours will depend in part upon the individual's estimate of the cost-benefit payoff. Preventive behaviours have value in protecting an individual against future illness but they also have costs associated with them, and in the absence of perceived personal risk individuals may estimate that the costs of safe sex are greater than the benefits. The costs associated with condom use include perceived loss of pleasurability, and for some contravention of a religious code. The alternatives to condom use of monogamy for non-infected partners or celibacy offer complete protection of course, but their costs are clearly unacceptable for many individuals.

These costs mitigate against the adoption of effective preventive measures. Effective health education should maximize that payoff by emphasizing the positive aspects of safer sex and must avoid mixed messages. Publicity surrounding the recent postponement of a planned advertising campaign promoting safer sex aimed at homosexuals, may adversely affect individuals' assessment of the relative benefits and costs.

However there is evidence that behaviour change is possible. This can be seen in the behaviour of both gay men and idus. There is substantial evidence of change among gay communities that is both self-reported and also confirmed by evidence from HIV seroconversion rates and reduction in sexually transmitted diseases. The shifts in behaviour that are reported to underlie these changes include reductions in number of sexual partners and adoption of safer sex activities and avoidance of high risk activities. Among idus there is evidence of a reduction in the sharing of syringes and needles, although their sexual behaviours have not altered. The successful changes among these groups were not due directly to public information campaigns, but in the first case to self-education within the community, and in the second to harm minimization programmes promoted by drug services such as the introduction of syringe exchange services. The changes among the gay communities emphasize the importance of social networks in determining behaviour. The theory of reasoned action incorporates this.

The theory identifies intention as the immediate determinant of behaviour. Intentions are themselves a function of privately held attitudes towards the particular behaviour and socially determined subjective norms that represent a person's belief that others think she or he should behave in a certain way. The model attaches values to each of these factors. The particular values attached to each of these factors will depend upon the individual's beliefs and thus in this way the theory is similar to the health belief model.

One difficulty with the reasoned action model is that it identifies a direct link between intentions and behaviours, but intentions are not always translated into actions. Even when an individual holds an intention towards some behaviour, action does not necessarily result. When considering sexual behaviours and safer sex practices there may be one or several reasons for individuals' failures to carry out intentions to act in ways that are perceived as beneficial. An action may not be possible in a particular situation or at a particular time, it may be difficult or time-consuming, or it may simply be suppressed, e.g. if intoxicant drugs accompany the behaviour. Greater consideration needs to be given to the impact of situational influences of this kind. Adherence to intentions for safer sex may be particularly vulnerable since sexual relationships involve a partner. What happens when one partner's intentions for sex do not coincide with those of the other? The social interactions that occur may involve one partner abandoning their intentions and accepting the wishes of the other.

In order fully to dissect the effects of situational variables upon adherence to intended precautionary measures, longitudinal studies of intentions and diary reports of actual behaviours are necessary. Such studies provide powerful tests of the robustness of the health models. They require considerable commitment on the part of researchers and their volunteer respondents and raise important issues concerning confidentiality, e.g. the legality of some practices reported and the reliability of self-reporting of private behaviours. Additionally, surveys of current sexual and drug-using behaviours are essential though not always supported. In

1989 a planned survey of the sexual habits of 20,000 Britons was postponed after opposition by the government on the grounds that it would be an intrusion of privacy despite evidence from a pilot study of 1,000 people that they were willing to cooperate with the survey. It could provide a comprehensive picture of sexual habits as well as providing data upon AIDS and other health issues such as sexually transmitted diseases and cervical cancer. There has been a similar postponement of a National Survey of Health and Sexual Behaviour of Americans. Recognizing the importance of such data, however, the World Health Organization has launched a survey in twenty different countries to establish why there are wide differences in the spread of the virus among different populations.

What are the alternatives to broadly based public education campaigns? There is little doubt that the principal dimensions identified by these models, perceived risk, perceived severity of the disease, perceived effectiveness of precautions, and cost-benefit payoff are important predictors of preventive health behaviours of many kinds. Until our psychological models are refined further, psychologists and health educators continue to offer pragmatic solutions. In the short term it may be that rather than aiming for educational messages suitable for all, which inevitably will be unsuccessful, a social marketing approach should be adopted which stratifies groups and develops messages that are tailored to the needs, interests and existing knowledge and beliefs of specific communities. Two examples of this approach are the introduction of community programmes and school-based interventions.

Community Programmes

Community groups with local social networks are suitable for the introduction of programmes for adolescent and adult groups. Following the intervention there is then the possibility of individuals adopting new ideas or practices that can be spread further by social diffusion. A model derived from communication studies predicts that the adoption of new ideas such as 'safer sex' takes time. Following introduction of the innovation its adoption is influenced by the way in which it is perceived, the availability of social networks to transmit the message, and its compatibility with the prevailing social norms of that community. The characteristics of the community, its social structures and social norms, will determine the response to the innovation and whether it becomes adopted by the majority within the community. Each community will differ, and advocates of innovations should take account of this and present their messages accordingly. It may be that particular communities (e.g. prisons) require special initiatives and it may be that sections of a community could become more involved in promoting educational messages (e.g. the workplace, trade unions, health clinics, church organizations).

Studies of HIV prevalence in American cities point to the need for intervention programmes that recognize cultural differences and the need for appropriate educational strategies and messages that are compatible with the social representations that exist within those communities. For example, Hispanic and black idus are at greater risk than their white counterparts. It is unlikely that this reflects any differences in genetic susceptibility, but rather their relative health and economic deprivations and their perception of AIDS as a homosexual problem.

Homophobia within black and Hispanic communities acts as an obstacle to the adoption of precautions by heterosexuals.

Idus and the subculture that supports their behaviours present a major challenge for those involved in AIDS prevention, but innovative policies that decriminalize drug use in favour of public health education for safer drug use can be effective. The potential impact of this approach can be seen by comparing HIV prevalence in Glasgow and Edinburgh. In both Scottish cities it is legal for pharmacists to sell syringes and needles to idus. However in Edinburgh police pursued a policy of arrests for those found carrying injecting equipment, whereas in Glasgow no such policy existed. Sharing of equipment occurs in both cities but because of this difference in policing, sharing occurs in small local groups in Glasgow, whereas in Edinburgh sharing exists between many more drug users in so-called 'shooting galleries' (places where drugs are sold and buyers share the injecting equipment with several others). In Glasgow the rate of HIV infection among idus at the end of 1986 was around 5 per cent, while in Edinburgh the rate grew from 3 per cent in 1983 to 50 per cent in 1984 and is now endemic among the city's idus.

Community-based interventions can be effective in reducing risk. In San Francisco there have been changes in the drug practices of idus following community-based initiatives such as the use of 'outreach workers' to distribute condoms as well as bleach for sterilizing injecting equipment, and to disseminate information about HIV/AIDS and effective precautions that can be taken. Higher order policies including decriminalization of aspects of drug use may encourage injecting drug users to use drug services within their local communities.

As reported earlier homosexual groups have altered their behaviours towards safer sex. These changes have spread through social diffusion as a result of the well-organized social networks within gay communities. In many instances the changes in behaviour had begun before the AIDS public education campaigns. There remain problems, however, since not all individuals have modified their sexual behaviours; some continue to engage in high risk practices. Others who generally practice safer sex may on occasions lapse. Recidivism of this sort is frequently encountered in preventive health behaviours. To be effective precautions must be maintained over time.

Social norms that encourage safer sex and discourage high risk conduct will depend upon community-based projects and educational interventions with messages targeted to users of specific risk activities, e.g. injecting drug use, engaging in unprotected penetrative sex.

AIDS Education in Schools

In the USA it is recognized that HIV infection is gaining prevalence among adolescents aged 15 years and above. Young people are not particularly skilled in managing their sexual and drug-taking lives and this places them at risk for HIV infection. Consequently adolescents are a particularly important group for future AIDS education campaigns. However they need more than information alone. They additionally require opportunities for learning about relationships and the social skills required to manage the dynamics of social relationships. Intimacy involves social interactions between partners, and negotiations about sex may not be equitable. For example, coercion or compliance may cause an individual to disregard his or her intention to allow sexual intercourse or to use a condom during intercourse. Information encouraging safer sex must be accompanied by education about adhering to intentions for preventive health.

Schools provide a suitable community with extensive formal and informal networks for delivery of health messages. Health education should be included in the school curriculum. Young people's beliefs, values and attitudes to health may be malleable unlike the more firmly held attitudes of older groups. If so, appropriate attitudes towards individual social responsibility can be encouraged that enable appropriate precautions against AIDS to be taken. Learning experiences of this type could make use of person-centred approaches rather than simple exposure to information. This would allow youngsters to develop their own knowledge structures, at their own rate and within the context of experiences within their own lives. It is quite clear that adolescents do require more information about HIV and AIDS, but information is not enough; they also need the opportunity to make use of that information for risk assessment and decision-making, and most importantly they need to acquire social skills that allow them to adhere to their decisions even in social contexts that exert pressures against those decisions. Education in schools should be a major aspect of campaigns against AIDS.

Tutorial Discussion Questions

We have introduced some of the issues around HIV/AIDS, but many remain, including paediatric AIDS, reactions to persons with AIDS, and the psychological reactions of AIDS patients to their own condition. We hope that you will explore these in your own discussions, as well as considering some of the questions below.

1 Should surveys of sexual practices be undertaken?
2 Should drug use be decriminalized in favour of health education approaches?
3 When researching HIV/AIDS, sexual practices and drug use, what ethical issues other than confidentiality should researchers be aware of?
4 Are our images of AIDS inevitably distorted by stereotypes presented by the media?
5 Do the existing psychological theories offer useful insights for encouraging safer health behaviours?
6 To what extent are individuals responsible for their own health?

You might find it helpful to focus your discussion around the situations facing the characters in the two vignettes described below. Why do you think we selected cases which both required a woman's decision?

Pauline, a 19-year-old artist, has been injecting heroin for three years since leaving home. Since becoming aware of the risk of HIV through sharing of 'works' two years ago, she has resolved to avoid sharing, although there have been occasional lapses. She has not been able to buy heroin for a day, but while at a party she is offered the chance to score. However she can only do so by sharing a friend's 'works'. Later she meets a man who is eager to screw, but he objects to the idea of using a condom.

Given her history would sharing 'works' be riskier than having unprotected sex? Who is at greater risk if they do have sex, him or her?

> Charlotte has been married for ten years, and entirely faithful to her husband, Jim. They are voluntarily childless, but are now trying to conceive. Jim confesses that while on a recent visit to New York he had sex once with a long-standing woman friend. Charlotte is now afraid that she will have contracted HIV and is considering what to do.

Should she have a test for HIV, abandon the idea of having children, cease her sexual relations with Jim, go to a clinic for the worried well? What would you advise?

Further Reading

AGGLETON, P., HART, G. and DAVIES, P. (1989) *AIDS: Social Representations and Social Practices*, London, Falmer Press.

AGGLETON, P., HOMANS, H., MOJSA, J., WATSON, S. and WATNEY, S. (1989) *AIDS: Scientific and Social Issues. A Resource for Health Educators*, Edinburgh, Churchill Livingstone.

KELLEY, J. A. and ST LAWRENCE, J. S. (1988) *The AIDS Health Crisis: Psychological and Social Interventions*, New York, Plenum.

MULLEADY, G. (1987) 'A review of drug abuse and HIV infection', *Psychology and Health*, 1, pp. 149–63.

PHILLIPS, K. C. (1989) 'The psychology of AIDS', in COLEMAN, A. and BEAUMONT, J. G. (Eds) *Psychology Survey No. 7*, London, British Psychological Society, Routledge, pp. 257–78.

PHILLIPS, K. C. (in press) 'The primary prevention of AIDS', in PITTS, M. K., and PHILLIPS, K. C. (Eds) *The Psychology of Health*, London, Routledge.

Chapter 9

Problem Drug Use

Moira Hamlin

'GRAVE ILLNESS & TERRIFYING SOCIAL EVIL'

The Daily Telegraph

'COCAINE SEIGE'

The Guardian

'TEENAGE TORMENT'

Daily Mirror

'GLUE TRIP PUNK IN DEATH LEAP'

Islington Gazette

Current newspaper headlines might lead us to think drug misuse is a modern phenomenon. Yet drug use to alter states of consciousness is a behaviour which has been with us throughout history. The first known brewery operated in Egypt in 3700 B.C., but there is evidence that people used alcohol as far back as the Stone Age. Many cultures have been able to assimilate drug use into their way of life, with few apparent problems. Substances are endemic in particular regions, such as coca leaves in South America, opium in the Indian subcontinent, and alcohol in the West. Opiate use without addiction has been fairly common in China for centuries. Problems occured only following the introduction of tobacco in the 1600s. In Europe patent medicines often contained opiates and were taken legally without prescription for a variety of ailments. However, when no cultural tradition for a particular drug use exists, the reaction of governments has generally been to prohibit use by law. Subcultures using the substance outside the law have sprung up, without the moderating influence of social or legal norms. The result has often been idiosyncratic or excessive drug use.

In Victorian times opiates were probably more widely used than today and before the 1920s various preparations of opium could be bought freely from a chemist. After such practice became illegal doctors were still able to prescribe heroin and cocaine to treat people who were addicted. The result was a group of people who were maintained on long-term prescriptions, but who were able to lead fairly stable lifestyles as long as they continued to use drugs. Consequently there was less need for people to turn to black market supplies. This situation remained unchanged until the late 1950s and early 1960s. From the 1960s onwards drug misusers became less respectable characters, often involved in crime and less in touch with mainstream society. In response to what the British Medical Association called 'a grave system of social disorder' in 1967, prescribing of heroin and cocaine was limited to doctors with a special Home Office licence. Sniffing cocaine became increasingly popular in the mid-1970s. Sniffing one powder made sniffing another (heroin) appear a small step. 'Chasing the dragon' or smoking heroin further opened the door to a wider range of users.

Extent of Use

Current trends in illegal drug use in the UK are a source of considerable concern for the authorities. At the prospect of the UK becoming a new target for cocaine exporters, the government Home Affairs Committee in 1985 saw this as 'the most serious peacetime threat to our national well-being'. The actual size of the problem is a matter of much conjecture and debate. Unfortunately there is more rhetoric around than hard facts. Information from various sources suggests that heroin is freely available in most areas of the UK. Whether this is linked to a ready supply at international level, through the increasing involvement of criminal organizations, or to increased demand for the drug is unclear.

Although exact figures are unknown, the incidence and prevalence of illegal drug use in the UK appears to have increased in recent years. It is thought that some five million people in the UK have taken cannabis, with at least a million taking the drug in a year. Amphetamines are probably the next most popular drugs, though a long way behind cannabis. Available data suggest that surprisingly small proportions of the population have used heroin and most occasional users sniff or smoke the drug rather that inject it. There are indications, however, that there has been a rapid increase since the late 1970s.

In 1976 the Home Office figures for those receiving notifiable drugs for treatment was 1,876. By 1986 the figure had increased to 8,445. The majority were using heroin or other opiates. Official figures alone cannot accurately assess the extent of use as many users do not come into contact with the medical profession. Various studies suggest that for every notified person between 4 to 10 other dependent people exist.

While they provide guidelines, all such figures should be treated with caution. Problems exist in estimating drug use, including definition of problem drug use, access to people involved in illegal activities, and so on. The only satisfactory way of estimating the number misusing drugs would be to conduct large-scale representative surveys of the general population and no such survey has been done in the UK. To put the debate on numbers into perspective, annual deaths from all illegal drugs amount to approximately 200. By contrast deaths due to alcohol misuse amount to 6,500 annually, and at least 100,000 die prematurely each year from cigarette smoking.

In the last decade it has been increasingly common for young people to use more than one drug. Multiple or polydrug use is the current problem facing treatment services. A common finding is illustrated by a research study in London of drug use by residents of a treatment centre. They found that multiple drug use was prevalent. Only 17 per cent reported current use of just one type of drug. Alcohol features heavily in polydrug use among the under twenties and a recent BBC TV *Panorama* programme calculated that 15 to 18 year olds spend around £277 million a year on alcohol.

Moira Hamlin

What Is a Drug?

Can you identify the following drug?

> The sufferer is tremulous and loses his self-command; he is subject to fits of agitation and depression; he loses colour and has a haggard appearance. His appetite falls off and symptoms of gastric catarrh may be manifested. The heart also suffers, it palpitates or it intermits. As with other agents a renewed dose of the poison may give temporary relief, but at the cost of future misery.

Reading this many people suspect it refers to a heroin or cocaine user. The drug in question is, in fact, coffee. Deciding what is a drug is not the simple task it first appears. The word 'drug' traditionally means something which a doctor prescribes to treat an illness or something which can be bought from a chemist for the same purpose. Alternatively, the word 'drug' conjures up an image of an illegal substance abused by stereotyped 'addicts'. The picture is complicated by the fact that substances not considered drugs can function as drugs under particular circumstances, e.g. foods or solvents and aerosols. Implicit in this notion of a drug is the role or function of the substance for an individual. Whenever a substance is used primarily for its psychological or physiological effect, it can be considered a drug. For example, heavy use of drinks containing caffeine produce effects on the nervous system and therefore can be viewed as drugs.

Why Do People Use Drugs?

Drug use must be viewed within a context — it is not something separate from the rest of a person's life and the culture we live in espouses 'instant cures' and a 'pill for every ill'. Whether someone takes drugs or not is influenced by many factors. These include psychological factors such as personality, the availability of a substance, the method of administration and the prevailing attitude towards its use. It also needs to be acknowledged that the effect of the substance itself is not necessarily the prime consideration. Some people would argue that drugs can be used occasionally for recreational use without significant psychological or social problems.

Models seeking to explain drug taking as a form of illness or disease imply qualitative differences between those who suffer the disease and those who do not. Their emphasis lies on pharmacological factors and with the substance itself. Acknowledgment that genetic factors may exert an influence in, for example, alcohol misuse does not rule out the contributory influence of environmental factors. It is an out-of-date argument to postulate that it is either genetics or environment which influences behaviour. The extent of the interaction must surely be the interesting equation. Psychological models which emphasize social learning approaches see drug taking as being on a continuum of behaviour, similar to a normal curve of distribution. Excessive use of substances is only quantitatively different from occasional or regular use. Misuse or abuse occurs when any substance which is self-administered has seriously adverse consequences for the user.

Young people often begin to experiment with drugs whilst at school. In 1985 (Plant *et al.*) reported a survey of 15–16 year olds conducted in 1979. They found that 15 per cent of the boys and 11 per cent of the girls reported using illicit drugs at some time. Four years later the figures had risen to 37 per cent and 23 per cent respectively. The most common drugs used were cannabis, amphetamines and LSD. Although the youngsters had experimented, most were not regular users.

Certain factors seem to promote the use of drugs among young people. Drug use is higher among those who live in areas of social deprivation and with few prospects of advancement. In addition young people with lowered self-esteem appear to be more vulnerable to taking drugs. Initial experimentation can then slip into recreational use, occasional use and finally into dependent use. Repeated experience with a drug can produce changes that increase its attractiveness. As more time is given over to drug use so the commitment to it increases. Within a broad social learning framework the individual is considered to balance the rewards and punishments of drug use, rather like an accountant's balance sheet. Through a gradual process the pleasures and rewards must outweigh any negative consequences that may occur. Initially drugs may help to blot out problems or increase excitement, and the adverse consequences such as involvement in a criminal activity and monetary cost may play a minor role. Gradually, physical health problems increase, involvement in criminal acts gets greater, and as economic consequences weigh heavier, the balance shifts. Tolerance to some drugs might also develop and the individual may need to escalate the dose to achieve the same effect. By then physical dependence on the drug may have developed and continued use may be maintained by negative reinforcement: the individual now takes the drug in order to avoid the unpleasant effects of withdrawal.

The reasons young people themselves give for taking drugs can be categorized under four headings:

1 *Peer pressures.* 'All my friends take drugs.' Some young people begin misusing drugs out of curiosity or to be part of the 'in-group'. Those with low self-esteem find it particularly difficult to resist peer pressure.
2 *Young people with problems.* 'I wanted to get away from this lousy world.' Adolescents who have trouble coping with the problems and changes in their lives may use drugs in an attempt to escape. Those from families which have marital problems, divorce or alcohol abuse may fall into this category.
3 *Boredom.* 'I needed a thrill.' Young people who see little value in school or have access to few leisure facilities are also vulnerable. Sometimes they are brighter than average, but have poor relationships with teachers and other significant adults.
4 *Loneliness.* 'There was no one to turn to.' Lack of family cohesiveness and poor parent-child relationships are at the root of this problem. If the young person feels they have no one to turn to when problems arise, drugs can seem the only answer.

An opposing viewpoint exists to counter the idea that drug use must always be seen in a negative light. Preble and Casey (1969) argued that in some respects heroin use can be seen as anything but an escape from life. In their description of life on the street they point out that users 'are actively engaged in meaningful activities and relationships seven days a week . . . they are aggressively pursuing a career that is exacting, challenging, adventurous and rewarding'. It might also be argued that heroin use is located with the informal or fringe economy in the UK. It is partly a response to economic recession and unemployment problems. For some users it gives them an active role in the working life and social life of the community: 'to be a user of heroin is to be someone who is typically more or less tightly enmeshed in a supportive social network whose members are keeping each other busy; and the appeal of being a heroin user is in part a function of this'.

Attitudes and Myths About Drugs

> I see no hope for the future of our people if they are dependent on the frivolous youth today, for certainly all youth are reckless beyond words. When I was a boy we were taught to be discreet and respectful of elders, but the present youth are exceedingly wise and impatient of restraint (Hesiod, eighth century B.C.).

Every so often societies appear to be subject to periods of moral panics. A group of people or condition emerges as a threat to societal values. The threat is portrayed in a stereotyped way in the mass media; the coverage and hysteria reach a peak and then subside when 'solutions' and 'ways of coping' are found. Such moral panics can be seen in society's response to drug issues.

Alcohol and tobacco are more widely available than heroin but public concern has focused on the latter. Heroin users are typically seen as weak, lying, cheating and concerned only with pleasure. The government's anti-heroin advertising campaign employed images of users as prostitutes, vomiting down toilets and stealing mum's housekeeping. Few would argue that heroin has become more available in the UK in the last twenty years, but does it justify the 'War on Drugs' waged by the US and UK governments?

In the 1960s and 1970s the popular view was to dismiss all concern about drugs as merely a moral panic. Drug use was only a problem because society perceived it so, largely through the efforts of the media. It is not possible, however, to dismiss all the media coverage on heroin as being without foundation. There *are* dangers in use, particularly as increased use is seen in an earlier age range. But it should also be appreciated that some of the problem with heroin lies in society's nervous reaction to it. Such a reaction generates distortions and myths about the drug's true nature which exacerbate existing hazards. Many first-time users hate the experience and never use heroin again. It usually takes regular use of several weeks before a habit develops. Some people can take it for years, even via a needle, and stay healthy by using clean equipment and spreading out hits.

The dangers of crack have come to the fore recently. The popular view is one of a drug so powerful that one smoke equals instant addiction. Closer to the truth there is no doubt crack is a powerful drug. As the high lasts only 5 to 10 minutes the following rebound encourages users into damagingly repetitive use. Potentially fatal toxic reactions are likely as the drug is of uncertain purity. Nevertheless instant addiction or even death are not an automatic consequence of use.

The rise and fall of the glue sniffer illustrates another example of moral panic. Glue sniffing rose to the fore in the UK in the late 1970s. At first it was not linked to any particular youth subculture, but sniffing was adopted by punks because public perceptions of sniffing fitted in with their self-image. Originally used experimentally and as a cheap high, adult disgust and hostility encouraged punks to use glue sniffing as a way of shocking society. Further, the use of readily available household products appealed to punks who saw themselves as rejecting consumerist values. The more adults emphasized dangers of solvents the more attractive they became. Glue deaths afforded the media ample opportunity for sensational stories. Exaggerated warnings of dangers were given with media campaigns promoting calls for legislation. Too much crying wolf and the lack of new angles to cover led to the panic dying down. Youth culture, too, moved on and developed new concerns. Although solvent misuse was a significant and serious problem, the panic generated helped to obscure the real issues and probably increased glue sniffing in the punk subculture. Drug problems require appropriate constructive and rational solutions. Panic is not part of an appropriate response.

UK Government Attitude

Since the early 1980s the UK Government has taken a strong interest in drug problems. *Tackling Drug Misuse: A Summary of the Government's Strategy* (Home Office, 1985) describes its policy in the field. Significant amounts of money have been allocated to treatment services as well as to education and prevention measures. The present government attitude is best summed up in an extract from the following report:

> Western society is faced by a warlike threat from the hard drugs industry. The traffickers in hard drugs amass princely incomes from the exploitation of human weakness, boredom and misery ... the ruthlessness of the big drug dealers must be met by equally ruthless penalties once they are caught, tried and convicted ... The American practice, which we unhesitatingly support, is to give the courts Draconian powers ... Drug dealers must be made to lose everything, their homes, their money and all that they possess ... (House of Commons, 1985).

Prevention Strategies

Prevention with regard to drug use, in its widest sense, would mean stopping people ever using drugs. To work only towards this ideal goal is to attempt the unattainable. As there are probably millions of people involved in problematic drug use in the UK, with a multitude of factors initiating and maintaining use, it is unlikely that simple preventative approaches will work. Clarity is needed about what a particular initiative is trying to prevent and whether the chosen strategies are appropriate in relation to the stated aims.

The pharmacological treatment for most heroin users involves substitution of methadone followed by withdrawal of methadone. Critics of the method argue that it is too rigid and inflexible, taking insufficient account of individual need. An alternative is to give higher doses of methadone and 'maintain' the user until he or she is ready to withdraw. Maintenance prescribing has been termed the 'British system' to differentiate it from the American approach which is abstinence-orientated.

Maintenance prescribing lost favour during the 1970s and it was assumed that users would be willing to work towards abstinence. The risk of HIV/AIDS through needle sharing has been a major factor in reassessment of treatment policy. From a pragmatic public health viewpoint it is better to adopt a policy which lessens the risk of AIDS, even though the consequences may be for individuals to continue taking drugs. Ironically it may turn out to be a policy which proves more beneficial to the drug user in the long run.

The idea of 'harm reduction' became popular, though controversial, in the mid-1980s, particularly with drug agencies in the non-statutory sector. Underlying the concept is an acknowledgment that for some people stabilizing use may be a first step which allows the opportunity to develop positive relationships with drug workers while examining alternative options to drug use.

Harm reduction, or damage limitation strategies, fit nicely into the model of drug careers outlined by Prochaska and DiClemente (1986). In this model users are considered to pass through a number of stages from precontemplation of change through to maintenance of change and possible relapse. At the precontemplation stage harm reduction is useful because the individual is not yet ready to give up drugs, but there is much that can be done to reduce the number of risks they take.

Examples of harm reduction strategies are wide-ranging but include some of the following:

1 Changing from sharing needles to own needles.
2 Sterilizing needles.
3 Switching from injecting to another route of administration.
4 Information about high dose levels.
5 Safe sex education.
6 Involvement in non-drug activities and relationships.
7 Vitamin supplements.
8 Food and shelter for the homeless.

For some users the benefits which accrue from damage limitation will precipitate a move into the next stage of Prochaska and DiClemente's model — contemplation. By now the user is likely to experience considerable conflict about drug taking, may glimpse the possibilities of change, and be ready to make a decision to change the behaviour.

Prevention in the UK has mainly been targeted at secondary school pupils. Early attempts focused on the substances themselves, using didactic treatment methods. More recently drug education agencies have produced packages which emphasize decision-making in relation to health decisions, using role-play and other experiential teaching methods. There is no evidence, however, that behaviour change is effected by any of the educational strategies. This is partly because many of the approaches assume a simple linear relationship between knowledge, attitudes and behaviour. It has been assumed that by providing accurate knowledge attitude shifts would then occur, which in turn would lead to behaviour change. Behaviour change is, however, more complex and subject to a range of interacting factors. The 'Just Say No' campaign championed by Nancy Reagan in the USA is a good example of an approach which failed to consider whether this was an appropriate response in the context of an individual's culture, age and background. It also failed to comprehend the influence of peer pressure for diffferent age groups and to acknowledge the level of assertive skills required to 'Just Say No'.

It should also be acknowledged that while we have information about drug misusers attending treatment services we know almost nothing about those who do not. There may be many differences including those due to substance. For young children involved in solvent misuse it might be best prevented with earlier detection and intervention to deal with family or school problems. To remedy the problems of long-term benzodiazepine use a major culture change is needed. Most tranquillizers are prescribed for anxiety symptoms and social stresses. There is no evidence of their effectiveness in the long term; instead they lead to problems of dependence. An attitude shift is required which recognizes that medication is of little benefit for minor affective problems and that it is social support, counselling or therapy that provide more effective and lasting solutions.

Substance misuse within inner cities, in broken homes and already abusing families suggests a connection between social factors, psychological stress and the misuse. Clearly there are no easy preventative approaches in this sphere, although it is evident that economic and social policies which include more people within mainstream society are needed. Future approaches are likely to switch from individual approaches to include greater involvement with local communities in determining their own needs for information, services and education for drugs.

Drug Knowledge Survey

Use the answers to the questions as a basis for discussion.

Questions

1 If you have a substance that is a fine, bitter-tasting white powder it is most likely to be:

(a) amphetamine; (b) heroin; (c) THC; (d) quinine; (e) no way of telling by sight or taste.

2 Methadone when used in the treatment of heroin addiction is:

(a) a cure for addiction; (b) similar to heroin in its potential for physical dependence; (c) a type of stimulant; (d) incapable of providing a heroin-like euphoria; (e) usually given by daily injection.

3 The drug most frequently responsible for serious disability to health and to intellectual and social performance is:

(a) heroin; (b) alcohol; (c) marijuana; (d) cocaine; (e) LSD.

4 Are the following statements TRUE or FALSE?

(a)	Cocaine is always snorted.	TRUE/FALSE
(b)	Codeine is an opiate.	TRUE/FALSE
(c)	Paracetamol is an opiate.	TRUE/FALSE
(d)	The withdrawal effects from tranquillizers (benzodiazepines) last for 2 to 3 weeks.	TRUE/FALSE
(e)	Dependence can only develop when drugs are injected.	TRUE/FALSE

Answers

1 (e). Amphetamine, heroin and quinine can all be found in the form of fine, bitter-tasting white powders. There is no way to identify a drug by sight or taste.
2 (b). Like heroin, methadone produces physical dependence. When used on a daily basis as an oral substitute for heroin it does not produce the euphoric 'high' as heroin does. Methadone plays an important role in the treatment of heroin dependence, but does not in itself act as a cure for dependence.
3 (b). Alcohol is the drug most frequently responsible for health and social damage. This is largely because it is used by a high proportion of the population.
4 (a) FALSE. Cocaine can be injected.
  (b) TRUE. Tolerance and dependence may occur with prolonged use.
  (c) FALSE. Paracetamol is a non-opioid analgesic, although overdose is particularly dangerous.
  (d) FALSE. Long-term users commonly report symptoms for up to eighteen months following withdrawal.
  (e) FALSE. The route of administration does not affect the development of dependence.

Drug Use

Make a list of your own drug use for a day including tea, coffee, aspirins, cigarettes, alcohol and so on.

Time	Drug	What you were doing at the time	Effect

Notice any patterns in your drug use. What do you think the function of the drug was? Examples might include habit, to relax, to combat boredom, to feel better.

Case Histories

Case One. Jane is 22 years old and she has been using heroin since she was 14. There had been problems at home for as long as she could remember. Her parents had frequent violent arguments, particularly when her father had been drinking. Jane's mother smoked heavily and she had been taking tranquillizers since Jane was 5. Her school years had not been particularly happy and she did not have many close friends. She became interested in boys when she was 13 and started going to parties without her parents' knowledge. Cannabis was freely available at parties and eventually she smoked heroin too. Her live-in boyfriend is also a heroin user. For the last six years Jane has injected heroin.

Case Two. Robert is 14 and lives in a large industrial town with a high unemployment rate. His father is unemployed as are his two older brothers. Robert is fairly bright, but sees little point in school. He has frequent clashes with the teachers and for the last two years has been in trouble for his high absenteeism rate. There are few leisure and recreational facilities in the town and Robert thinks 'youth clubs' and similar groups a waste of time. He generally hangs out with his mates on their estate. He has been in trouble with the police several times for petty thieving and vandalism. When he was 10 he joined some older boys who sniffed glue. He didn't believe all the stories about how dangerous it was and enjoyed himself with his mates when he was high. Now he is 14 he is able to obtain alcohol more easily and is frequently drunk.

Case Three. Simon is 30 and lives in London. His home was in Surrey but after doing very well at school he left to go to University. Simon always worked quite hard and, following a good degree, got a well-paid job in London. The company had a 'fast-track' scheme for promising graduates so Simon was promoted rapidly. He had to work long hours but he did not mind, although it left little time for a social life. He has had many girlfriends but no long-term relationships as he found they bored him after a while.

For the last two years Simon has been feeling vaguely dissatisfied but could not identify anything specific that was wrong. Many of his friends use cocaine regularly but he has always resisted, sticking to moderate amounts of alcohol. Recently someone persuaded him to try it and he found it a fantastic experience. He had nagging fears about becoming addicted at first but now feels he can handle it. Cocaine features regularly in his life outside work.

Read the case studies above and discuss with the following points in mind:

1 What major role did drugs play in each person's life?
2 What were the background factors which made drug use more likely?
3 Can you identify any psychological factors which might have predisposed the user to take drugs?
4 Can you identify any social factors which predisposed the users to take drugs?
5 Chart the stages and progression of drug use in each case. What do you think the future holds for each?

Tutorial Discussion Questions

Attitudes play an important role in our perceptions of problem drug use. Use the following questions as a basis for discussion, noting differences in attitudes.

1 Should smoking be banned in all public places?
2 Is an occasional smoke of cannabis possible without any harmful effects?
3 How might teaching safer injecting techniques to drug users reduce the risk of AIDS?
4 Is abstinence the only feasible treatment goal for anyone dependent on drugs (including alcohol)?
5 Under what circumstances might cannabis be legalized?
6 Do women need tranquillizers more than men?

References

HOME OFFICE (1985) *Tackling Drug Misuse: A Summary of the Government's Strategy*, London, Home Office

HOUSE OF COMMONS (1985) *Fifth Report of the Home Affairs Committee. Misuse of Hard Drugs (Interim Report)*, Session 1984/5.

PLANT, M. A., PECK, D. F., SAMUEL, E. and STUART, R. (1985) Alcohol, drugs, and school-leavers, London, Tavistock.

PREBLE, E. and CASEY, J. J. (1969). 'Taking care of business — the heroin user's life on the street', *The International Journal of the Addictions*, 4, pp. 1–24.

PROCHASKA, J. O. and DiCLEMENTE, C. C. (1986) 'Toward a comprehensive model of change', in MILLER, W. R. and HEATHER, N. (Eds) *Treating Addictive Behaviour*, New York, Plenum. pp. 3-27.

Further Reading

FIELD, T. (1985) *Escaping the Dragon*, London, Unwin.

HELLER, T., GOTT, M. and JEFFREY, L. (Eds) (1987) *Drug Use and Misuse: A Reader*, Chichester, John Wiley.

ORFORD, J. (1985) *Excessive Appetites: Psychological Approaches to the Addictions*, London, John Wiley.

Chapter 10

Alcohol Abuse: The Ins and the Outs

Clive Eastman

The purpose of this chapter is to consider what 'problem drinking' is, how one can become, remain and cease to be a problem drinker and how problem drinking might be prevented. In this context, the terms 'problem drinker' and 'alcoholic' are treated as overlapping but not identical concepts. The latter is here taken to signify someone who is physiologically dependent on alcohol; the former is not.

Definitions

Most people have a vague idea of what terms such as 'alcoholic' and 'social drinker' signify, but we need to do better than that, if we are to communicate effectively with one another.

Probably the most important step in this direction was the wide acceptance of the World Health Organization (WHO) definition of the term 'alcoholic'. In 1952 an Expert Committee decreed:

> Alcoholics are those excessive drinkers whose dependence on alcohol has attained such a degree that they show a noticeable mental disturbance or interference with their bodily or mental functioning or who show the prodromal signs of such development. They therefore require treatment (World Health Organization, 1952).

The Expert Committee clearly saw alcoholism as a disease, hence the use of the term 'prodromal' (the early signs or symptoms of an illness) and of 'treatment'. This view was enthusiastically espoused by the fellowship of Alcoholics Anonymous, not least because it appeared to explain what had previously been a puzzle: namely, why it is that alcoholics continue their excessive and destructive drinking despite the personal, interpersonal, social and financial harm it so obviously causes. Alcoholics are the victims of an illness that causes them to drink to excess, regardless of the consequences of so doing. It may seem surprising that, in recent years, the majority of workers in this field have given little credence to that definition.

However, one difficulty with the 1952 WHO definition is that it appears to confuse dependence with disability, where the former refers to what is commonly known as 'addiction'. Roughly speaking, dependence is the physical and/or psychological state in which the individual feels compelled to drink, to maintain that state, and sometimes to avoid the consequences of not drinking, that is 'withdrawal symptoms'. In addition, 'tolerance' may also be present, with the result that progressively greater amounts of alcohol need to be consumed to achieve the effects originally attained at much lower doses.

The WHO provided a possible solution to the definitional problem in 1977 with the introduction of the concept of the 'Alcohol Dependence Syndrome' (ADS) (World Health Organization, 1977). The crucial elements were that alcohol dependence was distinguished from alcohol-related disabilities, and acknowledgment was given to the fact that alcohol dependence exists in degrees, rather than as an all-or-nothing phenomenon. This new conceptualization was able to cope with the undoubted existence of alcohol dependent individuals who, despite their dependence, exhibit few if any signs of alcohol-related disabilities.

Inevitably, the value of the ADS conceptualization has been questioned, not least on the grounds that it is still underpinned by an 'illness' or 'disease' model of alcoholism. Indeed, in 1979 it was included in the International Classification of Diseases, thus becoming 'officially' recognized and accepted. How, then, can one account for a widespread resistance among researchers and therapists to accepting the disease explanation of alcoholism? The reason is simply that there is incontrovertible evidence that some alcoholics can and do return to (controlled) social drinking, something that, according to the disease model, should be impossible.

The Financial and Other Costs of Problem Drinking

The costs of problem drinking can be roughly divided into two categories: human and financial. The former, in terms of personal, interpersonal, familial and social misery cannot be quantified but is unquestionably vast. However, a variety of tangible costs can be quantified. There is the personal financial cost of supporting problem drinking. It does not come cheap. Less directly, the employed alcoholic is likely to cost the employer money in the form of reduced efficiency, poor decision-making, mistakes, absenteeism, accidents and so on. A large proportion of moving traffic accidents involve drivers who have been drinking: police, fire, medical and maybe legal costs are involved, perhaps in excess of £100,000. The cost to society of providing treatment services for alcoholism including in-patient and out-patient facilities is considerable, as would be the cost of providing first-class preventive measures. The real cost is unknown but in 1981, the cost in this country was estimated to be between about £700 and £1,100 millions per annum. One way and another, those costs are met by consumers and taxpayers.

Maybe it is worth noting that government revenue from alcohol is measured in thousands of millions of pounds per annum, not to mention a large export trade in spirits, in particular.

The major point to understand is that vast sums of money are involved in these issues and as we all know where large sums of money are involved, there tend to be vested interests.

Drinking is typically a social phenomenon, in the sense that it is learned from and practised in the company of other people. Except for cultures in which there is a total ban on alcohol, becoming a drinker 'of some sort' is the norm in Western society, teetotalism being a minority stance. So although we may be unable to identify some of the many routes by which individuals become 'drinkers', the crucial question is whether we can likewise discover the routes to and reasons why a significant minority (about 1 per cent) of people develop into 'problem drinkers'? Put simply, how does it happen and, for that matter, to whom does it happen?

'Professional' Explanation of Acquisition and Maintenance

The Disease or 'Medical' Model

The central thesis of this model is that alcoholics are, from a medical viewpoint, 'ill' and are suffering from a disease. Part of this explanation involves the suggestion that some drinkers either become susceptible, or are born susceptible to developing alcoholism. According to this view, once the individual has been introduced to alcohol, the onset of the disease may occur without warning and at any time in the individual's lifetime. The basic question is whether the child follows the parent(s) in becoming an alcoholic, i.e. is alcoholism an inherited trait?

This question, simple as it may appear, is a complex one. Factors other than heredity could also be operating in a family setting: factors such as learning from the parent(s) how to drink in such a way that alcoholism results. Somehow, the possibility that the alcoholic offspring might have 'learned to become alcoholics' has to be ruled out, or technically 'controlled for'. This has been accomplished, and the best available evidence so far is that heredity probably does play a tiny role in alcoholism but only in the case of the male offspring of alcoholic parents. There is not even this weak evidence in the case of the female children. It is extremely important to be clear what this means, namely that the contribution played by heredity in the development of alcoholism is tiny. It would be absurd to imagine that the children, particularly the male children, of one or more alcoholic parents were doomed to live with the threat of alcoholism hanging over them. It is not the case that such individuals dare not drink alcohol for fear of becoming alcoholics. Immensely greater importance must be given to factors such as age, sex, education, occupation, culture and religion, but this takes us from the medical to the social learning model of alcoholism.

The Social Learning Model

At its simplest, the social learning model suggests that people learn and develop patterns of drinking that result in alcoholism. They learn from the example of other drinkers (modelling) and from talking to others about drinking (information). For example, there is a great deal of evidence that the group in greatest danger of developing damaging drinking habits (and by implication alcoholism) is younger males between the ages of about 18 to 24 years, although this range may extend up towards 30. Similar drinking patterns among males over 50 years of age are far less common. Why should this be so?

The answer will certainly have to incorporate the fact that the late teenage years, and those of the early twenties as well, are traditionally the ones in which the individual is likely to be 'separating' from parents and parental values. It is the period when adult 'styles' are becoming more clearly established and it is a time when the peer group increasingly provides the support and moulds the personal values that, in younger years, were the domains of the parents and family. This is the time when the individual 'experiments' with relationships, with interests and with values. Being an integral part of a peer group provides both the matrix for such experimentation and models or examples. The individual is likely to be strongly influenced by the peer group. If that group happens to include some influential heavy drinkers, they may set the norm that others attempt to emulate. Being 'one of the boys', 'standing your round' and being able to 'hold your drink' are particularly important for males. Likewise, the most potentially damaging drinking patterns occur in females in the same age range, although population surveys consistently indicate lower consumption levels than among males. Significantly, admissions to treatment facilities for serious drinking problems have shown a marked increase in the younger age groups, as have convictions for drunkenness. The implication is that younger people are drinking more alcohol, partly because a larger part of their disposable income is likely to be available for this purpose than for older 'family' people.

It is clear that age and sex are but two of the relevant factors. Religious background also plays a role. It has long been known that Jews have a generally lower rate of alcoholism than, for example, Anglicans. The explanation usually advanced is that, among Jews, alcohol is typically consumed in the family setting, it is usually drunk at mealtimes, it is an important component in religious observances, and drunkenness is strongly condemned. These factors encourage the moderate use of alcohol.

As mentioned above, some occupations influence the drinking practices of their members. Alcohol producers and retailers have ready access to alcohol and, as one might anticipate, tend to have higher overall consumption levels than the general population. Members of occupations characterized by high stress levels, such as business managers, entertainers, journalists and travelling sales people, tend to be among the heavier drinkers, as do those whose work is so heavy that they lose large amounts of water (e.g. steel workers). Since alcohol is a well-known 'lubricant of the social wheels', some occupations tend to support heavier drinking in order to facilitate social interactions. Again, none of this should be taken to mean that members of these occupations will display damaging drinking habits, only that they are at greater risk of so doing by virtue of the pressures and requirements of their occupations.

It is worth bearing in mind that particular styles of drinking do not suddenly appear and are not necessarily static over time. For example, the ambitious and competent business person is likely to be promoted through a series of career steps, including changing companies. By and large, the higher one ascends a company hierarchy, the more socializing one is expected to engage in. Add to this the extra responsibilities, the longer working hours, the reduction in non-working time available to relax and to pursue other interests, the greater the risk is of resorting to alcohol to 'wash away one's problems'. Unfortunately, beyond a certain limit, which will vary from person to person, alcohol disrupts judgment and performance, so that alcohol fails to 'wash away' the original problems and, as an entirely negative 'bonus', it creates problems of its own. Notice that the individual is quite likely to be unaware of the increase in the frequency of drinking and of the quantity consumed at a sitting. The process can be insidious, as anyone will testify who has suddenly become aware that their alcohol consumption has been on the increase over the last few months or year, or whatever time period is involved.

This would seem to suggest that almost anyone could develop drinking problems. How far this might develop would again depend on a wide variety of personal factors, including at least the balance of benefits versus penalties for continuing on the same drinking path, the availability of alternative ways of coping with the factors that led to the problem drinking, the availability of assistance for dealing with the precipitating factors and drinking problems, and so on.

As two final examples of sociocultural influences on drinking practices, one can cite national and regional factors. Thus, in Europe, the *per capita* consumption of alcohol is at least twice as high in France as in Britain and 4 or 5 times that in Norway. In general terms, the higher the *per capita* consumption, the greater the risk of alcoholism. At a regional level, a 1980 survey by Wilson showed that Wales, the North West and North of England had the highest proportions of heavy drinkers.

The single most important point to emerge from this section is that alcohol consumption, and hence alcoholism, are influenced by a very wide range of factors and that the picture is anything but static.

Alleviation of Drinking Problems

There is a wide variety of professional and non-professional approaches to alleviating established drinking problems, ranging from Alcoholics Anonymous (which is a community-based organization run for and by alcoholics) to hospital-based or unit-based alcoholism programmes run by health care professionals. For the current purposes, and rather than simply describing a list of approaches, it is more useful to consider the goals of alleviation together with some of the means used to attain those ends.

The Goal of Abstinence

There are essentially two therapeutic goals available to the problem drinker: abstinence and controlled drinking. The former speaks for itself, in that the goal is typically lifelong total abstinence from alcohol of any sort. The term 'controlled drinking', again, is largely self-explanatory. The aim is to inculcate drinking control so that, to all intents and purposes, controlled drinking is equivalent to unproblematic social drinking. Different therapeutic agencies offer one or both goals, depending on the model of drinking problems espoused by the particular agency. Probably the best-known exampe of an agency offering a single goal is that of abstinence offered by Alcoholics Anonymous. Since that organization strongly and uncompromisingly adheres to the medical model of alcoholism, it believes the only solution for those suffering from the disease of alcoholism is total lifelong abstinence from alcohol. Indeed, so strongly does that fellowship believe the medical model that contrary evidence is explained away. Thus, the incontrovertible fact that some former alcoholics have been able to return to continuing unproblematic drinking, is discounted on the grounds that they were not 'real' alcoholics in the first instance.

The fellowship is a peer group approach in which 'recovered' (abstinent) alcoholics gather at least once a week to provide mutual support and encouragement within a programme whose emphases are on honesty about one's drinking, advice on changing one's lifestyle from that of drinking alcoholic to recovered (non-drinking) alcoholic, counselling by peers if one is tempted to relapse, and support programmes for partners and children. From this incomplete description, it can be seen that Alcoholics Anonymous attempts to provide a comprehensive community-based therapeutic programme whose aim is no less than altering the very lifestyle and outlook of the alcoholic and family. For a sizeable minority of alcoholics, these ambitious goals are achieved. The fact remains that, for a variety of reasons, the fellowship does not appeal to the majority of problem drinkers.

Other methods are also available for achieving the goal of abstinence including, for example, the highly structured 'community reinforcement' approach of Hunt and Azrin (1973) to the 'aversive conditioning' intervention of Voetlin and colleagues. Briefly stated, the former involves setting up a broad and complex community-based package of reward and reward withdrawal, whose objectives are abstinence and satisfactory family, marital, social and vocational functioning. A wide range of individuals is involved in the programme, including family members, friends, work colleagues and employers. Hence, like the AA approach, Hunt and Azrin's programme is comprehensive. In contrast, Voetlin and colleagues used a simple classical conditioning approach to inculcating abstinence in over 4,000 alcoholics in the 1940s. Using a nausea inducing drug injection, they repeatedly arranged that, immediately after smelling and tasting alcohol, the alcoholic patient vomited. This quite rapidly resulted in an aversion to alcohol, an aversion that still existed for almost 60 per cent of treated patients over a thirteen year follow-up period. Subsequent replications of this large study by other researchers have produced abstinence rates between 30 and 80 per cent.

The Goal of Controlled Drinking

The alternative treatment goal is controlled drinking. The basis for this approach is the social learning model of problem drinking acquisition and maintenance. Put simply, proponents of this treatment goal claim that, if problem drinking is learned (as they believe it is), it can be 'unlearned' and replaced by controlled drinking.

The pioneers of controlled drinking are the husband and wife team of Mark and Linda Sobell. Like Hunt and Azrin, they worked within an operant conditioning paradigm which rests on the fundamental observations that behaviour is largely influenced by its consequences. Thus, if drinking alcohol (the behaviour) gives me enjoyment (the consequence), I am likely to repeat that behaviour. If conversely drinking makes me feel ill, I am less likely to drink. In real life, most if not all behaviour results in a more-or-less complex set of positive and negative 'payoffs'. In these terms and from the problem drinker's viewpoint, the balance of advantages and disadvantages of drinking is tipped towards the former — despite any appearance to the contrary.

The Sobells (1979) constructed a hospital-based programme in which the problem drinker is helped to identify the circumstances that typically result in that individual drinking to excess. Alternative and more adaptive responses to those circumstances are then generated with the individual and, finally, (electrical) aversive conditioning is used to teach the person to drink only dilute alcohol ('long' drinks), to slowly sip rather than hastily gulp, to limit the number of drinks consumed at any sitting, and to refuse pressure from others to exceed that limit. Although this description does scant justice to this complex and comprehensive 'Individualized Behaviour Therapy' package, it illustrates the lengths programme providers must go to if the probability of success is to be maximized. The Sobells' package has been thoroughly tested and found to achieve its objectives in about 70 per cent of cases. This is excellent by any normal standards. Having said that, it is essential to understand this does not mean that comparable outcomes can be achieved with all problem drinkers. This caveat is also true for the Voetlin, and for the Hunt and Azrin interventions.

The Voetlin, the Hunt and Azrin, and the Sobell and Sobell studies were all carried out with problem drinkers who were almost certainly 'good bets', in that they were not impoverished, they were still functioning at the interpersonal, social and family levels, and for the most part they were in stable employment. The outcomes of these studies would almost certainly have been quite different had more severely and more globally affected problem drinkers been involved. The reason is to do with the depth and breadth of the problems involved. For long-standing problem drinkers, whose interpersonal, social, occupational and financial functioning has been severely disrupted, the magnitude and extent of changes necessary to support controlled drinking are so great that the chances of success can be relatively tiny. Hence, the archetypical, elderly, vagrant meths drinker is unlikely to benefit from any of the approaches mentioned. In such a case, the personal, interpersonal and social cost to the individual of again attempting to control his or her alcohol intake is likely to be too great for that person to sustain and maintain. Life for the vagrant meths drinking alcoholic revolves around drink and drinking. As some sociologists have expressed it, the individual develops and maintains a drinking 'career'. Having said all that, there are no doubt a few isolated exceptions to the general rule.

Interestingly, many controlled drinking programmes require of the potential client that they maintain a state of total abstinence from alcohol for a specified period of weeks, before they are accepted into a controlled drinking programme. One reason for using this is to select into controlled drinking programmes only those problem drinkers who can demonstrate a significant degree of control over their drinking, albeit a dichotomous 'on/off' control.

Quite apart from the extreme case of the vagrant meths drinking alcoholic, it is far from clear what proportion of long-term alcoholics could achieve the goal of controlled drinking. Currently, it is general practice to take a restrained view and to offer the opportunity of attempting controlled drinking only with 'good bets'. For the remainder of problem drinkers, the safest option is total abstinence although, as the reader will appreciate, that is often not easy for a former problem drinker to sustain, given that drinking plays an important part in many formal and informal activities in Western societies. Prevention of drinking problems, rather than their amelioration, is by far the best option for society at large, given the massive tangible and intangible costs of uncontrolled alcohol consumption.

The Prevention of Drinking Problems

The classic approach to preventing health problems is health education. The 'drink-drive' campaign that has been operating in Britain for a number of years now is a prime example. The assumption that once informed of the risks and dangers associated with a particular activity, the public will respond appropriately and the original problem will at least be greatly reduced. The evidence is that such campaigns need to be run on a continual basis and must be updated with new ways of presenting the essential 'messages', if they are not to pall. When an effective approach is used by a campaign (what is effective only becomes clear over time), ground may be gained with an initial reduction in the scale of the target problem, followed by some loss of that ground. At that point, the campaign needs to revitalized if it is not to lose impact. Naturally, this would be a multi-media campaign and back-up services would be in place before that campaign was enacted. In the case of drink-driving, legislation had been enacted, the police had been supplied with and trained in the use of Breathalysers, and so on. The harsh fact is that, in the case of drink-driving and problem drinking, the impact of the associated public health campaigns has been significant but only to the extent of 'nibbling away at the iceberg'. Public health campaigns can do so much, but legislation is also required.

The major means of preventing drinking problems among young people has been to establish ages below which it is illegal for the child to drink alcohol, and another below which it is illegal to provide the child with alcoholic beverages. Although under age drinking could never be completely prevented in this way, it is kept at a relatively low level by this widely respected legislation. Preventing adults from developing drinking problems is quite a different, and far more difficult, matter. The futile, North American attempt to establish Prohibition is too well known to require description. Incidentally, even in those cultures that for religious reasons expressly forbid the consumption of alcohol, drinking problems are not unknown.

The relative cost of alcohol has lagged far behind the increase in disposable income in this country. In real terms, alcohol has probably never been cheaper. It requires nothing more than common sense to expect that, as the real cost of alcohol has declined, *per capita* consumption has increased. It is also available from a wide variety of shops where, at one time, there were far fewer retail 'outlets'. In addition, the cost of spirits, with their high alcohol content, has increased at a slower rate than the cost of the various types of beer and wine, with the inevitable result. Evidence from this and other countries shows that cost per unit of alcohol is a major weapon in the fight against the acquisition of problem drinking. The cost of alcohol needs to be pitched at a level that does not encourage a significant increase in home-made alcohol, but that does render it very expensive to develop drinking problems. As a crude analogy, it would cost far less to become overweight on everyday foods than on caviar and truffles! In the same way if the real cost of alcohol were to be increased to the point that, for the average person, it became excessively expensive to develop drinking problems, fewer people would go down that path. It would mean an increase in the cost of all alcoholic beverages, the greatest increased being on those that contained the highest percentage of alcohol.

The sort of increases discussed in the academic and professional literature would make today's prices look like absolute bargains. For example, taking the average cost of a pint of beer as £1, the cost of one millilitre of alcohol in that beer is 3.52p. The cost of one millilitre of alcohol in spirits is 2.67p. If the alcohol in a bottle of spirits cost the same as that in beer, spirits would cost around £11 per bottle. Since fiscal measures would need to be aimed at reducing alcohol consumption, regardless of the type of beverage, all prices would need to rise while still ensuring that the cost of a unit of alcohol remained the same, regardless of the beverage in which it appeared. The final cost that would reduce the average *per capita* alcohol consumption could only be determined by trial and error. Those people with above average disposable incomes would probably not be as affected by price increases in the way that those in less favourable financial situations would be, but that is a global fact. The other side of the balance sheet is more difficult to quantify, since it involves intangibles such as human happiness and unhappiness, personal rights, vested interests, and so on.

Tutorial Discussion Questions

1 If alcoholism is a metabolic disease, it makes little sense to blame alcoholics for their plight. What if alcoholism is not a disease?
2 Is the ability to consume large quantities of alcohol at a sitting, without falling on one's face, a useful measure of an individual's maturity?
3 Do you believe anyone could potentially develop drinking problems, or do you think some people are immune from that possibility?
4 What do you think distinguishes the minority of drinkers who do develop serious drinking problems?
5 Can you identify the costs and benefits of your own abstinence or, if you do drink alcohol, of your drinking?
6 Since governments derive a significant income from the duty on alcohol sales what, if anything, might cause a government to take strenuous fiscal steps to reduce consumption?
7 Under what circumstances, if any, might society be prepared to condone the compulsory treatment of problem drinkers?
8 The conviction is currently gaining ground that those who pollute the environment should have to pay the costs of cleaning up their mess. Is it reasonable to argue that the drinks industry should bear some of the responsibility and costs of problem drinking?

References

HUNT, G. M. and AZRIN, N. H. (1973) 'A community-reinforcement approach to alcoholism', *Behaviour Research and Therapy*, **11**, pp. 91–104.
SOBELL, M. B. and SOBELL, L. C. (1979) 'Individualized behaviour therapy for alcoholics', *Behaviour Theraphy*, **4**, pp. 49–72.
VOETLIN, W. L. and BROZ, W. R. (1949) 'The conditioned reflex treatment of chronic alcoholism: X. An analysis of 3,125 admissions over a period of ten and a half years', *Annals of International Medicine*, **30**, pp. 580–97.
WORLD HEALTH ORGANIZATION (1952) *Expert Committee on Mental Health Alcohol Sub-committee Second Report. Technical Report Series, No. 48*, Geneva, World Health Organization.

WORLD HEALTH ORGANIZATION (1977) *Alcohol-Related Disabilities*, (Offset Publication No. 32), Geneva, World Health Organization.

Further Reading

EASTMAN, C. (1984) *Drink and Drinking Problems*, London, Longman.

HEATHER, N. and ROBERTSON, I. (1985) *Problem Drinking: The New Approach*, Harmondsworth, Penguin.

MILLER, P. M. (1976) *Behavioural Treatment of Alcoholism*, Oxford, Pergamon.

SPECIAL COMMITTEE OF THE ROYAL COLLEGE OF PSYCHIATRISTS (1979) *Alcohol and Alcoholism*, London, Tavistock. (The report of the Special Committee).

Chapter 11

Government and Tobacco: Economics, Ethics and Epidemics

Allan Norris

When I first met Wendy she looked a remarkably well woman in her late thirties, in spite of the fact that she was in a hospital bed awaiting radiotherapy and chemotherapy for cancer. Wendy had been referred to me by her oncologist because he felt that she was psychologically extremely distressed and was not coping well with her illness and its prognosis of only a few short months. However, Wendy not only looked well, she felt well. A short time before, she had visited her doctor only because she had noticed a small lump which had appeared on her back. This small lump proved to be a secondary tumour from the primary cancer in her lung.

Wendy died a few months after I first saw her. She did not see her first grandchild which her daughter was expecting; she did not enjoy the rewards of the hard work she and her husband had put into their small family business; she did not see her younger daughter reach maturity. She left a caring family grieving for her.

Wendy was not a heavy smoker; she was one of at least 100,000 smokers who die each year in the UK from a smoking-related disease (Royal College of Physicians, 1971). Nor was she terribly unlucky to suffer a smoking-related disease: 3 out of 4 smokers suffer from such an illness, and 1 of those 3 will be killed by it. This scale of death and disease has been compared by the Royal College of Physicians (1971) to the great epidemic diseases of the past.

Why Don't Smokers Stop?

More than one recent survey has shown that about 90 per cent of smokers know that smoking causes lung cancer, and that about 75 per cent believe that it causes heart disease. Why then do they not stop smoking?

This apparently simple question is not easily answered. First, it is really two questions: 'Why don't smokers try to stop?' and 'Why, when they do try, do they find it so difficult?' A government survey of smoking attitudes and behaviour (Marsh and Matheson, 1983) has provided interesting information which goes some way to answering the first question. It indicated that smokers who believe that smoking causes fatal and disabling diseases do not suffer the psychological discomfort of cognitive dissonance, because they believe that they will not suffer these consequences. For example, they think that it is only heavy smokers who are at risk (and they define heavy smokers as people who smoke more than they do). Similarly, they think that it is only people who smoke cigarettes of a higher tar content than theirs who are at risk. Many smokers believe that somehow they will know when to quit in order to avoid fatal illnesses. Unfortunately, the principal smoking-related diseases of heart disease and cancer give no such warning.

The second problem of why smokers find quitting so difficult is also a complex matter, but it is worth outlining some possible explanations, since these also have a bearing on questions of public policy on smoking.

The reasons are psychosocial and physical. Psychosocial factors underlying continued smoking include habit, classical conditioning, social pressure, the commercial promotion of smoking, and the cheapness and availability of tobacco.

The influence of habit may be gauged by the frequency and consistency of smoking behaviour. Most smokers smoke about 15 to 20 cigarettes a day; while some smoke very many more than this, very few smoke only a few cigarettes a day (the reasons for this are explained below). Smokers rarely experience a day without smoking, and they tend to smoke their cigarettes at the same time and in the same relaxing or pleasurable situations every day. Thus, with about ten puffs from each cigarette, they draw on a cigarette maybe 200 times a day. Perhaps any behaviour performed so frequently, so regularly and so persistently would be difficult to stop. However, the consistent and repeated pairing of smoking with work breaks, with food and drink, and with social contact may condition the smoker unconsciously to associate cigarettes with these other pleasures.

Social pressure from friends who smoke may also weaken a quitting smoker's resolve: small groups are held together partly by real or perceived shared qualities, such as common beliefs, attitudes and behaviour. A group member who renounces one of these commonalities (such as smoking) may thus threaten the group's cohesion. The group may then try to restore the previous situation by trying to entice the smoker back to the habit.

Cigarettes are cheap and are heavily promoted in all countries which permit tobacco advertising. In the UK, they have gone down in price in real terms over recent years, and at the time of writing, the duty on tobacco has not been increased sufficiently, even to keep pace with inflation.

If the above psychosocial factors were not enough of a problem for quitting smokers, the less conspicuous physical factors would provide sufficient obstacles.

The addictiveness of nicotine from cigarettes has long been recognized by clinicians, and tobacco dependence is included as a diagnosis in the American medical profession's view of dependency disorders (American Psychiatric Association, 1987). Similarly, tobacco withdrawal symptoms have been extensively documented by researchers in this field. Moreover, comparisons of relapse rates of addicts in treatment suggest that smoking is as difficult to withdraw from as heroin. Much physiological research data also support the conclusion that nicotine in cigarettes is addictive, but the evidence is complex and does not lend itself to brief summary. However, the principal relevant findings are as follows.

Smokers have been found to reduce their *ad libitum* smoking when they are given nicotine in another form; and people who are not permitted to smoke may find other sources of nicotine. For example, when British coal miners (who for safety reasons are forbidden to smoke underground) went on a prolonged strike in 1984, the snuff industry had a lean year, too. (Snuff is ground tobacco, and also gives its users a dose of nicotine with each sniff.) Studies of blood nicotine levels in smokers indicate that people smoke to maintain their accustomed blood nicotine levels: it is known that when smokers are switched to lower nicotine cigarettes, they will increase the number of such cigarettes they smoke, or will smoke them in such a way as to achieve their usual blood nicotine levels. Again, the data on the number of cigarettes smoked by the average smoker have shown a small increase when manufacturers have gradually reduced the nicotine content of cigarettes. Finally, the most successful current pharmacological treatment for smoking withdrawal is based on replacing the smoker's regular nicotine through a special nicotine chewing-gum which allows the smoker to concentrate on breaking the habit aspects of their dependency, while the gum allows a gradual weaning off nicotine.

Nicotine from a cigarette is rapidly and efficiently absorbed, taking only 2 to 3 seconds to travel from alveolar air to the brain. It travels to the brain in a bolus, that is, concentrated in a limited segment of the bloodstream flow, arriving at the brain in a single rush, even before it can be diffused around the cardiovascular system. Thus, the smoker gets the effect of the cigarette almost immediately and, in contrast to other drugs such as alcohol, there is immediate feedback of its effects. Nicotine is then broken down quickly (its half-life in the body, though complex, is around half an hour). Since, as we have seen, it is the nicotine which smokers smoke for, and since smokers regulate their smoking to achieve and maintain blood nicotine levels which they find comfortable, then it is not surprising that most smokers are ready for another cigarette within an hour of the previous one. This perhaps explains one of the most striking features of smoking behaviour: its consistency. Smokers vary their daily intake very little, especially in the direction of reducing it. Very few smokers indeed smoke only a few cigarettes, and even they may actually be *en route* to developing the more characteristic pattern of smoking behaviour.

Thus, in summary, smoking is a complex dependency. Smokers may try to protect themselves from the psychological discomfort which comes from the discrepancy between their knowledge and their behaviour. When they try to quit, both psychological and physical obstacles may frustrate their intentions.

These factors are important background to any consideration of smoking policy, but are especially so to a consideration of issues of freedom of choice. For example, choosing to smoke or not to smoke may be too simplistic a view of the decision process. Surveys indicate that about two thirds to three quarters of smokers say that they do not want to be smokers, and most of them have tried unsuccessfully to stop, often many times. Thus, choosing not to smoke is not like choosing, say, whether or not to wear brown shoes; for many it is more like being a hard drug addict.

Government Reaction to the Discovery of the Health Consequences of Smoking

Lung cancer was a rare disease before this century; increasing public concern about an apparent epidemic led Oxford epidemiologists Richard Doll and Austin Bradford Hill to research for possible causative factors. Doll did not suspect smoking, but thought that some other twentieth-century development would prove to be the culprit. Their results were striking and conclusive, however: cigarette smoking and lung cancer were unmistakably linked. When the cabinet learned of the link, it discussed what the government should do, especially since the government's own experts urged that young people at least should be warned of the danger.

Cabinet papers released under the 30-years secrecy rule (reported in *The Times*, 7 January 1985) reveal that the government of the day considered the matter (in February, 1954), but decided to play down the research findings and reassure smokers. (Thus, the initial impact which the news might have had with strong govenment support was irredeemably and permanently dissipated.) The cabinet's reasons were a fear of losing tax revenue, and because the tobacco industry had given a grant of £250,000 to the Medical Research Council. Although Iain McLeod, the Minister of Health, was reported as declaring in cabinet that there was no doubt in his mind about the link, in his statement to the House of Commons he played down the scientific evidence and asserted that 'There is no firm evidence of the way smoking may cause lung cancer, or of the extent to which it may do so'. He apparently timed his announcement to the House for the convenience of the Imperial Tobacco Company who wanted to be able to make reference to it in their forthcoming annual report.

The dilemma faced by the British government in 1954 has confronted every Western government to this day. Each has had to weigh the welfare of their population against financial considerations. Indeed, tobacco tax has been a predicament ever since James I first imposed it: he disliked smoking and taxed it heavily, but then reduced the duty when it looked as though it might jeopardize the burgeoning trade.

Tobacco duty is liked by government exchequers: it is easily collected by relatively few officials (unlike, say, income tax, poll tax or value added tax); it is widely regarded as justifiable as a deterrent to health threatening behaviour; and it is thought to be voluntary, since those paying it are not obliged to smoke.

As well as tax, another major concern of governments is the welfare of the industry which provides employment, and whose products bring in the revenue. Moreover, depending on the political leaning of the government, it may be sympathetic to lobbying either by labour unions who represent tobacco workers or by tobacco industry organizations.

The situation is further complicated by the fact that different government departments bring different priorities to the issue: health departments may urge curbs on smoking out of a concern for the health of the population, while the treasury may prefer a thriving, revenue generating industry, and departments of employment and trade want to see jobs secured and markets flourish. A recent example of the consequences of such conflict is provided by the case of the United States Tobacco Company who were given substantial government money to help them to set up a plant in East Kilbride in Scotland to manufacture 'Skoal Bandits' (small paper bags of ground tobacco for sucking). The Department of Health, concerned about medical evidence that these cause oral cancer, eventually succeeded in banning the product from sale in the UK, in spite of pressure from American politicans who argued that a ban would restrict free tade.

Such conflicting interdepartmental priorities were considered by the government in 1971, following a recommendation of a recently published report from the Royal College of Physicians (1971). The government set up a working party of senior officials from different departments to consider the likely economic consequences of significant reductions in smoking. Their report was kept secret by the government, but was leaked to *The Guardian* newspaper (6 May 1980) nine years later. The main conclusions of the report were that a reduction in smoking would result in hundreds of thousands of lives being saved over the coming decades. A reduction in prevalance of 20 per cent would cause a significant drop both in the number of days lost to industry through illness, as well as bringing about a fall in the cost of treating smoking-related disease. However, the economic consequences were thought to be undesirable. In particular, the cost to the government of paying pensions to the people who would live longer would more than offset the financial gains resulting from a healthier workforce. Similarly, the loss of tobacco duty was unlikely to be matched by the income from taxes on other goods or services on which consumers might spend their spare moeny. Finally, the working party feared that significant reductions in smoking might seriously damage the tobacco industry's health, with a consequent loss of jobs, especially in parts of the country which were already suffering economically. It seems they were particularly concerned that two tobacco companies, one South African and the other American, might withdraw from the UK. No apparent action was taken by the government following the report.

Governments are also subject to pressure from interested groups on both sides of the argument. The tobacco industry has developed a very effective parliamentary lobby: it retains the services of a number of members of parliament as its paid consultants. It also provides sympathizers on both sides of the House with selective information to support its case, and these members are well placed to bend the chancellor's ear in the run-up to the budget. It has the resources to buy goodwill: just as the cabinet were swayed by a grant to the Medical Research Council in 1954, the Minister of Health in 1982 said he was 'pleased to announce' a grant of £11,000,000 from the tobacco industry to establish the Health Promotion Research Trust. Its terms of reference required that it promote health in the UK through research to encourage people, especially the young, to take responsibility for their own health, and to promote research into factors which might affect the consequences of a more responsible attitude to health. However, the terms of reference specifically excluded 'studies designed directly or indirectly to examine the use and effects of tobacco products . . .'. Thus, while the Trust may promote much worthwhile research, in so doing, it will also inevitably shift public attention away from smoking as a cause of illness and death, by the emphasis which its work will give to other, relatively less important factors.

The anti-smoking lobby is a pauper in comparison to the tobacco industry. It is led by ASH (Action on Smoking and Health), which was set up in 1971 by the Royal College of Physicians and depends on an annual grant from the government for most of its funds. It relies on the enthusiasm and commitment of a very small number of staff, although it has a large number of subscribing supporters.

When the tobacco industry approaches senior civil servants, it is direct and effective. An investigative journalist, Peter Taylor, has given a detailed and disturbing account (Taylor, 1985) of this aspect of the industry's activities. He notes that the industry approaches all government departments which may be influential in their case, and they entertain officials at major sports and arts events which they are involved in sponsoring. The events include the tennis championships at Wimbledon, the cricket cup finals at Lords, formula one grand prix racing, and the opera at Glyndebourne. While there is no suggestion that in accepting such invitations, civil servants are transgressing their employer's conditions of service, and the officials themselves may believe that they can remain immune from their hosts' influence, nevertheless a psychologist might be more sceptical, knowing that attitudes, beliefs and behaviour are interdependent. And the tobacco industry presumably thinks it an effective strategy, or it would not do it.

The Tobacco Industry's Reaction to the Discovery of Smoking-Related Disease

Before Doll and Hill published their findings in 1952, the tobacco companies could believe themselves to be honourable people engaged in an industry which provided revenue for governments, secure employment for workers, and pleasure for its consumers. The Doll and Hill reports (and the flood of medical and scientific research which followed) confronted the managers of the industry with a dissonance provoking dilemma: they were manufacturing, distributing and promoting a product which kills or harms the majority of its users. They could resolve the dissonance in one of three ways. First, they could decide that they were not honourable and carry on their trade with little regard for their customers; second, they could decide that they were honourable, and should therefore run down their industry and discourage new smokers from starting; or finally, they could reject the research and continue to trade in the same beliefs they held previously.

Given the alternatives, it will come as little surprise that the managers chose the latter course. And, like any individual suffering dissonance, they first tried to refute the disconcerting research results. Thus, the tobacco industry in the USA, UK and Europe established or funded research laboratories to examine the effects of smoking on health. The laboratories were closed down when — like the British laboratories in Harrogate — they found that cigarette smoke contained carcinogens, or — like the German laboratory in Hamburg — they found that smoking caused cardiovascular disease.

Instead, the companies took a position which they have held to this day: their stance is that they are not doctors, but a causal link between smoking and disease has not been established to their satisfaction. At the same time, and somewhat inconsistently, the companies embarked on the production and promotion of lower tar cigarettes.

They also began the development of a 'safer' cigarette (although they still did not accept that there might be such a thing as more dangerous cigarettes). This research culminated in the production of two types of substitute tobacco with trade names 'Cytrel' and 'NSM' (New Smoking Material) in the 1970s. Following guarded approval by the government's Independent Scientific Committee on Smoking and Health, a range of new cigarette brands was launched (with a good deal of publicity and promotion) in 1977. The new brands were still made mainly of tobacco, with the synthetic material making up only a proportion of the filling. Every single new brand flopped disastrously, not least perhaps because the 'safer' cigarette would not deliver the nicotine dose which smokers were used to, and therefore would not produce the smoker's comfortable blood nicotine level. These 'safer' cigarettes were all quickly withdrawn.

The next major obstacle the industry faced was the growing movement for non-smokers' rights, first in the USA, then in the UK. Smoking has always caused some discomfort to non-smokers, and has affected the health of vulnerable individuals, but in the 1970s and 1980s medical and scientific reports of effects on the health of normal non-smokers exposed to tobacco smoke began to appear. This led to a number of small groups of voters in the USA using state legislation to introduce referendum proposals for the restriction of smoking in public. It would be expected that such propositions, if successful, would worry the tobacco industry considerably, not least because it might be the thin end of a wedge which could lead to smoking being regarded as unacceptable social behaviour. Taylor (1985) gives an account of the industry's response, which in essence was to set up opposition groups, and fund them on a massive scale. The industry also ensured that voters were saturated with propaganda which did not argue the case proposed, but spread fear and doubt with misinformation about the consequences of such proposals.

The industry had discovered the tactic of deliberately arguing the wrong case. Unless recognized, this has the advantage of giving the appearance of winning the argument, while at the same time discrediting your opponents by attributing a weak or foolish stance to them. It also takes attention away from the issues which caused the concern in the first place.

The tactic was developed and refined with the establishment of permanent pressure groups, largely funded by the industry, which would be able to keep the industry's message in the public eye, and would be available to fight on its behalf whenever any new initiative on smoking was suggested. In the UK, the industry helped to set up and support FOREST — the Freedom Organization for the Right to Enjoy Smoking Tobacco. (While the words 'Freedom', 'Right' and 'Enjoy' may have been carefully chosen, the memorable acronym is somewhat inappropriate since tobacco growing and curing is a major source of deforestation in many developing countries; see Madeley, 1986.) The intention of the strategy appeared to be to shift attention away from public concerns about smoking and health (and especially about passive smoking) by casting the smoker in the role of a persecuted minority — thus building on associations in the public consciousness of civil rights campaigns and other popular causes for social justice.

The industry also keeps a wary eye on those doctors and scientists in the forefront of research on smoking and health by, for example, sending anonymous delegates to their conferences. At the Sixth World Congress on Smoking and Health in Tokyo in 1987, it was noted that about 10 per cent of the delegates were tobacco industry spies, and it was decided not to make the next such conference in 1990 so welcoming to them. Tobacco industry conferences have never been open to outsiders.

In the UK, the tobacco industry has another major problem to face which is also a consequence of the research on smoking and health: smoking has been in a slow but steady decline since the mid-1970s, since about ten million smokers have given it up. And in addition to smokers who quit, the industry loses a further 100,000 of its customers each year through smoking-related disease. The industry also knows that, in general, adults do not start to smoke; much research into the matter has shown that smokers usually start during adolescence. The industry must be very well aware of this vital marketing information, the implication of which is that, if it is to win new customers, it must recruit them from the young if it wants to have any future home market. However, the sale of cigarettes to children is against the law (although it is a law which is rarely enforced), and the tobacco companies' voluntary agreement with the government on advertising prohibits tobacco promotion to children.

The industry's stance on this is quite clear: the companies assert that their advertising is intended only to protect the market share of their brands, not to recruit new smokers, and that their advertisements only affect those over 18 years of age. Research on children's awareness of cigarette brands following the televising of tobacco-sponsored sporting events, however, suggests that this assumption may not be justified. One researcher (Chapman, 1986: 84–5) has noted that if cigarette advertisements do not help to attract new customers, then they must be unique in the whole world of advertising, where every other advertisement attempts to do just that.

The industry also appears to have targeted women as one market section where it might slow the decline in sales. It has even been able to exploit the feminist movement of recent years: cigarettes have been promoted to women through a curious mixture of appeals to women's aspirations on the one hand, and of traditional — and arguably sexist — promotion of 'women's cigarettes' on the other. That is, advertisements have promoted images of independent women, while still reinforcing stereotypes: one example used a picture of a slim, attractive and self-assured young woman alongside the slogan, 'You've come a long way, Baby', to launch Virginia Slims (and the last word of the brand name is significant).

Cigarette brands designed for the female market have been heavily promoted in women's magazines, and there is good reason to believe that many of their editors and writers have underplayed smoking in their coverage of women's health issues (Jacobson, 1986). This omission is all the more significant since smoking plays an especially important part in women's health. In addition to all the risks which male smokers run, women who use the contraceptive pill are at special additional risks, and pregnant women who smoke also jeopardize the health of their unborn baby.

But it is not only through advertisements that tobacco companies may be able to promote smoking to women and young people. Public relations agencies or other 'information' providers are also used. Such activities have the merit of not being obvious advertising. Both FOREST and the Tobacco Advisory Council (the industry's mouthpiece) carry out such work by providing highly selective information, arguments and suggestions for the media. At the time of writing, for example, a glossy magazine aimed at the young (*Blitz*, February 1990) devotes its cover and the main feature to what looks very much like industry propaganda. The cover shows a photograph of a film star smoking, against the headline, 'Smoking is good for you'. The feature inside could have been composed by industry public relations writers: after suggesting to readers that smoking is 'cool' and listing 'cool smokers' (film and other personalities, living and dead, who smoked), the article goes on to offer instructions for initiation into smoking, how to look 'cool' while smoking, and to attack the health lobby as puritan killjoys. The article, which does not mention the disease caused by smoking, ends: '. . . the more we find to celebrate in the act of smoking and the rich, colourful culture that surrounds it. Anyone got a light?'

Marketing managers of many industries have used a technique called 'product placement': in return for investing in the production costs of a feature film, for example, the film makers agree to include the manufacturer's product in the script, either by name or in image. This strategy has particular advantages for tobacco manufacturers: it offers convenient and influential role models for the young, both through the characters of the story and the actors portraying them. Films offer the young person a view (which may seem authoritative) of the adult world and adult behaviour. Again, the technique has the advantage of not being an overt advertisement. It also allows promotion without concern for the standards which the advertising industry enforces, or the rules which have been agreed with government on the advertising of cigarettes.

An alternative to trying to slow the decline in the home market is to seek markets abroad. Undoubtedly, the market with the greatest growth potential for the industry is the third world. Here the industry promotes cigarettes in ways which would not be tolerated in developed countries, ironically often associating their products with images of Western success, pastimes and technology to appeal to the aspirations of people, many of whom already have problems of health and poverty.

At a more responsible level, tobacco companies have diversified their commercial interests. The major British companies have acquired interests in insurance, hotels and brewing, for example.

The companies have also bought good relations through their sponsorship of major public events (many of which, such as tennis, motor-cycle racing, grand prix racing, rugby football, cricket and snooker, have an enthusiastic following among the young). Such sponsorship may not be pure altruism; the sponsor's brand names, colours and logos are inescapable at such events. Indeed, some events or teams have come to be known in abbreviated form by the name of the cigarette. For example, the one-day cricket competition is often called 'the Benson and Hedges', and the Lotus formula one racing car was known as 'the JPS' until John Player withdrew from the sponsorship (to be replaced by Camel).

However, there is another possible reason why the tobacco industry might want to sponsor popular events. The industry particularly fears a ban on advertising and promotion; through sponsorship, the industry is paying a sort of insurance premium against its worst fear. It is assembling ready-made supporters who might be counted on to protest against measures which could affect their sport, their arts or their team. The industry used exactly this tactic when state legislation against tobacco promotion first appeared likely in Western Australia in 1983.

Another industry tactic is to market other products with their cigarette brand names. Silk Cut and Peter Stuyvesant holidays, and Marlboro and JPS rally jackets are among the better-known examples. Apart from associating their cigarettes with certain lifestyles, this strategy also muddies the waters for any future legislator intending to curb tobacco promotion.

The above is not a complete list of the range of the industry's responses — that would be difficult, not least because the companies are secretive about many of their activities — but it clearly illustrates the ingenuity, determination and vigour which characterize their approach.

What Should Government Do about Smoking?

The sum of action which successive British governments have carried out to reduce smoking is not impressive. It might be concluded that governments have been less than wholehearted in their efforts to reduce the number of deaths due to smoking.

Much of the decline in smoking which has continued since the early 1970s cannot be attributed to government measures. On the other hand, the publication of reports on smoking and health by the Royal College of Physicians in 1963 and 1971, together with the attendant publicity, was followed on both occasions by sharp falls in cigarette consumption in both men and women. Other factors may also have had an effect: the campaigns by various health lobbies, such as ASH, the British Medical Association (BMA), and the National Society of Non-Smokers (who initiated the annual 'National No Smoking Day' in the UK), have probably helped to change public attitudes to smoking. And at an individual level, as non-smokers have become a majority in both sexes and in all social groups, they have perhaps felt more confident to ask for smoke-free areas in enclosed public places — something which would have been unthinkable twenty years ago, when the majority of men and nearly half the women smoked. At that time, wherever smokers and non-smokers were not segregated, it was the norm that smoking was permitted.

Before a government considers what it might do, it will first question whether it should do anything at all. Perhaps its answer to this question will reflect its view of its own role and responsibilities in governing the nation, and hence, its priorities when it comes to formulating policy. Only then can it decide which of its responsibilities should take precedence: the health of its subjects or the health of an industry? Alternatively, it might put the question in other terms: should not governments expect people to take responsibility for their own health behaviour? And therefore, might not government action on smoking be unfair interference in the rights of people engaged in perfectly legal behaviour?

The view of the BMA is that governments have some responsibility for the health of their subjects, and quite simple action could reduce the holocaust of deaths due to smoking, currently averaging nearly 300 a day in the UK alone — equivalent to the loss of life in a very major disaster every single day of the year.

The view of the industry, on the other hand, as expressed by its parliamentary supporters, is that government action is unwarranted since its products are safe, and that any such action is undesirable as it is 'nannying' the population and interfering with people's freedom to choose to do what they want within the law.

A different view might be that both the law and most governments' policies were established before our current knowledge about tobacco and its consequences. Neither policy nor the law has kept pace with medical and scientific research. Tobacco is a lethal drug of addiction. If tobacco and its problems were discovered today, no responsible government would permit it. Yet current policies appear to be based mainly on premises which the tobacco industry promotes: that the health case against smoking is unproven, or at least that smokers have been warned, and have only themselves to blame if they choose to start smoking or to continue to do so. That is, evidence on the age of onset of smoking and the addictiveness of nicotine are apparently overlooked by government policies.

Arguments based on the freedom of the individual to choose also disregard research findings on nicotine addiction. In any case, governments have always curbed some individual freedoms to protect the individual and others from harm: they do not permit people to take other addictive drugs which may damage them.

One particular body of research is especially important for governments considering these matters: it is the increasing evidence that it is not only the smoker whose health may be at risk, but also those who share indoor space with them. Freedom of choice to do what one wants cannot be unrestricted when it affects the health of others. Thus, there is no legal right to drink and drive, and there is no legal right to discharge pollutants into water supply reservoirs. In any case, it is also a matter of fact that there is no general right in law to smoke. The exception to this is under Army and Navy Regulations: a traitor condemned to death has a legal right to the last rites, a visit from his family and a final cigarette! (Howard, 1989)

Tutorial Discussion Questions

1 Could governments take action to reduce the number of people who become ill or die from smoking, without undermining any fundamental rights of the individual?

2 Tobacco is a legal product; should there be any restrictions on its marketing and promotion? (Currently, most tobacco advertising in the United Kingdom is regulated by voluntary agreement between the government and the industry; it is monitored by a joint committee of representatives from each side. See Chapman, 1986, for further information and discussion on this topic.) The tobacco industry might argue that any restriction would represent a curb on freedom of speech; the health lobby might say that there should be no freedom to promote a lethal and addictive drug.

3 Should governments legislate on the subject of smoking in public places? Would restrictions infringe the rights of smokers, or impose undue and unnecessary stress on them? Are these considerations more or less important than the right to breathe clean air and freedom from involuntary smoking?

4 To what extent should governments inform, persuade or cajole its subjects about smoking, disease and death? Should governments offer help to smokers who want to give up, or is this the responsibility of the individual, and unjustified when there are other acute demands on the health services?

5 Would it be justified to use taxation as a means of controlling the prevalance of smoking, or in order to reduce the number of children and adolescents who start to smoke? Taxation has been shown to have an impact on both, but the industry argues that its products are already heavily taxed, and further taxation may differentially affect the least well-off in society.

References

AMERICAN PSYCHIATRIC ASSOCIATION (1987) *Diagnostic and Statistical Manual of Mental Disorders*, 3rd ed., revised. Washington, DC, American Psychiatric Association.

CHAPMAN, S. (1986) 'Cigarette advertising and smoking: a review of the evidence', in BRITISH MEDICAL ASSOCIATION (Ed.) *Smoking Out the Barons: The Campaign against the Tobacco Industry*, Chichester, John Wiley. pp. 79–97.

HOWARD, G. (1989) 'Some legal issues of smoking at work', unpublished paper.

JACOBSON, B. (1986) 'When smoke gets in your eyes. Cigarette advertising policy and coverage of smoking and health in women's magazines', in BRITISH MEDICAL ASSOCIATION (Ed.) *Smoking Out the Barons: The Campaign against the Tobacco Industry*, Chichester, John Wiley. pp. 99–137.

MADELEY, J. (1986) 'Tobacco: a ruinous crop', *The Ecologist*, 16, pp. 124–29.

Allan Norris

MARSH, A. and MATHESON, J. (1983) *Smoking Attitudes and Behaviour*, London, HMSO.
ROYAL COLLEGE OF PHYSICIANS (1971) *Smoking and Health Now*, Tunbridge Wells, Pittman Medical.
TAYLOR, P. (1985) *The Smoke Ring: Tobacco, Money and Multinational Politics*, London, Sphere Books.

Further Reading

ASHTON, H. and STEPNEY, R. (1982) *Smoking — Psychology and Pharmacology*, London, Tavistock.
BRITISH MEDICAL ASSOCIATION (1986) *Smoking Out the Barons: The Campaign Against the Tobacco Industry*, Chichester, John Wiley.
JACOBSON, B. (1986) *Beating the Ladykillers*, London. Pluto Press.
MADELEY, J. (1986) 'Tobacco: a ruinous crop', *The Ecologist*, **16**, pp. 124–29.
MARSH, A. and MATHESON, J. (1983) *Smoking Attitudes and Behaviour*, London, HMSO.
TAYLOR, P. (1985) *The Smoke Ring: Tobacco, Money and Multinational Politics*, London, Sphere Books.

Chapter 12

Animal Experiments in Psychology

Glyn Thomas

Animal experiments have occupied a central position within psychology for many years, but have recently become increasingly controversial. On the one hand, animal rights campaigners represent psychologists' use of animals as sickening cruelty carried out to answer pointless questions (Sharpe, 1985). Defenders of animal research, on the other hand, claim that it offers the best hope of curing afflictions such as depression and schizophrenia (Keehn, 1986). In this chapter, I will present some of the arguments for and against animal experimentation in psychology, and invite comparisons with other uses of animals by mankind.

Why Experiment on Animals at all?

One reason to do animal experiments in psychology is to find out about animals themselves and their behaviour. Understanding animal behaviour contributes to scientific knowledge and may have practical uses (for improving animal husbandry, for example). Many animal experiments in psychology, however, are performed ultimately to increase our knowledge about human behaviour and mental functioning. This requires some justification, because the obvious way to learn about people, surely, is to study people, not animals.

When psychologists choose animals rather than people as subjects it is because in several important ways they are *easier* to study in a scientifically rigorous way. Firstly, it may be easier to isolate the underlying principles of behaviour in an animal than in a man, because the behavioural processes are usually simpler in the animal. Secondly, many of the animals usually chosen for study (e.g. rats, mice, gerbils) are small and have short life cycles so that it is relatively easy to exert precise control over the conditions of the experiment. Finally, experimenters can do things to animals which they would not nowadays be allowed to do to human subjects.

Of course, none of these advantages of animal experiments would be of any account if the results obtained with animals could not be applied to human beings. A strong Western religious tradition holds that man is absolutely unique, but this is increasingly an untenable position. The structure and functioning of our bodies in breathing, feeding and reproducing, for example, are similar to those of many other mammals. Furthermore, the human brain has a similar basic structure to other mammalian brains. At a behavioural level it is increasingly difficult to identify qualitative differences between people and animals. Achievements such as some use of tools and language are now known to be within the reach of chimpanzees, and not, as was once thought, unique to mankind. What we know of the selection of genetic adaptations by environments suggest that these similarities are the result of the evolution of people and animals from a common ancestor. According to this view, we are not just very *like* animals, we *are* animals. Indeed, in this chapter I am using the term 'animal' as a shorthand for 'non-human animal'.

What Experiments are Carried Out?

A survey conducted by the British Psychological Society (1979) found that in 1977 approximately 43,000 animals per year were being used in research in UK psychology departments. Mice, rats and birds accounted for over 92 per cent of this total. Mesirow (1984) found a similar pattern of use in a survey of graduate departments of psychology in the USA. In the UK, the number of animals used by psychologists was relatively small compared with the total of five and a half million animals used for all scientific purposes in 1977.

With regard to procedures, in 1977 the British Psychological Society survey found that per year in UK psychology departments approximately 4,000 animals were exposed to electric shock, 6,850 to drugs, 4,700 were subjected to surgery, and over 8,000 were deprived of food or water for a period to motivate them. To appreciate what these procedures involve it may help to consider selected experiments in some detail.

Experiments involving drugs or surgery are usually performed to study the physical structures and processes underlying behaviour. In an early experiment of this kind, Maier (1935) located the part of the cerebral cortex needed for skilled movement in rats. He surgically destroyed part of the rats' brains on one side only. After the animals had recovered from the operation, Maier looked for signs of hemiplegia (one-sided paralysis) in the rats when they tried to walk along a narrow 'catwalk'. After he had assessed the degree of paralysis, he killed the rats and dissected their brains to discover the precise areas which had been destroyed by the earlier operation. In this way, Maier was able to correlate damage to different parts of the cortex with the extent of paralysis found in the walking test. It hardly needs to be said that such an experiment could not be legally carried out with human subjects.

While animal experiments involving surgery and death of the animals seem severe, they have one mitigating feature; that is, every attempt is made to minimize suffering by the use of anaesthetics and humane killing methods. Experiments to study the effects of stress, however, lack this redeeming feature because the aim of the experiment cannot be achieved without exposing the conscious animals to the stressors.

Experiments on *learned helplessness* in animals provide a good example of this kind of research. Seligman and Maier (1967) restrained dogs in a harness and gave them repeated electric shocks. The shocks were painful, inescapable and unavoidable, but not physically damaging. The dogs were subsequently tested in a 'shuttle box', an oblong cage with a low barrier across the middle, in which they were given further electric shocks which they could avoid by jumping the barrier.

Dogs without prior experience of uncontrollable shocks generally learn quickly to jump the barrier and thus avoid most of the shocks. In contrast, the dogs that Seligman and Maier had first treated with uncontrollable shocks in the harness found it very difficult to learn to jump the barrier to avoid the shocks in the shuttle box. After some initial frantic struggling and running, the pre-exposed dogs usually just gave up and lay down. Seligman has called this failure to avoid shocks 'learned helplessness', and has suggested that it represents a universal reaction to traumatic but uncontrollable events.

It must be said, however, that many animal experiments in psychology involve treatments which are far less severe than those just described. Many experiments on learning, for example, involve only limited restriction of food intake to ensure that the animals will be motivated to work for food rewards. Such restriction of food intake should not prevent the animals from receiving adequate nutrition for good health, or else the animals would be of no use in the experiment. Indeed, the level of deprivation produced might not be so different to that commonly experienced by many animals living in their natural environments.

We should note that psychologists (and other scientists) in the UK are not free to perform any animal experiments they choose; they have to operate within the restrictions imposed by the Animals (Scientific Procedures) Act 1986. Under this act, anyone wishing to carry out research that potentially entails harm to animals must first obtain a Project Licence from the Home Office for the specific procedures to be used. Project Licences are granted only to suitable qualified people and only for work that can be adequately justified. All laboratories in which animal experiments are conducted have to meet minimum standards for housing animals, and are inspected from time to time to ensure compliance with the law.

Of What Value is Animal Experimentation in Psychology?

Collectively, animals themselves have undoubtedly gained significantly from studies of animal behaviour. Experiments on animals have produced the detailed information (on their feeding habits, social and sexual behaviour) necessary for the conservation of species in the natural environment, and for successful breeding of captive animals in zoos. The fate of entire species may depend on these efforts, and the breeding of captive animals may sometimes be a necessary step towards re-establishing wild populations of threatened species.

There have, in addition, been substantial benefits to humans from psychological experiments on animals, over and above the many benefits from medical research using animals. One long-established tradition of animal research has provided fundamental information on how people learn, and this information has led to some of our more effective treatments for anxiety (Smith and Glass, 1977).

The experiments on learned helplessness, described above, are widely considered to be a possible model of human exogenous depression. Depression is a common problem, and in its extreme forms leads to intense suffering and even suicide. Research into learned helplessness, therefore, offered the hope of reducing human suffering by improving our understanding of depression and helping to develop effective treatments for it.

Much animal research in psychology, however, is not performed with an immediate practical benefit in prospect. Maier's experiments, described above, to locate the motor cortex in the rat fall into this category; and it is tempting to dismiss this research as cruel and unnecessary. Nevertheless, the basic knowledge gained from studies such as these proved to be important many years later in developing treatments for hemiplegia in human stroke patients (see Feeney, 1987).

Of course, not all experiments will turn out to be useful, but what can be done about that situation? Part of the problem is that we cannot always tell in advance which experiments and which items of information are going to be of most value. In the past, some of the most important scientific discoveries (penicillin, for example) have been the results of happy accidents. Furthermore, it is easy to find instances where the importance of a piece of research has only been recognized many years later. Consequently, if research were to be limited only to experiments of immediately obvious practical benefit, then we would likely forgo, or at least delay, some important discoveries.

Why Concern Ourselves with Animal Welfare?

Do Animals Feel Pain?

To suggest that animals feel pain is sometimes branded as unscientific anthropomorphism. The modern idea that animals have no feelings probably originated with the views of Descartes, who argued that animals were biological machines, responding automatically and unfeelingly to stimuli. Some people take a less extreme view, concede that monkeys, cats and dogs might experience pain, but deny feeling to 'lower' species such as fish and insects. Let us look at the evidence.

We can, of course, never observe an animal's feelings directly, any more than we can directly observe in anyone else the feelings we have ourselves. We can in general be sure that other people experience pain much as we do, because they cry out when injured and report pain in circumstances that seem appropriate (following a blow, for example). The same meaning can reasonably be attributed to similar signs of pain from animals. If an animal squeals when injured, then it seems reasonable to infer that it is in pain even though it cannot talk to us about the pain.

Furthermore, there is evidence from neuroscience about responses to noxious stimulation, which seems to me to be compelling. When someone is injured, part of their physiological response is the production of special hormones by the brain. These hormones, called endorphins and enkephalins, are similar to morphine and have pain-killing properties. It has been suggested that the release of these natural hormones serves to mask chronic pain resulting from severe injuries. Consequently, the discovery of these hormones in many different species of animal (even earthworms) suggests that they too feel pain, even though their experience of it, like everything else, will not be exactly the same as ours.

Squeamishness, Corruption and Compassion

Many city-dwellers (that is, most of us) encounter animals mainly as pets, as appealing and interesting exhibits in zoos, or as subjects of wildlife programmes. Given these limited and predominantly pleasurable experiences with animals, it is perhaps not surprising that many of us are repelled by the thought of hurting or killing animals. Is this revulsion mere squeamishness, an emotional indulgence which only the well-fed and affluent can afford? It is unlikely that our hungry hunter-gatherer ancestors were much troubled about the suffering of the animals they killed for food. It may be that some people today do show an excessive degree of concern for animals (see discussion of motives on p. 130). Nevertheless, there are several arguments, weightier than mere squeamishness, why we should care about the welfare of animals.

The first argument to consider is that based on religious authority. Many religions, including Hinduism and Buddhism, have taught compassion for animals and the sanctity of all forms of life. Not surprisingly, the belief that one's soul might be reincarnated in the form of an animal naturally encourages respect for all forms of life, no matter how lowly.

In contrast, traditional Jewish and Christian teaching has not, on the whole, been kind to animals. For centuries, Christians have asserted that only people have immortal souls, and that animals are not so blessed. Let us put aside the issue of how this distinction could ever be tested, and consider what its implications might be for our treatment of animals. The crucial question is whether its presumed lack of an immortal soul excludes an animal from moral concern? It is hard to see why it should. On the contrary, one Roman Catholic theologian, Cardinal Bellarmine, argued that we ought to treat animals *better* than we treat our fellow human beings, because unlike us they cannot look forward to an afterlife in which all earthly wrongs will be rectified.

Another moral argument against mistreating animals is that enjoyment of cruelty against an animal may corrupt the perpetrator. This argument played an important part in securing legislation against bull and bear baiting in the early nineteenth century.

Yet another moral argument deployed against cruelty to animals is that it desensitizes the perpetrator and makes cruelty against humans more likely. Given that mistreatment of fellow humans is wrong, then any action which facilitates it, such as cruelty to animals, must also be wrong.

Quite regardless of the effects of animal cruelty on its perpetrators, many humanitarians argue that we also have a duty of compassion towards the animals themselves. We may need to kill animals for food and clothes, but we have a duty not to subject them to needless suffering in the process. Put another way, animals may have a right not to be mistreated, and it was this view which largely inspired early-nineteenth-century legislation to prevent excessive cruelty to domestic animals.

Do Animals Have Rights?

We are concerned here with the kind of rights to fair treatment set out in the constitution of a country like that of the USA, or in the European Court of Human Rights. Do animals have any rights of this kind? It makes little sense to give animals the right to vote, or the right to a free trial, but it might be appropriate to acknowledge their right to humane treatment.

The fact that animals cannot speak or vote or understand the law should not necessarily debar them from having such rights because there are human beings who are equally as incapable of obeying laws or speaking or voting, to whom we extend rights without hesitation. I am thinking particularly of infants, of the severely mentally retarded, and of the insane. I think it will be fruitful to consider whether there are any grounds for excluding animals from the rights that we grant to these particular groups of human beings.

In the past, use of language has sometimes been set as a criterion to distinguish humans from other animals. Regardless of the chimpanzees who have learned sign language, I think it doubtful that use of language is relevant to the issues of rights. The *ability* to use language fails to distinguish animals from human infants. The *potential* to learn language fails to distinguish animals from severely mentally retarded human beings. The ability to tell right from wrong fails to distinguish animals from children (at least in a legal sense). Finally, as we have seen above, the capacity to suffer pain seems not to distinguish animals from human beings. If it is difficult to find reasons to discriminate between human beings and other animals in such ways, then it is hard to resist the idea that animals too have related rights. As one eighteenth-century British philosopher put. 'The question is not, Can they reason? nor, Can they *talk*? but, *Can they suffer?*' (Bentham, 1982: 283).

The acknowledgment of animals rights need not depend on a claim to an absolute truth; rather it is a recommendation about the kind of values that our culture should uphold. These sets of claims and values are not static; they have changed in the past and may yet change again in the future. The original authors of the revolutionary declarations of human rights in the eighteenth century did not for one moment intend these rights to be enjoyed by *women*, only be men. Women in fact were thought of as *property*, as were black slaves and animals. Eventually, people began to think it unreasonable to deny to women any of the rights that men enjoyed, and unfair treatment on the grounds of gender is now described as 'sexism'.

Recently, Peter Singer has used the term 'speciesism' to describe similar unfair treatment on the basis of species. He argues in the utilitarian tradition of Jeremy Bentham that animals should be considered our equals with respect to their rights of life, happiness and to the avoidance of suffering. It should be pointed out, fairly quickly, that Singer neither meant that all animals were entitled to exactly the same treatment, nor that the interests of all conscious beings should have equal weight. Quite obviously, a treatment which would cause suffering to members of one species could be inocuous for another. Furthermore, Singer took into account the capabilities of the animals in question. He suggested that 'no matter what the nature of the being, the principle of equality requires that its suffering be counted equally with the like suffering — in so far as rough comparisons can be made — of any other being' (Singer, 1976: 27). Interpreted with respect to life (as distinct from pain), this claim means that the survival of bacteria and viruses should be counted as precious as that of human beings — a position that can raise some difficulties with conflicts of interest, to which we now turn.

Conflicting Interests

There is, it seems to me, a fundamental conflict of interests at the heart of the debate on animal experiments in psychology. On the one hand, I am convinced that animals can suffer in experiments, and that they have a moral right to compassionate treatment at our hands. On the other hand, animal experiments in psychology have produced knowledge which has helped to reduce human suffering, and also increased our understanding of ourselves and other animals. Furthermore, we have every reason to believe that animal experiments in the future could continue to produce useful information. Do we not have an obligation to the disabled and the mentally ill to conduct experiments which may help to develop new therapies to reduce *their* suffering? So, against the rights of animals to be free of pain and suffering we must set the rights of those human beings who will be helped by the results of animal experiments.

A similar conflict of interest arises when humans use animals for food and clothing, or when animals threaten humans. The cattle we rear for beef, for example, presumably have rights to continued existence which are violated when we kill them.

There have been several attempts to arrive at a principled resolution of this conflict of interests; none in my view is entirely satisfactory. As noted above, Singer argued that it was 'speciesism' and as morally objectionable as sexism or racism to discriminate unfairly among species. The alternative position is that we give some sort of preference to our own species. Of course, to give preference to our own species need not mean that all human interests, however trivial, outweigh those of an animal. In reality, I think that there are many people today who will (reluctantly) accept animal suffering if it helps a good cause (finding a cure for cancer, for example), but who reject the killing of animals for more trivial reasons (such as testing cosmetics). The point at which this balance is struck is a personal decision for all of us.

Alternatives to Animal Experiments

A natural response to the dilemma that animal experiments reduce human suffering, but only at the cost of animal suffering, is to search for alternatives to animal experiments. In medicine and in toxicity testing it has been possible to partly replace animals with cell cultures.

For psychology, however, the prospects for replacing animals are rather limited. Cell cultures are unlikely to be appropriate, simply because the aspects of behaviour of most interest to psychologists require some form of nervous system operating within a whole organism that interacts with an environment. Some replacement of animal experiments may be possible through the use of computer modelling, but the results obtained with a computer model still have to be checked against the behaviour of living animals.

There is, however, evidence of a decline in the number of experiments in an area in which animals have traditionally been used extensively, namely the study of learning processes. A report by the editor of the *Journal of Experimental Psychology*: Animal Behaviour has shown that since 1977 there has been a drop of over 17 per cent in the number of articles appearing in the four main American journals publishing research into animal learning. There are signs that there has been a similar decline in the use of animals in other areas of psychology, with the implication that more research is being undertaken with human subjects instead.

It is important to remember, however, that psychologists are unlikely to be pursuing the same research questions with human subjects as they would have done with animals. It is impossible to tell whether we may fail to make some important discovery as a result of this switch, or whether diverting our efforts to human research may pay better dividends. Brigid Brophy (1971) has made a similar point when she noted that we often do not know whether the undoubted knowledge and benefit gained from an animal experiment could not have been obtained in some other way, without causing suffering to animals.

The Conduct of the Argument

Questions of animal suffering seem often to arouse great passion. I am led to think that animals, particularly cute furry ones, trigger some parental protective instinct in many of us, so that we are not entirely rational in our handling of these matters. Nevertheless, at the centre of the issues there lies a real conflict of interests to which there is no easy answer. The achievement of a reasonable compromise is inevitably a matter of argument and debate. I think that we are more likely to resolve matters wisely if we are aware of some of the misleading and erroneous claims that have been put forward.

It is not, I think, helpful for those in favour of animal experiments to simply claim that all is well, and that regulation of animal research is an unnecessary hindrance to scientific progress. Some animal experimenters in the past have been barbarically insensitive to the suffering of animals. Claude Bernard, the great French physiologist, was notorious for his disregard of animal feeling. His operations on un-anaesthetized animals were an important factor in the rise of the anti-vivisection movement in England in the nineteenth century. Indeed, Bernard's work so revolted his own wife and daughters that they started an animal protection society of their own.

More recently, Alice Heim (1971) noted that animal experimenters often adopt 'hygienic' terminology, which serves to minimize the emotional impact (to the human reader) of what may be very painful procedures (for the animal subject). It does not sound so bad, for example, to say that an animal 'vocalized' than that it 'screamed'.

'Loaded' language has also been used by those who oppose animal experiments. It is misleading, for example, to describe as 'starvation' the regulation of food intake used in many experiments on animal learning. It is common for opponents of animal experiments to cite examples involving cats or dogs as subjects, because such animals are familiar to us as pets and most likely to elicit feelings of compassion. In reality, however, cats and dogs are used in only a tiny percentage of animal experiments in psychology.

Another debating strategy used by opponents of animal experiments is to suggest that the research questions investigated using animal subjects are essentially trivial. This suggestion is made either by careful selection of examples, or by direct misrepresentation of the purposes of the experiments and the value of the results.

All these debating strategies, however, pale into insignificance against the direct action adopted by some of the animal liberation organizations. Over the past ten years confectionery has been deliberately poisoned, stores (selling furs) have been fire-bombed, and scientists and their families have been intimidated and threatened. Laboratories have been invaded to liberate the animals, with much accompanying destruction of property and records (Henshaw, 1989).

Without doubt, these attacks have publicized the cause of animal rights. By making animal research more risky and more expensive this campaign may be partly responsible for the recent decline in animal research that we have noted above. It is less certain, however, whether anyone has been persuaded to join the cause as a result of the terrorism. It seems to me, as to many others, that there is something strange about a moral position which sanctions risking the lives of innocent human beings (including children) in the cause of reducing suffering in cats, dogs and rats.

Last Words

By our mere existence we kill or cause suffering to countless other animals, even if we are careful vegetarians. Worms are undoubtedly killed, for example, when farmers plough their fields to grow crops for our food. Flies are squashed to death in their thousands against the windscreens of our cars, not to mention all the animals who die when their habitats are destroyed to create farms, golf-courses and towns. It is a hard fact of life that all animals, not just human beings, displace or exploit other animals in some way. That predators kill and eat their prey is fairly obvious, but even herbivores are in competition with each other for food and living space. If it is impossible for us to live at all without harming other animals in some way, then it is hard to find reasons why all experiments on animals should be morally wrong while other uses of animals for our benefit are considered acceptable.

Acknowledgments. I wish to thank David Booth and Steven Cooper for their comments on earlier drafts of this chapter.

Tutorial Discussion Questions

1 Are there some kinds of information that can only be gained through experiments on animals?
2 Is it possible to tell in advance which experiments will turn out to provide useful information?
3 Do animals suffer as we do?
4 To what rights are animals entitled?
5 Is speciesism as morally and socially objectionable as racism and sexism?
6 Do we have a responsibility to the disabled and mentally ill to carry out research to discover new treatments and cures?
7 Is terrorism ever justifiable if the cause is sufficiently important?
8 Is the use of animals in experiments morally any different to killing animals for food?

References

BENTHAM, J. (1982) *Introduction to the Principles of Morals and Legislation*, edited by J. H. BURNS and H. L. A. HART, London, Methuen. (The First Edition of this work was printed in 1780, and first published in 1789 by T. Payne, London.)

BRITISH PSYCHOLOGICAL SOCIETY: SCIENTIFIC AFFAIRS BOARD (1979) 'Report of the Working Party on Animal Experimentation', *Bulletin of the British Psychological Society*, **32**, pp. 44–52.

BROPHY, B. (1971) 'In pursuit of a fantasy', in GODLOVITCH, S., GODLOVITCH, R. and HARRIS, J. (Eds) *Animals, Men and Morals*, London, Gollancz, pp. 125–45.

FEENEY, D. M. (1987) 'Human rights and animal welfare', *American Psychologist*, **42**, pp. 593–9.

HEIM, A. (1971) *Intelligence and Personality*, Baltimore, MD, Penguin.

HENSHAW, D. (1989) *Animal Warfare: The Story of the Animal Liberation Front*, London, Fontana/Collins.

KEEHN, J. D. (1986) *Animal Models for Psychiatry*, London, Routledge and Kegan Paul.

MAIER, N. R. F. (1935) 'The cortical area concerned with coordinated walking in the rat', *Journal of Comparative Neurology*, **61**, pp. 395–405.

MESIROW, K. H. (1984) 'Report on the Animal Research Survey', paper presented at the meeting of the American Psychological Association, Toronto, Canada.

SELIGMAN, M. E. P. and MAIER, S. F. (1967) 'Failure to escape traumatic shock', *Journal of Experimental Psychology*, **74**, pp. 1–9.

SHARPE, R. (1985) *Psychological and Behavioural Research*, London, Mobilization for Laboratory Animals Against the Government's Proposals.

SINGER, P. (1976) *Animal Liberation*, London, Jonathan Cape.

SMITH, M. L. and GLASS, G. V. (1977) 'Meta-analysis of psychotherapy outcome studies', *American Psychologist*, **32**, pp. 752–60.

Further Reading

COILE, D. C. and MILLER, N. E. (1984) Comment: 'How radical animal activists try to mislead humane people', *American Psychologist*, **39**, pp. 700–1.

FEENEY, D. M. (1987) 'Human rights and animal welfare', *American Psychologist*, **42**, pp. 593–9.

MIDGLEY, M. (1983) *Animals and Why They Matter*, Harmondsworth, Penguin.

SINGER, P. (1976) *Animal Liberation*, London, Jonathan Cape.

Chapter 13

Racial Prejudice

Raymond Cochrane

There are three linked concepts which it is important to distinguish in discussing the psychological basis of race relations in contemporary society. *Racism* is a particular kind of discrimination and refers to behaviour that stems from a belief that people can be differentiated mainly or entirely on the basis of their ancestorial lineage. In addition racism leads to the assumption that people are to be treated differently because some groups are considered inferior, and some groups superior, to others. *Prejudice* on the other hand is a negative attitude towards ethnic or minority groups held in the absence of evidence for these attitutdes, or in the face of contradictory evidence. While prejudice produces a tendency to respond to people in terms of their race or ethnic status rather than as individuals, it does not necessarily produce overt behavioural effects. *Race thinking* underlies both racism and prejudice. It is an assumption that race is an objective fact which can be used to explain differences between individuals and groups, rather than that race is an artificial, socially constructed, label which can be used in many different ways. Race thinking does not necessarily imply biological differences between groups and does not necessarily imply notions of inferiority and superiority, but race thinking often leads to these conclusions.

In this chapter we will be dealing mainly with the concept of prejudice, but we will also be considering racism as a result of prejudice. Racial prejudice in one form or another is very common. The exact extent of prejudice is uncertain and the level that is detected in various studies depends largely on the definition of prejudice that is used. What is important about the findings that prejudice is very common, however, is that any explanation for it must recognize that it is a statistically 'normal' psychological phenomena and not an aberration limited to a minority of unstable or disturbed people. Although theoretically prejudice can be manifested by any group or individual in society, most of the psychological research, and most of the political significance that surrounds racial prejudice, refers to that kind of prejudice held by the more powerful groups towards the less powerful groups in our society. Thus in contemporary Britain we are concerned with the prejudice of white against black people.

What is Prejudice?

Prejudice finds many forms of expression. The extreme manifestations such as attempts at genocide, political and legal systems which systematically discriminate against some groups in favour of others (such as found in South Africa), and physical assault or damage to property based on racial motives would be universally regarded as indicators of prejudice. So, probably, would incidents of open discrimination even where this is illegal, and the suggestion made by some extreme-right-wing political parties that certain people should be 'repatriated', or deported, without their consent purely because of the ethnic group to which they belong.

Then there is a middle band of behaviour and style of interaction which many objective observers would consider to result from prejudice, but which the person exhibiting these behaviours might well deny stem from prejudice. An example of this is 'disguised discrimination' where making decisions based on so-called 'objective criteria' lead to the consequence that some racial or ethnic groups are disadvantaged compared with others. In employment, for example, situations often arise where the choice between candidates for a job, or for promotion, is influenced by factors which are not directly relevant to that job or promotion. Thus an employer would not say, 'We are not going to employ you because you are black', but might say, 'I am sorry that we cannot offer you the post because your English is not good enough', or more likely would say, 'I'm sorry this post has already been filled', when this is not the case. A recent survey by the Manpower Services Commission of Job Centres in London showed that, on average, a white worker had to apply for 8 jobs before he or she was offered one. A black worker had to apply for 13 jobs before one was allocated, and an Asian worker had to apply for 16 jobs before he or she was taken on.

Another insidious manifestation of prejudice which those who engage in often deny is a result of prejudice is 'adjectival racism'. This is the attachment of a racial or ethnic identifying adjective to a person or group where this confirms a stereotype in terms of the behaviour being described. Certain sections of the popular media are past masters at playing this game and many of the stereotype-confirming incidents are absorbed into popular lore. Examples are referring to 'Jewish businessmen' or 'black muggers'. Then there are stories about homeless families being placed in expensive hotels while more permanent accomodation is found and where the families is identified as 'Asian' where this is totally irrelevant to the real point of the story.

The London *Evening Standard* on 22 February 1990 carried a story about Sir Ranulph Twistleton-Wykeham-Fiennes' attempt to walk unassisted to the North Pole. Sir Ranulph is reported by the paper as saying, 'Where I am going, my chances of survival are statistically higher than they would be on a London street'. Whatever Sir Ranulph actually meant, the *Evening Standard* took his comments as a platform to launch a supposedly humorous piece about the dangers of London streets. 'When', they ask, 'is some explorer going to conquer the North face of Brixton?' There is no doubt that the choice of Brixton as an example of dangerous parts of London was because it is identified in popular stereotypes with having a large black resident population. Later in the same piece the *Evening Standard* says that to guarantee safety in some areas of London at certain times of the night one needs protection from, among others, 'a drunken Irish friend carrying a chainsaw'.

An even more covert and likely to be denied form of prejudice is the making of racial jokes within one's own group and not directed at individuals of other groups. Thus the telling of West Indian stories or Irish stories in gatherings in a public house when no people from those groups are present is often regarded as harmless fun. Justification is often sought by reference to professional comedians who also peddle these types of jokes about their own ethnic group. Clearly the jokes are only funny because they are based on stereotypes and they confirm the prejudiced view that some groups are more stupid, more venial or more victimized than others.

Then we have a form of prejudice which is often described as tolerance or merely reporting objective 'facts' with no apparent question of opinion. In 1982, for example, the Metropolitan Police first released certain types of crime statistics broken down by suspected ethnic origin of the perpetrator. This could only ever be suspected ethnic origin, because only a very small minority of perpetrators were actually ever apprehended by the police. Not all types of crime were broken down by ethnic group, indeed it was only those categories of crimes where the police and public held stereotypes of ethnic involvement that were released in this way. Thus, for example, street robberies, commonly known as 'muggings', were broken down by the ethnic origin of attacker, but burglaries and car thefts were not. The day after the police released these data, the *Daily Mail* on 11 March 1982 carried the following piece:

> Britain faces the chilling spectre of an increase in the type of crime which plagues the Ghetto's of America. This was the blunt message from Scotland Yard yesterday as the extent of black involvement in violent crime was revealed for the first time.

These two sentences cleverly imply that black crime was increasing — when there was absolutely no evidence of this — and that these data had been available for some while but were only 'revealed' yesterday because of their serious nature. Neither the police nor the *Daily Mail* reported that black people in London are very much over-represented among the victims of violent crimes.

A further example is the way in which the various Immigration Acts introduced by governments of both political parties from the 1960s onwards have been justified. Defending the 1971 act Reginald Maudling, the Home Secretary, said that the main reason for restricting the number of non-white immigrants into Britain was to produce 'peace and harmony'. He went on, 'We must give reassurance to the people who were already here before immigration, that this will be the end and there will be no further large-scale immigration'. This gets very close to saying that it is immigration which is causing racial resentment and the solution is to prevent non-whites from entering Britain so that the psychological tranquility of the white indigenous population can be protected.

Recently the definition of prejudice has been extended by some people to those who resist positive discrimination, or 'affirmative action' as it is known in the USA. Thus arguing that all discrimination is bad, even that which is in favour of groups who have suffered disadvantage in the past, is now defined as a form of prejudice in its own right.

Explanation of Prejudice

There are many explanations of prejudice which have been suggested by psychologists and other social scientists. It is not possible to do justice to all of these, so some important accounts (for example, those based on the economic and social functions of prejudice) will be omitted. Instead I will concentrate on prejudice as an attitude held by individuals. This is consistent with our original definition of prejudice, and we can look to the large body of research and theory in social psychology that deals with attitudes to give us some clue as to why people may have this particular attitude.

We can start by drawing on an informal rule of inertia in psychology: namely that people will not do anything unless there is a reason to do so. This rule extends to the development, maintenance and expression of attitudes. The implication of the rule of inertia is that unless an attitude is serving a function for the person who holds it then they will not bother to do so. So the question becomes, what possible benefits can someone derive from holding prejudiced attitudes? Several distinguished social psychologists have described categories of functions that any attitude may serve for the person who subscribes to it. If, for example, holding and/or expressing an attitude results in receiving social reinforcement from other members of one's social groups, then these attitudes are more likely to be learned than those which are usually met by a negative response, or by being ignored. Just the mere expression of a prejudiced attitude can serve a valuable function for the person so doing, if it reinforces their membership of a particular social group which they value. Thus expressions of racial prejudice and hatred among groups of football fans supporting a national team may well contribute to the solidarity of that group of individuals. Perhaps by chanting racially biased slogans, or even by launching physical assaults on members of other groups, they establish that they really belong to their own group.

Prejudiced attitudes can also serve a valuable function by rationalizing behaviour that would otherwise be considered by the person themselves to be unacceptable. Thus if a particular group is defined as being inferior and unworthy, then causing them suffering or disadvantage is less difficult to justify because they 'deserve it'. This was clearly a rationalization for the persecution of Jews in many European countries over the last three centuries. The popular attitude was that Jews were in some way undermining the stability of the state, or the integrity of the culture, of the majority group among whom they found themselves. Therefore physical assaults, and confiscating property owned by Jews, was not seen as a reprehensible act, and this presumably helped the perpetrators avoid feelings of guilt and shame after they had indulged in these activities. The use of attitudes to defend self-image was undoubtedly a common phenomenon during Britain's colonial history. The exploitation of other human beings via slavery and by economic and military domination could only be justified by a society which identified itself as highly moral and Christian so long as those who were being exploited were considered to be subhuman. Either that, or if the colonized groups were acknowledged to have human characteristics, then they were regarded as being too primitive culturally to be allowed to shape their own destiny and needed guidance by a superior race until such time as they had matured into independence. No doubt there are a lot of hangovers of these colonial stereotypes which are still used today in Britain to justify economic exploitation and other forms of discrimination and oppression against ex-colonial people.

Another obvious function of an attitude which implies notions of inferiority and superiority is that it allows an easy contrast to be made by the person holding the attitude between himself or herself and the other group. Defining oneself as part of a superior group, and having that definition confirmed by those with whom one mixes, gives a ready, and perhaps much needed, boost to self-esteem. Thus the unemployed, the impoverished or the relatively disadvantaged members of the majority group can say to themselves, 'Well, I may not amount to much, but at least I am white, and therefore better than all black people'.

Neither should we underestimate the value of holding stereotypes of all kinds. In a vastly complex social world, where it is impossible to process all the information that we encounter, it is probably essential to have certain preconceptions about events and individuals in order to be able to respond to them at all. We all have modes of interaction which are brought into play at first encounter with a new person which reflect our stereotype. Thus without knowing anything more about them we tend to respond differently to an elderly person compared to the way we would respond to a younger one. We tend to respond differently on first contact with a strange man and a strange woman. We may not know it, but we probably are influenced by the way people are dressed when we first meet them and respond differentially to the smart or power dresser and to the shabby and scruffy. Prejudice serves a similar simplifying function. If we believe that all members of a particular ethnic group have some characteristics in common and some characteristics which differentiate them from other ethnic groups, then we already have a partial basis on which to judge new individuals who we might meet. To a certain extent this is inevitable, harmless and even necessary for normal social intercourse. Imagine being introduced to two people at a dinner party: one is a young man recently arrived in Britain after being born and brought up in Jamaica, the other is a middle-aged woman from the Republic of Ireland. When wondering about what topics of conversation might be of interest to these fellow guests we might think that cricket would interest the former but not the latter. This reflects both ethnic and gender stereotypes and so could be described as a manifestation of prejudice. It might also, however, oil the wheels of initial social interaction and allow the conversation to turn to topics which might genuinely interest the parties concerned. Stereotypes become problematical when they are resistant to change even in the face of consistent evidence that they are inappropriate. Not infrequently the power of the stereotype is such that reality is distorted by the holder. This resistance to change will interfere with the development of anything other than very superficial and unsatisfactory social interactions between the person who holds the stereotype and a member of the stereotyped group.

Important though attitudes are for determining our perceptions of other people, and our responses to them, they are only part of the whole psychological make-up of any one person. Attitudes are themselves embedded in a larger cognitive system and are related to the person's own self-image and personality. One of the most famous attempts to show how attitudes indicating prejudice serve basic personality needs was reported as The Authoritarian Personality Study (Adorno *et al.*, 1950). The theoretical model adopted by the researchers in the authoritarian personality study was that specific attitudes will only be a surface manifestation of a total personality complex which would have its roots in early experience and the child rearing practices to which the adults had been exposed. The study was very successful in showing that a specific attitude (in this case anti-Semitism) was indeed highly correlated with more general social and political views of a right-wing or conservative nature, views about personal relationships, value systems and personality structure. On the basis of in-depth retrospective interviews too, the researchers also purported to show a link between the way in which people had been raised by their parents and their adult personality and, hence, their adult prejudices. The basic characteristics of the authoritarian personality which distinguishes it from the non-authoritarian personality are as follows:

1 Rigid in outlook, intolerant of ambiguity or argument.
2 Strong emphasis on conventional / traditional values.
3 Admiration of power and 'toughness'.
4 Belief in importance of obedience to, and respect for, authority.
5 Only secure in a hierarchical structure.
6 Combines aggression with submission.
7 Exaggerated concern with sex.
8 Punitive orientation to those who differ.
9 Power orientated in family relationships.
10 Uses stereotypes — race, sex, age, class, etc.
11 Cynical about 'human nature'.
12 Does not like to look inwards and examine own feelings and motives.

These characteristics are believed to arise from being brought up in a strictly hierarchical family structure which also employed a lot, or the threat, of physical punishment as the chief means of controlling the child's behaviour. In these families parental love was said to be conditional upon the display of approved behaviour by the child and there was very exaggerated concern by the parents with the way in which the family would appear to outsiders. Parents, particularly fathers, are remembered as aloof, stern and punishing but are nevertheless romanticized and recalled as an idealized version of what parents should be like.

The suggestion was that a person who had been through this kind of up-bringing, and who had subsequently developed the authoritarian personality would be much more prone to see relationships between individuals and groups in power terms and to see clear differentiations between different segments of society. They would also be desperately searching for a secure hierarchy in which they could be located and in which they would know their place. This, according to Adorno and his co-authors, made them receptive to political ideologies which emphasized the importance of obedience and authority, the most obvious example being Fascism:

> Thus a basically hierarchical authoritarian, exploitative parent child relationship is apt to carry over into a power-oriented, exploitatively dependent attitude to one's sex partner and one's God and may well culminate in a political philosophy and social outlook which has no room for anything but a desperate clinging to what appears to be strong and a disdainful rejection of whatever is relegated to the bottom.

Such a person will be very likely to develop attitudes which imply the innate inferiority of members of groups other than his or her own, and over which he or she is entitled to exercise some degree of domination.

Although initially received as a breakthrough in the study of the aetiology of prejudice, the authoritarian personality study has been less kindly treated by more recent critics. Apart from some minor psychometric problems which have been put right since, the major criticisms of the study have been threefold.

First, there is the reliance on retrospective interviews in place of direct observation of child rearing practices. People's memories are notoriously faulty, especially when they are asked to recall events which happened 2 or 3 decades previously. Given that the researchers were dealing with a group of people who had already been identified as having a particular personality structure, it is not unlikely that their memories were influenced by their adult development.

Second, the original researchers failed to observe that both the child rearing practices and the adult personality which they assumed stemmed from these practices could in fact be related separately to a third variable — namely that of social class. Thus while there might well be a correlation between childhood experiences and adult personality, and hence with prejudice, this correlation does not indicate that one causes the other. Both might independently be caused by the social class milieu in which the person was brought up and in which their adult life was spent. This does not necessarily undermine the claim that prejudice is a manifestation of a particular personality type, but it does undermine the claim that this is produced by early experiences.

Third, Milton Rokeach pointed out that there was a basic confusion in the authoritarian personality analysis between the *content* and the *style* of thinking. Beginning with informal observations of those around him, Rokeach suggested that it is possible to hold any set of views, even those which are not prejudiced, in an authoritarian fashion. This approach defines authoritarianism as an unwillingness to even consider that alternative views might have any validity or be worth listening to. Thus in this interpretation it is possible even for those with strongly anti-racist views to be considered authoritarian. To avoid semantic confusion he called this cognitive style 'closed-mindedness' and contrasted it with 'open-mindedness' where, even if someone holds views firmly, they do not categorically reject the possibility of considering an alternative point of view or accepting that it may have some validity. Rokeach went further and suggested that the content of political and social views and the style in which they are held are completely independent of each other — technically speaking they are orthogonal to each other (Rokeach, 1960).

This leads us onto a third major conceptual scheme which has been developed to explain racial prejudice. According to Rokeach the closed-minded person will be prejudiced against those with whom they disagree about important issues. There would be no obvious or inevitable reason why they should be prejudiced against someone from a different ethnic group. Unless, that is, the closed-minded person assumes that people from ethnic groups different to their own also inevitably have different political and social views to them. Thus race prejudice would become a particular example of belief prejudice. The corollary to this is that when the closed-minded person discovers the true views of other individuals, he or she will respond to them in terms of their views and ignore their ethnic origin. Thus there might be extreme antagonism directed towards those who hold contradictory views whether or not they are from the same ethnic groups as themselves. Similarly there would be no prejudice directed at any individual from whatever ethnic background if they tended to agree with the closed-minded person. Rokeach quoted informal evidence that white civil rights workers in the USA in the 1960s were subject to vicious and often fatal attacks by white racists because they were expressing disagreement with their latter's extreme views. Equally white bigots did not attack or reject those black people who shared their views that blacks were inferior and who remained subservient. Thus prejudice was in fact directed against those who held different views rather than just against those who were of a different ethnic group.

The basic hypothesis of the theory of belief prejudice has been tested many many times. It is easy to construct an experimental situation where closed-minded people are asked to interact with a group of other people who they believe are also part of the experiment. Thus a white person may find himself interacting with 2 black and 2 white people where 1 from each ethnic group consistently agrees with his or her views while the other member of each ethnic group consistently disagrees. This situation is obviously artificially constructed — the only real subject in the experiment being the person under test, the other participants being actors. Results based on this kind of experiment, and several variants of it, have consistently supported Rokeach's view that, when sufficient information is made available, people drop prejudice based on race and ethnic group and take up prejudices based on belief differences.

This was an appealing theory to many social scientists because it offered an obvious way forward in the struggle to reduce racial prejudice in society. If people could be convinced that their belief systems were basically similar to other groups in society who happened to have a different skin colour, then racial prejudice as such should disappear. It is worth noting in passing that this would not necessarily produce a more liberal or tolerant society as prejudices would be redirected at those with whom the prejudiced person disagreed, rather than at those who happened to belong to a different group. Although this assumption of basic similarities in beliefs and values may have had some validity in the USA of the 1960s and 1970s which was eager to see itself as a pluralist society in which most people ultimately come to share a common value system, it is not easy to make that assumption about contemporary Britain. Here we are faced with a variety of ethnic and cultural traditions which do pride themselves on being, and remaining, distinct and different. Thus, for example we have no reason for assuming that, let us say, an elderly white Londoner will have basic belief systems in common with his next door neighbour who happens to be a young Bangladeshi woman. In this context increasing familiarity about belief systems could, according to Rokeach's model, produce increased rather than decreased racial prejudice.

Reducing Prejudice

Most people, even those who might recognize prejudice in themselves, would agree that prejudice is a negative aspect of their own cognitive system and of the society in which they live. Thus we might find a fair degree of consensus that prejudice is harmful and that, if at all possible, it should be reduced. There is, in fact, ample objective evidence that prejudice produces harmful effects on those against whom it is targeted. Numerous studies have shown that discrimination based on racial prejudice is widespread in contemporary Britain and affects many areas of life: employment, housing, education, politics, the law enforcement and legal systems, to name but a few. The psychological sequelae of prejudice for those people subjected to it has been less well researched but has been suggested to include under-achievement, resentment, lowered self-esteem, rejection of prevailing moral and political values, and heightened levels of frustration and hostility.

For the remainder of this chapter I am going to outline what a psychologist would recommend as the best means of reducing racial prejudice based upon psychological research and principles, and assuming that the reduction of prejudice had a very high priority in society. The latter qualification is necessary because some of the most effective attempts to reduce prejudice could well produce a clash with other cherished ideals and values. Most recommendations, however, will not be contentious except in so far as they require the expenditure of additional resources.

Increased General Educational Level

Surveys of the distribution of prejudiced attitudes within society consistently show that the extent of prejudice is negatively correlated with educational level: those who are better educated are much less likely to show any form of prejudice than those whose education has been terminated at an early stage or has been unsatisfactory for some other reason. Highly desirable for a whole host of other reasons, increasing the general educational standard across the whole of society would undoubtedly be the most effective way of reducing the level of prejudice. If only one recommendation could be implemented, then it should be this one.

Enforce Laws Which Make Discrimination Illegal

It is often said that prejudice cannot be reduced by legislation; in other words it is impossible to change people's attitudes by preventing them from behaving in a way which is consistent with their attitudes. This is not true. In many instances it is not the case that behaviour is developed on the basis of attitudes, but that attitudes are developed on the basis of the behaviour a person sees themselves performing. Thus enforcing a change in behaviour can also produce a change in attitudes, while at the same time showing society's extreme disapproval of certain kinds of behaviour by making them illegal.

Legislate for Equality

This clearly is a more contentious recommendation. However, if reducing prejudice is the first priority, then all the evidence seems to indicate that positive discrimination not only produces immediate benefits for the previously disadvantaged group, but also results in a long-term change in attitudes even among those who are racially prejudiced. Positive discrimination can take many forms, for example insisting that institutions like universities take quotas of students from various ethnic groups reflecting the numbers in the population at large or catchment area of the university. This policy could equally well apply to employing lecturers and other categories of staff in the institution. Thus, in an extreme example, government funding for a particular university would be reduced if, let us say, 10 per cent of the student body and 10 per cent of the academic staff were not black. This would force the institution to discriminate in favour of a previously under-represented group. This would directly conflict with another cherished value of our higher education system (some may say a sacred cow of the system) that universities, when selecting staff and students, should only discriminate on the basis of merit. However the predictable outcome of a positive discrimination would be that, by having more black students, members of staff and professors, this would come to be seen as normal and not as the exception to the rule. This would provide both a role model for future applicants which might mean that positive discrimination was no longer required, and also undermine the stereotype that may be held by many members of the white majority in society.

Censor the Press and Other Mass Media

Again this recommendation clearly conflicts with another very high priority in our society — namely freedom of the press. However it is undeniable that the frequent use of racial stereotypes and worse by the popular press in Britain, even if it does not cause prejudice, nevertheless is an important element in maintaining it at its high ambient levels. Headlines and stories such as 'Police Find 40 Indians in Blackhole', 'Black Power Take Over Plot' (which actually referred to the Labour Party selecting a black candidate for a local election), 'Scandal of Asian Immigrants Living in Luxury Hotels', and the infamous 'Immigrant Bites Man on Bus' are unacceptable. They are found alongside racist cartoons showing Indians lying on beds of nails, black people swinging from trees, and so on, which are not uncommon in the most despicable elements of the popular press. Of course their atrocious practices are not confined to racial prejudice; they employ other techniques of sensationalism and pornography in order to boost sales. Looking at this issue purely from the point of view of reducing prejudice, there is no doubt that banning this kind of activity would have a beneficial effect.

Encourage Intergroup Contact

This is a more complex recommendation than appears at first sight. It is a method of prejudice reduction that lends itself to experimental manipulation and has therefore been studied in great detail by social psychologists. Some circumstances have been identified where increased intergroup contact can actually lead to an increase in prejudice rather than its reduction. Intergroup contact appears to produce beneficial effects only where the following conditions are fulfilled:

1   Initial intergroup attitudes are not extremely negative. The more polarized the groups' views are of each other at the time the contact is initiated the less likelihood there is for positive change.
2   Contact has to be of a relatively intimate nature rather than just casual. It is essential that the members of the two groups actually do get to know each other to such an extent that their stereotypes of each can be seriously challenged.
3   A situation which requires intergroup cooperation in pursuit of a common goal, in other words the creation of a dependence of each group upon the other for the achievement of a desired outcome, is also a very effective means of turning intergroup contact into intergroup liking and respect.

4   The contact between the groups must be of equal status. This is important both at the formal level, that is in terms of those who are organizing the contact, and also in terms of the informal levels of the degrees of expertise and knowledge and leadership potential manifested by members of the two groups. Contact between two groups where there is clearly an inequality of status at either level may lead to confirming of stereotypes and prejudices.

5   Ideally, too, the individuals selected to 'represent' their groups in the intergroup contact situation should have salient values in common with each other. If intergroup contact just reveals basic and fundamental differences then it is unlikely to lead to improved relations.

6   The prevailing social climate to which the people will return, if indeed this is the case, must be in favour of improved intergroup relations. Intergroup contact at work, for example, is unlikely to produce such beneficial effects if the workers return to segregated and mutually hostile housing areas.

Reduce Environmental Frustrations

Although it has not been dealt with specifically in this chapter, the frustration-aggression model of prejudice suggests that levels of prejudice will increase as people become more frustrated by their social environments. Thus in times of high unemployment or economic recession, where there are high levels of poverty, poor housing and so on, frustrations will grow and this will produce a tendency to react aggressively. Because the aggression often cannot be directed towards the source of the frustration, it may find another outlet and be displaced upon a group which is relatively powerless to defend itself or strike back. Hence members of minority ethnic groups may bear the brunt of frustration-induced aggression, even though they were no way instrumental in producing the frustrations in the first place.

Uniform and Unambiguous Rejection of All Aspects of Racism by Political and Social Opinion Leaders

Mrs Thatcher's famous statement prior to the 1979 general election is often used as an example whereby a politician who does not unambiguously reject all aspects of prejudice can lead to prejudice remaining as a politically acceptable element in society:

> People are really rather afraid that this country might be rather swamped by people with a different culture . . . The British character has done so much for democracy, for law, and done so much throughout the world, that if there is any fear that it might be swamped, people are going to react and be rather hostile to those coming in.

While not directly expressing racist sentiments herself in this passage, Mrs Thatcher is expressing understanding for those who might be prejudiced. She is also explicitly contrasting the British character which has done so much for democracy, and law and so on with the character of those who might want to settle here, which presumably has not done much for these very areas. If instead she had rejected prejudice outright and not shown any tolerance for racist and prejudiced views she would undoubtedly have done much more to improve race relations in this country and to reduce the level of prejudice that exists. But it is not only politicians who should accept this responsibility. Entertainers, sportsmen and women, businessmen and women who have no obvious axe to grind and even Chief Constables should also be seen to go out of their way to reject and condemn any expression of prejudice.

There is a particular problem in Britain at present because of successive governments' 'soft' line on apartheid in South Africa. While all major mainstream political figures verbally reject apartheid as an unacceptable political system, they have also been seen to resist what many believe is the most effective means of bringing apartheid to an end, namely that of imposing and enforcing economic sanctions. This must result in a contradictory message being sent to both the black and white communities in Britain. This is confounded even further by the argument which is commonly produced when the sanctions issue is raised: that sanctions would hurt black South Africans more than they would hurt white South Africans. And this is despite the frequent claims by leaders of South Africa's black population for sanctions to be applied. The implicit message here seems to be that black people in South Africa do not really know what is in their best interests, whereas white politicians in London do know. It is clear that the majority of Britain's black population would be much more impressed by our leaders' rejection of apartheid and racism if this was backed by forceful action, even if it could not be proved to be totally effective.

Recently there have been heartening demonstrations by prominent and highly respected white entertainers, people from sporting fields, and others that they are concerned about racism and that they are willing to lend their talents to fighting it. Festivals such as the celebration of Neslon Mandela's seventieth birthday, and his subsequent release from a South African prison, must make it easier for members of non-white groups in Britain to feel part of this society and to identify with the larger cultural milieu in which they are embedded. This leads to the final recommendation and perhaps one of the most contentious of all.

Encourage Assimilation and Intermarriage

If Rokeach's theory of belief prejudice is correct, then the continued existence of distinctive cultural and religious views and practices by prejudiced-against groups in Britain will lead to the persistence of prejudice in both directions, at least among the more closed-minded members of society. Increasing educational levels should go some way to reducing the number of closed-minded people, but will probably not eradicate close-mindedness altogether. Continuing with Rokeach's hypothesis for a while longer leads to the inevitable conclusion that only when fundamental belief and value differences are eliminated will all forms of prejudice disappear and ethnic prejudice have no logical basis. The ultimate expression of assimilation is complete intermarriage and the disappearance of separate ethnic identities.

Clearly, as with some previous recommendations, this conflicts very heavily and directly with other important and socially desirable objectives. Why should Muslims, for example, be persuaded to give up their particular religious beliefs and practices in favour of a 'broadly Christian' tradition? Why should Sikhs be persuaded not to wear turbans and other distinctive items of dress? While these sacrifices may lead to a reduction in racial prejudice, they could also lead to adverse consequences elsewhere within and between communities. Whether this should occur or not depends upon the priority afforded to implementing policies designed to reduce racial prejudice.

Tutorial Discussion Questions

1 Is it a type of prejudice to wish to associate with people from the same ethnic group as yourself?
2 Do you support the idea of 'affirmative action' (positive discrimination)? Would you like to see a quota system at your place of education?
3 Should the freedom of the press be curtailed in order to promote better race relations?
4 Should ethnic minorities be encouraged to become assimilated and adopt traditional British values and morals?
5 Do you consider yourself to be entirely free of racial prejudice?
6 Has the increasing number of children being educated in mixed race groups at school decreased or increased the general level of prejudice?

References

ADORNO, T. W., FRENKEL-BRANSWIK, E., LEVINSON, D. J. and NEVITT-SANFORD, R. (1950) *The Authoritarian Personality*, New York, John Wiley.
HEWSTONE, M. and BROWN, R. (1986) *Contact and Conflict in Intergroup Encounters* Oxford , Blackwell.
ROKEACH, M. (1960) *The Open and Closed Mind*, New York, Basic Books.

Further Reading

CASHMORE, E. and TROYNA B. (1990) *Introduction to Race Relations*, 2nd ed, Basingstoke, Falmer Press.
EDWARDS, J. (1987) *Positive Discrimination: Social Justice and Social Policy*, London, Tavistock.
MCCULLOUGH, M. (1988) 'Are we secret racists?', *The Psychologist*, 1, pp. 445-7.

Chapter 14

Work, Unemployment and Mental Health

Graham Stokes

In the history of sociology and social psychology the question of whether there are types of societal and technological change which can affect the level of social and individual pathology is one which is well developed.

Since the Great Depression during the 1930s many researchers have been concerned specifically with the possibility that a decline in economic activity may produce a notable increase in the incidence of treated psychological disorder. Attempts were made to establish possible correlations between the annual rate of unemployment and the incidence of mental illness in the general population, as indicated by mental hospital admission rates.

The early studies in the USA suffered from a variety of methodological weaknesses which undoubtedly contributed to their equivocal findings. Even when the expected association between economic crises and mental hospitalization was established it was possible to argue that some artefact was responsible for the appearance of the relationship. The problem was that in the absence of modern sophisticated statistical techniques in the 1930s, efforts to identify the relative effect on mental hospital admissions of a change in the rate of unemployment were bound to be inconclusive. This relationship cannot stand in glorious isolation, for at the same time other social and economic trends are manifest which may also be exercising an effect on treated mental illness. For example, the impact of such short-term trends as alcohol legislation, the redefinition of diagnostic categories, and increased hospital bed capacity were consistently neglected.

Harvey Brenner (1973), in an exhaustive and statistically sophisticated study of first admissions to mental hospitals in New York State, went beyond considering only major economic changes occurring between 1914 and 1967. Because of the advanced statistical techniques he employed, he also avoided many of the methodological problems of earlier studies. Working with the hypothesis that mental hospitalization rates increase during economic downturns and decrease during upturns, Brenner found that when population groups were appropriately identified, and when the effects of external trends were controlled for, substantial inverse relations were revealed between economic changes and mental hospitalization rates.

Three years later, Brenner established that the national unemployment rate was a statistically significant predictor of several measures of social trauma, namely mental hospitalization, homicide, suicide, imprisonment, mortality and alcoholism. Brenner further reported that a sustained 1 per cent increase in unemployment produced a 3.3 per cent increase in mental hospital admissions five years later.

Replicating the work on mental hospitalization data, Stokes and Cochrane (1984) found that in England and Wales between 1950 and 1976 there was a positive relationship between the rate of unemployment and the rate of first admission to mental hospitals. While the relationship applied to both sexes, the correlation was statistically significant only for those men aged 25–44 years, and for women aged 20–54 years.

While ecological studies using archival data are interesting and indicative, they often seem to raise more questions than they answer.

Who is Affected by Increasing Unemployment?

It is important to realize that the relationships that have been established are at an aggregate level only. We have no evidence to suggest that any increase in the rates of mental illness and other deviant behaviours that appear to occur during periods of high unemployment is accounted for in whole, or in part, by those who actually lose their jobs. This point is illustrated in the finding that while working age populations are the most adversely affected by economic contractions as measured by their rate of admission to mental hospitals, the relationship actually holds for 'all age groups' — even those who are likely to be retired.

When considering how people who are not experiencing unemployment may have their psychological health affected by economic recession, it is important not to neglect the impact which unemployment has on family life. Fagin (1981) reported the onset of health problems in families of the unemployed. Cochrane and Stopes-Roe (1981) found that the level of psychological symptoms reported by married women was strongly influenced by their husband's employment status.

So we cannot assume that all those people of working age who are negatively affected at times of high unemployment are necessarily unemployed. Employed workers may become anxious over the possibility of losing their jobs. There may be an introduction of short-time work or a reduction of overtime, which will lead to a loss of income. Thus, there will be those who are 'economically injured', but who do not directly experience unemployment. With an increase in unemployment those who work in welfare services whose function is to assist the unemployed may experience involuntary increases in workload. Skilled and experienced people may be subjected to the frustration of having to accept jobs for which they have no desire and for which they are overqualified. Thus, there is the distinct possibility of an increase in work stress and a decline in life satisfaction among workers whose jobs are not threatened.

The Direction of Causation

Even if it were established that the unemployed were more likely to manifest pathological behaviour at a time of high unemployment, it is not possible to be dogmatic about the direction of causation in the relationship. The average rate of unemployment in the UK between 1949 and 1969 was approximately 2 per cent of the working population and poor health was just as likely to have been the cause of, as well as the result of, economically related life problems. Time-series studies do not, and cannot, establish causation for they are based on correlation which can only reveal the level of co-variation between variables, and whether or not these relationships are significant.

Time-lag

The probability is that there will be a time-lag between economic change and the appearance of mental disorder requiring treatment. This means that if the analysis does not take account of this, a serious obstacle to the measurement of the effects of economic stress is presented. Using a 'lagged', time-series approach, wherein the backward and forward shifting of the economic indicator in relation to the annual measure of mental hospitalization is examined, produces the best chance of linking the two indicators and therefore identifying the true relationship.

However, this methodology has been criticized because of the arbitrary nature of the time-lag examined and on the grounds that the correct approach should be to predict the time-lag *before* the study from the knowledge of the natural history of the disorders. The suspicion is that the empirical search for the optimum lag represents little more than a massaging of the data to obtain a significant outcome.

Are Mental Hospital Admission Data an Accurate Indicator of a Population's Mental Health?

When investigating the historical impact of economic change on psychological health, it is impossible to use an indicator of mental status in the population that includes all psychologically disturbed people regardless of whether or not they are in receipt of treatment. Thus, the true total incidence of psychological disorder can only be estimated indirectly. Using admissions data involves an assumption that they are a valid index of the general mental health of the population. Such an extreme measure of psychological reaction is not only relatively insensitive to the effect of economic change, it is also not typical of the experiences of most people affected by economic stress, and with the trend toward community-based models of care it will increasingly become an inappropriate, archaic measure of a population's mental health. A current issue is therefore to establish a more valid archival measure to employ in time-series studies.

Is There an Increase in Treated Mental Ill-Health?

Time-series methods using archival data cannot establish whether there has actually been a real increase in the incidence of mental illness. A heightened usage of health services may be identified, but this may simply reflect a relative intolerance by the population of mental disorder at a time of economic recession. The 'availability of treatment hypothesis' as a function of hospital bed capacity must also be considered.

Intolerance of Deviance Hypothesis

This hypothesis states that psychologically disturbed people are perceived, or dealt with, differently, at different times and in different social situations. It is argued that at a time of economic recession the emotional and material resources of a psychologically disturbed person's family may be diminished, and this might decrease their level of tolerance for his or her behaviour, thereby increasing the likelihood that the disturbed person will be brought into contact with mental health facilities. While it is unlikely that mental ill-health is totally unresponsive to economic change, the intolerance of deviance hypothesis is a tenable partial interpretation of time-series data.

Availability of Treatment Hypothesis

This hypothesis maintains that as psychiatric hospitals are nearly always operating at maximum capacity, any major increase in hospital admission must be a result of increases in the availability of inpatient resources. While this argument possesses historical validity and is supported by data from the USA during the 1930s, the current therapeutic climate which gives primacy to community care no longer means that all psychiatric hospitals are full to overflowing.

Traditionally, time-series methods have served the needs of econometricians and sociologists, but have held little interest for psychologists. One reason is that when studying the psychological reaction to economic change an indicator of the general mental health of the population is used which has no direct bearing on the psychology of individual mental illness. The use of hospitalization data cannot provide information concerning the psychological and social processes that lead to successful, as well as unsuccessful, adaptation to economically precipitated stress. Furthermore, the use of aggregate, retrospective data precludes the identification of the factors intervening between economic change and hospitalization.

If the results of time-series studies are to have a bearing on the psychology of mental illness, then as a necessary preliminary the nature of the intervening variables must be investigated. It has been shown that changes in macro-economic activity influence the level of economically related individual life stresses which have been empirically linked to the development of psychological problems in individuals. If the impact of economic change on personal well being is to be adequately explored, then epidemiological studies of individuals are needed to complement ecological studies.

Does Unemployment Damage Health?

Time-series analyses have demonstrated an association between the level of economic activity and health, yet can it be argued that unemployment *causes* ill health? Is there direct evidence that unemployment exercises a deleterious impact on psychological well-being?

Unfortunately, while the stigma and ill effects of unemployment have been recorded since the Great Depression of the 1930s, contemporary studies, many of which have reported similar findings, still adhere to a research design that many psychologists would regard as too descriptive, anecdotal and methodologically weak. The size of samples can be small. The frequently cited effects of unemployment such as alienation, social stigma and apathy do not facilitate the participation of unemployed workers in research studies and this difficulty of access may be the reason why unemployment research is predominantly small-scale. Thus, while such studies may provide a colourful and thought-provoking picture of life without work, they do not allow systematic and convincing judgments to be made about the impact of job loss.

As most studies have recruited their samples from individuals who have lost their jobs, a major weakness of research into the health costs of unemployment is whether an investigation is being made of antecedents or consequences of job loss. Thus, while there is substantial evidence of a high rate of health problems among unemployed people, the direction of causality in the relationship is unclear. In one study 55 per cent of the unemployed sample had either stopped work voluntarily, had been sacked or had never worked. Hepworth (1980) found that workers who had been dismissed or had left their last job voluntarily revealed greater evidence of potential psychiatric morbidity than did those who gave redundancy as their reason for being unemployed. There is also evidence that people in poor health and of advancing age are more vulnerable to periods of unemployment. Furthermore, workers from large families, disturbed backgrounds, and earning below average incomes are more likely to become unemployed. It is evident, therefore, that among the unemployed there are many people whose health and social background may place considerable strain on their psychological well-being regardless of their employment status. It may well be that these factors create personal distress and instability, which in turn is responsible for the experience of job loss and any subsequent health or social problems identified during unemployment.

The Study of Redundancy and Unemployment

The collection of valid data is more likely if the methodological advances proposed by George Brown and his colleagues (1973) are followed. They note that the issue of doubtful causality may be resolved if those events where there is a suggestion that they were produced by a disorder (called 'illness-related') were to be excluded from any analysis. This would leave two types of event: those events which on logical grounds would be very unlikely to have been generated by personal inadequacy or illness (termed 'independent'), and the remainder which would be classed as 'possibly independent' for which the same claim could not be made, even though there may be no reliable evidence of their being caused by the disorder.

Redundancy, as distinct from individual cases of job loss, offers the opportunity to investigate the effect of an 'independent' event. Unemployment via redundancy is out of the control of the workers involved and thus it cannot be argued that their misfortune was a result of poor health, extraneous social difficulties or personal weakness. Unfortunately, there have been few such studies. Kasl (1979) investigated the physical and psychological health impact of permanent factory closures in the USA. It was found that while the period of anticipation can be as threatening as the event itself, the overall impact of unemployment on physical and psychological well-being appeared negligible. Kasl found that the workers did not maintain a state of physiological arousal and psychological distress throughout the duration of unemployment. In fact, following an initial period of upset, those workers who remained unemployed could not be distinguished on the indicators of well-being used from those who had found re-employment. Kasl concluded, as a result of the ease with which the workers adapted to unemployment, that redundancy may not be the traumatic experience that it is often thought to be. In contrast, Warr (1978), in a cross-sectional study in this country found that redundant steel workers who remained unemployed for six months or more displayed higher levels of self-rated anxiety, life dissatisfaction and negative affect than those who regained employment. The extent to which employment was personally salient was a significant moderator of the negative consequences of unemployment.

Understanding the Effects of Unemployment Over Time

Kasl's study has the obvious advantage of being longitudinal so that changes could be observed over two years for the same group of subjects. A weakness with all unemployment studies which are cross-sectional is that the effects of job loss over time are based on interviewing *different* people who have been unemployed for *differing* lengths of time. Thus, we must be cautious in interpreting studies which have documented the progress of the 'individual' through unemployment, yet have employed a cross-sectional research design.

Many investigators have identified three distinct stages of reaction to unemployment, namely, an initial response, followed by an intermediate phase and a final period of settling down to unemployment. While the initial response to job loss, following a worrying phase of anticipation, is often positive with the thought of unlimited leisure time and the opportunity to do all those tasks that had been postponed due to work commitments, the unemployed soon enter the intermediate phase, which is characterized by boredom, self-doubt and distress. In the final stage there is a reduction in the level of anxiety, and the struggle for work and hope for the future both decline. While Kasl's study of unemployment failed to identify this process of adaptation, the optimism–pessimism–fatalism sequence has been supported in several cross-sectional studies. However, as a result of using cross-sectional methodology, and despite consistent findings, it cannot be said that a particular individual will inevitably go through all the stages in the expected sequence, or whether they will go through them at all.

Is Prolonged Unemployment a Traumatic Experience?

When levels of distress have been identified by recording observable 'illness behaviour', such as visits to the general practitioner, or drug usage for stress-related disorders, it can be argued that unemployed people have more time to bring their health and welfare problems to the attention of the medical or social services. Some researchers have avoided this uncertainty by using self-report measures which identify 'untreated' negative rsponses as well as those exposed for treatment. However, a more challenging point for discussion is not so much the possibility that levels of sickness are reported which do not represent actual pathology, but suggestions that unemployment does not exercise a deleterious effect on health at all.

The question of how long a period of unemployment has lasted is pertinent, for the relationship between the length of unemployment and reaction is not a simple linear one. Nihilistic attitudes with an acceptance that unemployment is not to be fought against but is to be tolerated as an inevitable fact of life are beliefs which are more likely to become apparent as unemployment progresses. The critical question is whether such an adjustment represents a long-term beneficial change in psychological health and well-being or indicates an inappropriate and damaging means of escape from a harsh and unrewarding reality.

In a study conducted by me (Stokes, 1983) the well-being and attitudes of a group of unemployed school-leavers was observed to change over a period of six months. On standard measures of psychological health they experienced an apparent *improvement* in their condition as the time without a job progressed; self-image improved, anxiety diminished and feelings of frustration and hostility were reduced. However, interview data revealed that this 'improvement' had occurred as a result of the young people redefining their position, subjecting expectations to a reappraisal, and restructuring beliefs about the value of work. As a consequence they had become resigned to their privation, hope for the future was restricted, and fatalistic apathy permeated everyday life. A clear deterioration in social and practical skills also accompanied what Anna Freud has labelled 'restriction of the ego'. While unemployed people do adapt, and as a result do not feel in perpetual crisis, the impact on psychological health cannot be considered negligible. A state of chronic semi-depressed resignation may ultimately be responsible for the development of psychological disorder. Thus, a case could be made that the disappearance of anxiety produces the 'demotivation' of the long-term unemployed which in itself is a cause for concern and should not be regarded as wholly benign.

The Unemployed Are Not an Undifferentiated Group

In general, when considering the psychological consequences of unemployment, it is inappropriate to regard unemployed people as an undifferentiated group. There are likely to be broad age, sex, occupational, as well as individual differences in the experience of unemployment.

Much of the concern about unemployment has been directed either towards the plight of unemployed men, or to the waste of talent as young people leave school without meaningful employment. Unemployment among adult women has not been considered a major issue. Traditionally, it has been widely accepted that women tend to view paid employment as being of secondary importance, rather obtaining gratification and self-expression through the roles of wife and mother. However, there is now an increasing literature which shows not only that paid work outside the home has positive health effects for women, but also that non-employment has negative social and emotional consequences. It is probable that the relationship is complex, being mediated by a woman's occupational involvement, and the quality of her employment relationship. It appears that employment status can no longer be regarded as being of only minor importance to women.

The large literature on youth employment has avoided many of the methodological weaknesses of adult studies, and used longitudinal data. There is little evidence for the stage model of unemployment, but there is support for the argument that very few young people enjoy being unemployed and there are indications that teenage girls have impaired psychological well-being much like their male contemporaries. Banks and Jackson (1982) showed that the link between unemployment and elevated symptoms of mild psychological disturbance was not explained by young people who are in poor mental health being unable to get jobs. Longitudinal analysis showed that the experience of unemployment was more likely to create psychological symptoms rather than the other way round.

Overall, when young people are unable to enter the labour market after leaving school, the evidence suggests that those individuals with inadequate or maladaptive coping strategies will experience adverse effects on psychological health, personal development and rewarding interpersonal relations, as well as the possibility that extreme political attitudes may well be fostered.

The Meaning of Work

From what has been discussed so far it is clear that being deprived of work can be a disturbing and threatening experience, yet how is it that a single life activity among many can have such emotional significance? What qualities does work possess that an inability to obtain it can result in psychological disturbance, self-doubt, guilt, boredom and loneliness?

In any society the economy is the instrument by which the basic requirements of life are obtained. However, in Western industrial societies direct participation in economic life enables a person to satisfy a variety of psychological and social needs, in addition to providing material benefits. Despite this, many investigators have drawn attention to the fragmented and depersonalized nature of work. For instance, during the period between 1950 and 1969 when the annual rate of unemployment in the UK was approximately 2 per cent — a figure commensurate with the concept of full employment — concern was not with the plight of the jobless, but with the nature and organization of work and the corresponding degree of job satisfaction. It was considered that for the majority of the working population, work had become meaningless and problematical. This led to an increasing involvement with the so-called 'private' sphere of life, and it was assumed that the prevailing mood of alienation had, for many people, resulted in work merely having an exchange value. People sold time in order to buy products and services that would enhance and add meaning to their leisure activities which were the real focus of their lives.

While such debate on the meaning of work is justified, alienation in the working environment is only an aspect of the work experience. As Marie Jahoda has observed 'alienation is a response to the organisation of work, not to work per se, not even to employment per se', and while pay and conditions may account for the negative feelings about employment, a job possesses 'latent functions' which accounts for a positive motivation to work. Marsden and Duff (1975) found that some of the 'workless' in their study held onto their desire to work even though their actual employment experiences had been harsh and unrewarding. Furthermore, it has been reported that 110,000 heads of families in full-time employment earn less than the state poverty line income, and thus would have been at least as well remunerated if they were in receipt of statutory benefits but instead they opted to continue in work.

When a person is deprived of a job, he or she loses both employment and work. Employment is an exchange relationship between an employer and an employee which occurs within an organizational structure, the employee receiving an economic reward as determined by market value. This is the individual manifest function of employment. On the other hand work is an activity, the expenditure of energy for a purpose, which can be performed inside or outside the employment relationship. Public concern about unemployment is a consequence of the increasing loss of work in employment opportunities, not with any reduction of activity in the large area of work conducted without organizational and/or financial structures. Thus, work is not synonymous with employment.

While a person may regard their job as having many negative aspects (e.g. stress), the availability of latent positive consequences might still allow for a favourable attitude toward job involvement. Work may provide a variety of social and psychological satisfactions, such as the acquisition of personal identity and self-worth, the imposition of a purposeful time structure, the attainment of goals and aspirations, the establishment of social relationships, and the provision of active interests. For these reasons being without work in employment can be psychologically destructive, while formal economic activity can be psychologically supportive even when conditions are bad. Therefore work in employment is meaningful beyond earning a living, and thus being without a job may deprive a person of additional meanings in life, even if it does not involve a reduction in the standard of living. While it is possible for the latent consequences of work in employment to be obtained through other forms of activity, none of these pursuits incorporate a dimension of social compulsion. They therefore require a degree of initiative which, in the opinion of Jahoda and Rush (1980), only a few 'psychologically privileged individuals can draw upon on a regular basis'.

Tutorial Discussion Questions

1 Discuss the view that among the unemployed there are people whose health and social background places considerable strain on their psychological well-being regardless of their employment status.

2 How could unemployment in a family create the conditions for ill health and emotional disturbance among its members?

3 What interpretation can be placed on the results of cross-sectional studies which have identified stages of reaction to unemployment?

4 How may unemployed workers cope with a situation of enforced leisure-time in order to avoid the psychological decay associated with unemployment?

5 Only 'psychologically privileged individuals' among the jobless have the initiative to regularly pursue activities which provide access to the latent functions of work in employment. Discuss.

6 Special government measures and schemes have been directed towards the plight of unemployed school-leavers and young people (for example, the Youth Training Scheme). Is this a wise use of scarce resources when it can be argued that relieving the hardship of adult workers with family and financial responsibilities should be the priority?

7 If large-scale unemployment is to remain a feature of our economic and social landscape, are there constructive alternatives to employment so as to

ensure that the social fabric of society is not undermined by the existence of an alienated 'class' of people denied access to the material and emotional rewards available to those who do have jobs?

8 Women draw psychological and social satisfactions from employment. Is this a recent development or the case of a long-standing psychosocial phenomenon only now being recognized?

References

BANKS, M. H. and JACKSON, P. R. (1982) 'Unemployment and risk of minor psychiatric disorder in young people: Cross-sectional and longitudinal evidence', *Psychological Medicine*, 12, pp. 789–98.

BRENNER, M. H. (1973) *Mental Illness and the Economy*, Cambridge, MA, Harvard University Press.

BROWN, G. W., SKLAIR, F., HARRIS, T. O. and BIRLEY, J. L. T. (1973) 'Life events and psychiatric disorders. Part I: Some methodological issues', *Psychological Medicine*, 10, pp. 115–24.

COCHRANE, R. and STOPES-ROE, M. (1981) 'Women, marriage, employment and mental health', *British Journal of Psychiatry*, 139, pp. 373–81.

FAGIN, L. (1981) *Unemployment and Health in Families*, London, Department of Health and Social Security.

HEPWORTH, S. J. (1980) 'Moderating factors of the psychological impact of unemployment', *Journal of Occupational Psychology*, 32, pp. 309–14.

JAHODA, M. and RUSH, H. (1980) 'Work, employment and unemployment', *Science Policy Research Unit Occasional Paper Series*, No. 12, September.

KASL, S. V. (1979) 'Changes in mental health status associated with job loss and retirement,' in BARRETT, J. E. *et al.* (Eds) *Stress and Mental Disorder*, New York, Raven Press, pp. 179–200.

MARSDEN, D. and DUFF, E. (1975) *Workless*, Harmondsworth, Penguin.

STOKES, G. J. (1983) 'Out of school — out of work: The psychological impact', *Youth and Policy*, 2, 2, pp. 27–9.

STOKES, G. J. and COCHRANE, R. (1984) 'The relationship between national levels of unemployment and the rate of admission to mental hospitals in England and Wales, 1950–1976', *Social Psychiatry*, 19, pp. 117–25.

WARR, P. B. (1978) 'A study of psychological well-being', *British Journal of Psychology*, 69, pp. 111–21.

Further Reading

BANKS, M. H. and ULLAH, P. (1988) *Youth Unemployment in the 1980's: The Psychological Effects*, London, Croom Helm.

EISENBERG, P. and LAZARSFELD, P. F. (1938) 'The psychological effects of unemployment', *Psychological Bulletin*, 35, pp. 358–90.

JAHODA, M. (1982) *Employment and Unemployment*, Cambridge, Cambridge University Press.

STOKES, G. J. (1983) 'Work, unemployment and leisure', *Leisure Studies*, 2, pp. 269–86.

WORLD HEALTH ORGANIZATION (1985) *Health Policy Implications of Unemployment*, Copenhagen, World Health Organization.

Chapter 15

Social Issues and Policing: Politics or Psychology?

Susan Phillips

The Police Service of the 1980s, its policies and practices, has generated television documentaries, public opinion polls and academic research in unprecedented volume. The reasons for this may be traced to a number of sources and events, some with a clear causal link, others more likely due to coincidence.

The riots of the 1980s — firstly those in Bristol in 1980, then Liverpool, Birmingham and London in 1981 — undoubtedly served to focus public attention on the police in a new way. The following wave of discontent in 1985 in Handsworth, in Toxteth and at Broadwater Farm, Tottenham maintained this focus. Major industrial disputes of the 1980s — the Coal Dispute of 1985, the NGA Wapping Printworks dispute of 1986–7 — again brought media attention to the police by showing their handling of the situation alongside the cases put by unions and management. Less high profile, but for a number of interlinked reasons consistently referred to in the public domain, are figures relating to volume of crime: police statistics showing crimes reported and solved; findings from the British Crime Surveys of 1983, 1985 and 1989, which as victim surveys uncover part of the dark area of crime; offender surveys and studies of offender behaviour. All these serve to maintain public interest in policing.

Responses to these stimuli come from a number of areas and derive from concern about how the police service behaves in the face of issues of social concern. To the service itself the amount of interest generated has posed a threat to its professionalism. Boundaries between politics and professionalism, good reporting and exploitative journalism, evaluation and well-intentioned justification are blurred. Scrutiny by academic researchers has produced some well-documented evidence that has challenged assumptions widely held within the police service itself. Academic interest in the police service has been aroused in a wide range of disciplines: law, social policy, criminology and psychology.

Concern has been expressed that the policing of political activity erodes personal freedoms. Police powers are wide, their potential for infringing personal freedoms in some places limited more by the exercise of discretion than by the law itself. But for the police to act as agents of social control there has to be a consensus about the boundaries within which they should operate. Some of the events referred to above have ensured that there is continuing debate about the nature and location of these boundaries.

Attempts to improve the relationship between the police and the public, particularly during the period following the riots of the 1980s, have proliferated. As a consequence there has been an increase in both measurement of public opinion of the police, and the monitoring of police performance.

Riots may be seen as an attempt by a marginalized youth subculture to be heard by an increasingly deaf society which, at the same time as denying them work, publicizes the advantages of consumerism. In this sense the riots may be seen as a form of political expression. The instrumental nature of the 1960s riots in the USA which drew attention to the needs of the black community has been widely acknowledged. To the extent that this was true of the 1980s riots in Britain, they may be seen as functional on a number of levels: economic — attracting government money to improve housing stock, provide incentives to businesses to move into the inner city, and develop youth training strategies; political — to provide a vehicle for expression for members of minority and marginalized communities; and through their powerful and sustained influence — to impinge upon a variety of social institutions, including the police.

Improving Police-Public Relations — The Task Defined

Viewing the Brixton Disorders, which generated the Scarman Report (1981), as a catalyst we will trace the development of three themes: the accountability debate; the re-emphasis on community policing; and the creation of social crime prevention strategies. The thrust of Lord Scarman's recommendations was a rapprochment of police and community. Those key events of the 1980s which served to keep policing in the public eye provided examples of police function which raised fundamental questions about who controls the police and fuelled the debate about to whom they are responsible. By following each of these themes we shall examine some of the practical outworkings of his recommendations and the kind of public discussion which has been engendered.

It is said that the police do their work of maintaining peace and tranquillity, detecting and preventing crime, by the consent of the populace. But what does that actually mean? What structures exist to facilitate the expression of discontent, if that is how the absence of consent should be described?

The Framework for Public Accountability

The police are accountable to the law for the legality of their actions. But because of the exercise of discretion the police do not enforce the law equally and evenly across time, among all sections of the community, and in relation to all laws. For example, you and I are more likely to be picked up by the police for a minor traffic offence at 2 a.m. than at 2 p.m.; are more likely to be arrested if we commit petty theft than for minor business fraud; and are more likely to be the subject of police attention if we purchase cannabis than if we drop an empty McDonalds package on the pavement.

Within London the police are answerable to the Home Secretary and elsewhere to local Police Authorities. However the extent of jurisdiction by these bodies is in practice quite small. In terms of the constitutional relationship between central government and local police forces there exist two sanctions which may be applied: central government provides half the policing budget, and therefore one sanction which could be applied to a police force which failed to satisfy the government of the day is fiscal control, i.e. the witholding of money; in addition the Secretary of State has the power to force the retirement of a Chief Constable. In practice influence is brought to bear through informal means via Her Majesty's Inspectorate of Constabulary (HMI) and Home Office circulars, which are used to underline good practice identified by the HMIs and to communicate the thinking of central government.

Police Authorities, which are composed of two-thirds elected representatives from the local councils and one-third non-elected members from the magistracy, provide the other half of the police budget and are responsible for maintaining an efficient public service in terms of expenditure and use of resources. They do not have any statutory control over police policies and practices; these are the domain of the Chief Constable who, in many Police Authorities, provides the necessary information for the balancing of the books in the form of an annual report but otherwise has relatively little contact with members.

The sphere of influence of individual police authority members, or even the Police Authority as a body, is very limited, and in terms of rapprochement between police and people little movement has occurred since 1981 (indeed, some would say that since the Police and Criminal Evidence Act was passed in 1984 the trend has been in the opposite direction).

However, the Police and Criminal Evidence Act did build upon one of Lord Scarman's 1981 recommendations by stating in section 106 'arrangements shall be made in each area for obtaining the views of the people in that area about matters concerning the policing of the area and for obtaining their cooperation with the police in preventing crime in that area'. As a result police forces have adopted one of two prevailing models for Police Consultative Committees: either the open forum type which is advertised in an area (police subdivision) as a public meeting, or the more focused type where representatives of local associations are invited to attend regular meetings, perhaps with an annual meeting open to the general public. Meetings are chaired by police authority members and held either in public buildings within the area or in police stations (for a discussion on these arrangements see Morgan, 1989).

These then are the constitutional and local arrangements for dialogue between police and public. The question of the need to develop and enhance police-public cooperation is one agreed by all political parties, although their methods for achieving this end differ: for example, the Public Order Act, introduced by the Conservative government, increased powers to control an unruly public; while inspired by the Left is a lobby to empower police authorities to determine policing policies and to establish a totally independent police complaints procedure. Control of the police is a live political issue, the debate is over the direction of control. Do we in practice have a national police force with control exerted by central government? Has the power vested in Chief Constables allowed them to develop an authoritarian style which will increasingly remove them from the public they are supposed to serve? And what about the sticky question of the function of Police Authorities? Should local policing policies be set by the Chief Constable? How local is local, and is there such a thing as a consensual public constituency?

To what extent Police Consultative Committees meet their intended goal of allowing the people who live in the area to express their views and concerns and cooperate with the police in preventing crime is also open to debate. From studies of the early days of police consultative committees it seems that in reality membership is frequently far from 'the people who live in that area', and either by accident or design, (depending on the model adopted) is composed of a select group of middle-class articulate people.

Community Policing as a Strategy

The second of our themes occupying a central place in the police-community relations debate of the 1980s and 1990s is community policing. Community policing is a term which is used to describe a whole range of measures, and its wide usage indicates a failure to properly define its meaning, but its central construct is that of positive communication between police and public. For the purpose of this discussion we will take it to refer to two particular types of initiative: the work of Home Beat officers, and that of specialist Community Liaison Officers (CLOs).

The development of community relations strategies based on fixed area foot patrol as a means of improving police-public relations is a reaction against two trends, both of which have an economic root. Low pay and poor working conditions meant that during the 1970s the police force was operating considerably under-strength. Foot patrol was seen as an extravagant use of manpower and a form of policing known as Unit Beat policing was introduced through Home Office recommendation and financial incentive. Panda car patrols and radios enabled a small number of officers to maintain a visible presence over a larger area than foot or cycle patrol. Conventional wisdom points to the unintended consequence of this dependence on vehicles as a deterioration in police-public relations resulting directly from reduced face-to-face contact between police and public (Weatheritt, 1986).

If the panda car and the radio provide the reason the police lost touch with the people who live in the area in which they work, the Edmund Davies pay awards of the late 1970s and widespread relaxation of rules governing where police officers should live exacerbated the situation. While there is no doubt that the awards effectively addressed the manpower problem, increased prosperity produced a further unintended consequence. No longer did police officers have to live in local authority housing, either on housing estates or in police enclaves developed among privately owned housing stock. They could choose where to live, and had the money to afford a mortgage in areas which matched their social aspirations.

Why is it important to develop and maintain good relations between police and public on this more individual level? If the police are professionals who should be trusted to get on with their job without political interference, which is the justification for resisting *control* and favouring *consultation* as the feature of constitutional relationship between police and public, then why not just let them get on with it as other professionals do? The argument of course is not as simple as that, for, without the cooperation and involvement of the public, the police cannot operate. They depend on members of the public to report crimes (and the British Crime Survey suggests that only 30 per cent of crimes do get reported, most reliably theft of vehicles and burglary). They also depend on the public for information to enable them to prosecute offenders. Crime-related information will not flow when there is little confidence in the police, either in relation to their competence or their trustworthiness (Kinsey, Lea and Young, 1986). Therefore, good police community relations are of paramount importance.

Intuitively, it would seem that a strategy which emphasizes contact between police and public should inevitably result in improved community relations. However, a number of factors exist which make both measurement and motivation in this area difficult. It is in fact extremely difficult to measure the impact of policing strategies which emphasize police community relations in terms of their effect upon crime figures, because of the circular effect of the argument which goes like this: when the police improve relations with the community, then the public supply more information about the amount of crime and the identity of offenders; as a result the crime figures increase and detections increase, but detections always increase at a lower rate than reporting so that the overall effect on the crime figures suggests that the police are being less effective in their fight against crime. Alternatively, if increased contact does not actually lead to improved community relations, and there is evidence to support this argument at least in the case of some sections of the community who may well be those who hold the most reliable information about offenders and offences, then crime may increase as a direct result of this contact. For example, if a police officer uses his or her powers to stop a member of the public, but does this in such a way that the person feels their personal freedom to be challenged, and so resists or refuses to cooperate, then the stop, rather than leading to information about a crime, may end up leading to the commission of an offence, i.e. obstruction of a police or even assault.

Police subculture defines 'real police work' in terms of the fast response, crime fighting function, whereas analysis of citizen-initiated contact with the police shows that 75 per cent is non-crime-related. Some say that the police force would be more efficient if it concentrated its efforts on reducing crime and delegated its service function to other agencies; but this would be at the expense of non-confrontational public contact, which overall is responsible for much of the public goodwill towards the police, while public reaction to adversarial, police-initiated, contact is more negative. Studies have shown that cognitive, attitudinal and behavioural differences exist between officers who operate fast response mobile patrols, and officers whose mandate specifically includes developing relationships in the community whether by foot patrol, i.e. Home Beat officers, or as Community Liaison Officers.

Following the riots, most forces which did not at the time have specialist community liaison departments developed in this direction, introducing specialist officers to improve police community relations. In practice, CLOs may interpret their role in various ways ranging from public relations to explaining the police role or informing members of the public about the rights and duties of citizens, or they may define their role in terms of a bridge function existing to facilitate two-way communication between members of the police force and members of particular subgroups in the community.

The words 'community policing' produce a comfortable feeling in those old enough to remember Dixon of Dock Green, but in practice what does the adoption of community policing policies actually mean? Crime statistics suggest that foot patrol officers are not likely to detect or prevent most crimes. The areas they patrol are very wide and the probability of just coming across a crime, e.g. a burglary while it is being committed, is very low. While seeing a police officer passing in the street may reassure many members of the public, it is actually unlikely that their chances of becoming victims of crime are reduced. However, fear of crime as an undesirable thing in itself is a powerful factor in this debate. Victims of violent crime are more likely to be male than female, more likely to be young than old, and in some areas more likely to be black than white. Elderly white ladies, however, are more likely to be reassured by exchanging a nod with a passing police officer than by examining criminal statistics.

Where these initiatives have been developed as a means of establishing and repairing a broken relationship, it has not been without cost to the police service. In financial terms the cost is probably very low. The economic advantages of panda patrol have been cancelled out by the increasing capital and fuel cost of the mobile patrol, but the psychological cost of attempts to reconstruct the friendly neighbourhood officer image in hostile neighbourhoods may well be considerable. To the shift inspector who described the demeanour of his foot patrol officers who were required to reintroduce community policing in an area notorious for the breakdown in relations between its residents and the police as having 'faces white with anger and spittle down their jackets', the psychological costs are too high. If such methods fail to restore a relationship, what will they in the end produce? And even if they are successful on the individual and personal level, as studies in the psychology of prejudice suggest they might be, what is the probability of their positive effect being transferred beyond the level of the individual either to the group or towards the police force as a whole, particularly as evidence indicates the existence of incompatible attitudes and behaviour between those who choose to adopt a service rather than a law enforcement role.

Preventing Crime

The third area to take our attention is that of crime prevention. Many of the arguments already raised will apply in this section, though the direction and cause of the changes which have taken place since the riots differs. Crime prevention has always been seen as a prime function of the police service. Recent developments, however, have widened the area of interest to increase contact with the public as collaborators in the crime prevention endeavour, rather than as consumers of specialist police advice on locks and bolts, known as 'target hardening'. 'Social crime prevention' includes looking at design factors ranging from introducing steering locks on cars to designing housing estates around the concept of defensible space. Cooperation in crime prevention then requires establishing contact: at the agency level, with local authority housing departments and housing associations, for example; with industry, as with designing steering locks where liaison has been effective; or at the commercial level where, for instance, pressure to consider the effect of store display on shoplifting has met with a mixed response.

At the more individual level Neighbourhood Watch schemes have proliferated. These schemes encourage a small group of neighbours to take an active role in protecting one another's property, and provide channels between police and community for information about 'suspicious incidents'. While strong support for these initiatives exists, and in some areas consumer satisfaction is high, there is little evidence to support Neighbourhood Watch as being effective in reducing the amount of crime which occurs. Displacement studies have failed to identify clear patterns, partly because in some areas studied there has been an overall increase in the type of crime which the schemes aim to reduce. It could be, of course, that, by providing definite channels of communication and encouraging the reporting of suspicious events, the police have instituted the cycle already described and the crime figures reflect an increase in reporting rather than in the actual incidence of such crimes. However, property crime — theft of motor vehicles and burglary of private dwellings — is the most reliably reported type of crime, so it would seem that Neighbourhood Watch in itself cannot be viewed as a genuinely preventive measure. Victim studies explain this by showing that most property crime occurs in areas of high density housing where victims and offenders live within the same geographical area, and could be described as 'neighbours'.

Psychological Effects and Interventions

What has been written above reflects some of the pressures and challenges to change which the drive for improved police-public relations has produced. In this final section we shall examine the potential effects upon the men and the women who wear the uniforms. We will note the evidence for psychological strain and examine the need for an acknowledgment by the police service as a whole of the psychological pressures upon individuals and the service as a whole. Finally, we will consider the organizational response which has been produced at least in part by the public demand for a more sensitive and accountable police force.

Records of sickness, accident and absenteeism are classic measures of organizational strain. If police forces were finding that there was an increase in the number of days lost as a result of sickness, then that could be taken as an indication that as a whole the service was suffering psychological strain. Similarly, if there was an increase in wastage during service or in early retirement the same conclusion could be reached. In fact over the past few years the levels of sickness, accident an ill-health retirement have beeen causing concern to police managers, and as recommended in an Association of Chief Police Officers (ACPO) working party report, forces have been taking steps to address this problem.

The working party identified four major sources of stress which might impair individual and organizational effectiveness: management systems; management styles; management support; and traumatic incidents.

Taken at face value these areas do not appear to link with the earlier argument about the direction of change within the police service being towards a more community sensitive policing. It is certainly true that during the same period of time there have been pressures of quite a different nature impinging upon the service. The drive towards increased public accountability has, for example, been matched by a drive towards greater financial accountability, with an emphasis on effectiveness, efficiency and value for money. Cost-centre accounting, civilianization and a reducion in overtime are some of the results. Where the links arise between those areas identified as the most potent stressors by police officers and the political pressures described earlier is in their demand for change. Coping with change makes emotional demands on all human beings, be they police officers, teachers or students. Life Events scales which measure stress always include numerous items related to change, whether that be anticipated as a positive experience (e.g. getting married, moving house) or as a result of personal tragedy (e.g. death of a loved one, loss of a job). Change in the work situation is a frequently cited source of occupational stress irrespective of occupation. In this respect the police service as an organization is probably no more under stress than the teaching profession. However, that does not invalidate the point that organizational strain is an important issue and one which needs to be addressed if the police service is to rise to the challenges of the 1990s.

Support Through Counselling

Clearly, no single initiative could deal effectively with the four stressors identified by the ACPO working party, but there is evidence to suggest that the service is at least attempting to address these issues. For example, a number of forces have set up some form of counselling service. Developments in this area have been accelerated by a series of public disasters in which the police took a major role, for example the Bradford fire, the Hillsborough disaster, the Kegworth plane crash. Following these events a small number of officers experienced acute post-traumatic stress disorder (PTSD), and were referred for specialist help to experienced counsellors. The police are not unique in their attempts to address either traumatic stress or psychological strain, but for the police service these developments are particularly significant in view of the generally macho culture which prevails within the service, with its tendency to reject, or even penalize, any demonstration of vulnerability.

Traumatic stress, however, is perhaps easier, in organizational terms, for the service to address than the other areas which emerged from the working party report, for these relate to an insidious malaise within the organization rather than within particular vulnerable individuals; therefore, to address them involves an admission that the organization as a whole is flawed. Dealing with problems at the management level may involve the risky business of balancing public confidence with internal credibility, as demonstrated in the recent controversy over the very public decision by the then Chief Constable of the West Midlands to disband the Serious Crime squad and subject its members to an enquiry. Some senior police managers believe that they have made definite headway in overcoming the internal stressors by management decisions and strategies, albeit with a less public impact than Geoffrey Dear's, but others believe that the emphasis on managerial competence has been just another demand taking the officers lower down the hierarchy closer to overload.

Support Through Training

There is evidence of a tendency within the service as a whole to respond to any perceived deficiency by making adjustments to its training programme (Southgate, 1988). This response is so marked that it could almost be described as a reflex. Since the riots of the 1980s there have been various attempts to introduce training packages aimed at improving police-community relations by addressing the psychological capacity of the police to produce a more community sensitive service. Probably the best researched is the new Police Probationer training programme. Police recruit training follows a centrally prescribed curriculum and is carried out at Police District Training Centres which serve a wide geographical area and take recruits from a number of different forces. During the past decade police training in general has been widely scrutinized from both within and outside the organization, and enormous changes have been made to move from what ten years ago was an almost entirely didactic style of teaching, using traditional classroom methods, with a strong emphasis on rote learning, to a more student-centred approach employing a wide range of teaching methods. But the most comprehensive analysis of police training focused on recruits, and during the 1980s a team of educationalists from the University of East Anglia conducted a thorough evaluation of recruit training culminating in the introduction of a radical new approach in the summer of 1989.

The changes have not been without controversy, and it remains to be seen whether the new training can indeed be implemented in the way in which it is intended, and whether officers trained under the new methods are in fact more able than their predecessors to respond to the demand for improved police-public relations. The 'Reflective Practitioner' model of the police officer on which the training is based highlights 'the importance of self and social awareness for high quality operational performance' (Elliot, 1988). It aims to produce a more reflective self-confident individual, who is resistant to pressures to conform to the powerful effects of police occupational culture, and able to operate as a problem solver in the face of the social and legal dilemmas which police patrol work presents. By using a case-study-based curriculum, in which periods in the training school are interleaved with periods of patrol work, the new training is designed to address the complex psychological and social factors which officers need to consider when making decisions about how to enforce the law.

Studies of police selection and training have shown a pattern which includes a liberalizing effect on recruits during the early stages of training which is then dissipated by the experience of 'real police work', exposure to 'canteen culture', and job-related cynicism. There is evidence to suggest that an initial idealistic approach to police work is followed by an instrumental, pragmatic phase, which replaces idealism with a sense of policing being 'just a job' (Fielding, 1988). Yet this is followed by a more mature phase in which each individual having been exposed to the many influences of police work and training finds his or her own personal perspective in harmony with their personal identity. This maybe is the point where the political and the psychological meet — the point of the individual. For all of us, whether police or 'public', there is the need to reconcile the political and the personal pressures inherent in the exercise of social control, and the maintenance of personal freedoms in the real world of social inequality and greed.

Tutorial Discussion Questions

1 What does the idea that riots can be functional say about how the government should react to such events?
2 Given that the police cannot respond to every infringement of the law, either because they are not informed of an incident or because of competing calls on their attention, how should policing priorities be determined?
3 Should local policing policies be set by locally elected representatives of the community, by the Chief Constable, or by the Home Office?

4   Is it inevitable that consultative machinery will be used predominantly by middle-class articulate people? How would you design a consultative procedure to involve a wide section of the population?

5   What would be the advantages and disadvantages of the police force delegating its service function to other agencies? Would you favour such a change?

6   Consider how crime prevention initiatives could enhance the fear of crime. What role could the police play in reassuring those who are unnecessarily fearful of becoming victims of crime?

7   Do you expect that those recruits with the most comprehensive knowledge of the law will necessarily make the most effective police officers?

References

ELLIOT, J. (1988) 'Why put case study at the heart of the police training curriculum?', in SOUTHGATE, P. (Ed.) *New Directions in Police Training*, London, HMSO, pp. 148–69.

FIELDING, N. (1988) 'Socialisation of recruits into the police role', in SOUTHGATE, P. (Ed.) *New Directions in Police Training*, London, HMSO, pp. 58–73.

KINSEY, R., LEA, J. and YOUNG, J. (1986) *Losing the Fight against Crime*, Oxford, Basil Blackwell.

MORGAN, R. (1989) 'Policing by consent: Legitimating the doctrine', in MORGAN, R. and SMITH, D.J. (Eds) *Coming to Terms with Policing*, London, Routledge.

SCARMAN, LORD (1981) *The Brixton Disorders 10–12 April 1981: Report of an Enquiry by the Rt. Hon. the Lord Scarman, OBE* (The Scarman Report), London, HMSO.

SOUTHGATE, P. (Ed.) (1988) *New Directions in Police Training*, London, HMSO.

WEATHERITT, M. (1986) *Innovations in Policing*, London, Croom Helm.

Further Reading

BROGDEN, M., JEFFERSON, T. and WALKLATE, S. (1988) *Introducing Policework*, London, Unwin Hyman.

HOLLIN, C. (1989) *Psychology and Crime*, London, Routledge.

SOUTHGATE, P. (Ed.) (1988) *New Directions in Police Training*, London, HMSO.

Chapter 16

Lie Detection: Lies and Truths

Douglas Carroll

One day in 1978, in Toledo, Ohio, Floyd Fay was arrested for robbery and murder. Before dying, the victim, who was an acquaintance of Fay's, had said that one of his masked assailants looked like Floyd. Fay was held in custody for two months while the police searched in vain for additional incriminating evidence. Finally, he was offered a deal. He could take a polygraph lie-detection test and if he passed, all charges against him would be dropped. However, if he failed the results would be presented in court.

Floyd Fay agreed and failed the test. A second test, conducted by another examiner, also pointed to the same conclusion: Fay was guilty. The evidence of the polygraph test results was duly presented to the court and Fay was found guilty of aggravated murder and sentenced to life imprisonment. Two years later, the actual perpetrators of the crime confessed and Fay was exonerated.

David Lykken of the University of Minnesota purports to have collected hundreds of such cases. In cold statistical terms, they are all 'false positives': individuals who are actually innocent but are pronounced guilty on the basis of a polygraph lie-detection test. How does this test work? Just what did Floyd Fay fail? Is it really such a hit-and-miss procedure? Why might psychologists have an interest? These are the questions that this chapter will try to address.

The last of these questions is relatively easy to deal with. In its aims, the polygraph lie-detection test is a psychological test. While its focus, as we shall see, is an individual's biological reactions to a series of questions rather than their written or verbal answers — the usual psychological test format — polygraph lie-detection shares the common purpose of attempting to divine a person's mental state from a sample of their behaviour. Accordingly, psychologists should have something to say about it. Further, in those countries in which it is used, particularly the USA, it is used heavily. The area of criminal investigation is but one of its applications. By far its largest use is in the area of job screening and security vetting. In the USA for example, it is estimated that around two million people per year are subjected to polygraph tests to detect actual or likely security or employment risks. Approximately 25 per cent of major American employers routinely use such tests. A number of countries, such as the UK, have so far largely resisted the polygraph. Nevertheless, many employers in these countries have registered an interest and ideas which originate in the USA have a tendency to get caught up eventually in westerly air currents.

The Polygraph Lie Test

A polygraph is simply a flat-top pen recorder that charts variations in an individual's breathing, blood pressure and skin electrical activity. Measurements are taken while an individual is posed a series of questions structured to yield yes/no answers. The underlying assumption is that the reactions to some questions relative to others will signal deception or truthfulness. It is perhaps worth stressing that none of these measures constitutes a unique index of lying. There is nothing in our biology akin to Pinocchio's nose. At best, changes in breathing, blood pressure and skin electrical activity signify the body's registration of emotional arousal. Thus, it is possible to gauge which questions were more arousing, but, of course, not the nature of the arousal, which might be due to guilt, fear, anger, embarrassment or any other emotional state. Nor can we discern the source of that emotion: fear of being found out when guilty, or fear of being implicated though innocent.

The usual questioning technique applied in criminal investigation is the control question test (CQT). In the CQT there are three sorts of questions posed: neutral questions, such as 'Are you 25 years old?'; accusatory questions relating to the crime at issue, such as 'Did you kill Fred?'; and so-called control questions, such as 'Before the age of 20, did you ever hurt anyone on purpose?' This last type of question is designed to be emotionally arousing, but unrelated to the current investigation. The assumption is that innocent people will react at least as much, if not more, to such control questions as they react to the specific accusatory questions. The guilty, on the other hand, should find the accusatory questions much more arousing than the control questions, and display their most emphatic biological reactions to those. In screening and vetting tests though, since no specific crime has been committed, the CQT cannot be applied. Instead, the examiner is asked a series of neutral questions and a series of more general accusatory questions such as 'Did you lie on your application form?' Thus, guilt in such circumstances is deduced from the relative strengths of the biological reactions to just these two sorts of questions.

While the theoretical foundations of polygraph lie-detection may be rather primitive, its status is likely to be determined by more practical concerns, i.e. does it work? Does the polygraph help us in making substantially accurate judgments of truth and deception? Our everyday language suggests that not all of us are particularly astute in social encounters at detecting whether or not we are being lied to; words like dupe, sucker, mug and so on have few equivalents on the other side of a gullibility dimension. However, are we really that insensitive in such matters? You can test this out. Have a fellow student make 10 brief biographical statements, 5 of which are true and 5 of which are false, and then try and divine the truths from the falsehoods. Having checked your success rate, repeat the exercise. Research demonstrates wide individual variation in detection accuracy. However, it also shows that with practice and feedback of success and failure, individuals improve substantially in judging truth from fiction. The central issue surrounding polygraph lie-detection is whether the polygraph adds anything to such traditional methods of sorting the false from the truthful, the guilty from the innocent. Two major sorts of evidence are available to us on the accuracy of polygraph lie-detection: first, laboratory studies, and second, field tests; both have focused on the CQT in a criminal investigation context.

The Evidence

Recently I reviewed five laboratory studies, choosing those which most closely mirrored CQT practices in the real world and were methodologically sound. In the main these studies had guilty subjects engage in a mock crime (e.g. steal a small amount of money from a desk drawer); other subjects were aware that a crime of this nature had been committed, but were innocent of it. Guilty subjects were usually instructed that if they were not detected by the polygraph interrogator as guilty, they would get to keep their ill-gotten gains. Innocent subjects were usually promised a reward if the test pronounced them innocent. *Table 1* summarizes the overall outcome of these five studies. While accuracy rates varied among the studies, the average success rate at detecting guilt means that out of every 20 guilty individuals, 17 were correctly judged to be guilty. This is a not an unimpressive hit rate. However, the average rate for correctly identifying the innocent is somewhat lower; out of every 20 innocent subjects, 15 were correctly determined. This figure has to be set aside a chance level of 50 per cent, i.e. 10 out of 20 innocent subjects would be judged so by tossing a coin.

One other feature of these studies is worthy of mention. Although the polygraph interrogator in each case was ignorant of the subjects' actual guilt or innocence, they did have access to information other than that conveyed by the polygraph recordings of the subjects' biological reactions to the different sorts of questions. Since the people making the assessment were also those who conducted the questioning, they had access to a possibly rich source of clues as to guilt or innocence in the subjects' behaviour and demeanour during interrogation. What one would like to know is the accuracy of judgments based solely on the information available from the polygraph recordings. It is this question which brings us closer to a determination of the polygraph's particular contribution to accurate judgments of guilt and innocence. Only one laboratory study yields useful data on this issue. Hammond's (1980) study compares the accuracy of judgments made by the original examiner (who had access to the polygraph recordings plus the full range of the subjects' conduct during questioning) and those made by a 'blind' assessor (who had access only to the recordings of subjects' physiological reactions to the questions asked). The results are summarized in *Table 2*. Ignoring the inconclusive cases for a moment, there would appear to be no overall drop in accuracy from the original examiner to the 'blind' examiner. However, it is also apparent that the 'blind' examiner offered far fewer definite judgments, particularly in the case of innocent subjects. Whereas the original examiners correctly identified 12 of the innocent subjects, the 'blind' examiner was able to provide a definite judgment of innocence for only 4 of them. This would seem to imply that there was sensitive information available during the original examination that was simply unobtainable from the polygraph recordings alone.

Laboratory studies of field CQT practices, then, suggest aggregate global accuracy rates of somewhere between 80 and 85 per cent. There are more false positive errors (innocent classified as guilty) than false negative errors (guilty classified as innocent). Further, the evidence, such as it is, indicates that reliance on information solely from the polygraph would not appear to affect accuracy unduly; it also suggests, though, that in reaching a decision the original examiner makes considerable use of non-polygraphic sources of information, particularly in the case of innocent subjects.

Table 1   Laboratory studies of accuracy

Study	Status of Subjects	Number of Subjects	% Accuracy	% Aggregate Accuracy	% Guilty Classified Innocent (False − ve)	% Innocent Classified Guilty (False + ve)
Barland and Raskin (1975)	Guilty Innocent	26 21	88.5 71.4	80.0	11.5	28.6
Raskin and Hare (1978)	Guilty Innocent	21 23	100.0 91.3	95.6	0	8.7
Hammond (1980)	Guilty Innocent	24 18	95.8 66.7	81.2	4.2	33.3
Waid, Orne and Orne (1981)	Guilty Innocent	40 34	72.5 76.5	74.5	27.5	23.5
Barland (1981)	Guilty Innocent	26 21	80.8 76.2	78.5	19.2	23.8
Average Accuracy			87.6 76.4	82.0	12.5	23.6

163

Douglas Carroll

Table 2   Hammond (1980): Summary of results for global and blind examination

	Original Examiners Actual		Blind Examiner Actual	
	Guilty	*Innocent*	*Guilty*	*Innocent*
Classification				
Guilty	23	6	21	2
Innocent	1	12	0	4
Inconclusive	8	12	11	24

Overall, though, there are good grounds for suspecting the utility of laboratory studies for the purposes of evaluating accuracy in the field. The most compelling concerns the emotional significance of accusatory questions for innocent people in the two contexts. In the laboratory such questions are of little psychological significance; only the subject's acquisition of some minor incentive is at stake. Guilty subjects, if they go undetected, generally get to keep the money stolen in a mock crime; innocent subjects, if asessed as innocent, receive a monetary reward of similar magnitude. In the real world, though, such questions hold enormous significance; the suspect's reputation, livelihood and liberty are most probably at stake. Given that our biology is sensitive to significance, one would expect innocent criminal suspects to show relatively more responsiveness to accusatory questions than innocent laboratory subjects. In short, an analysis of polygraph data from the laboratory will yield unrealistically high estimates of accuracy regarding the innocent.

Designing field studies that conform to the highest principles of experimental design is no easy matter. The main problem is finding a satisfactory criterion for assigning guilt or innocence. Many studies have managed this in only a small proportion of cases, and accordingly accuracy rates so derived may be unrepresentative of accuracy over the full range of cases. There is one very parsimonious explanation for why someone who has failed a polygraph test does not subsequently confess their guilt; they are, in fact, innocent! The crucial attribute of any criterion is that it must be independent of the polygraph examiner's judgment. Thus, retrospective comparisons of examiners' judgments against court judgments, where the polygraph examiners' decisions are part of the evidence contributing to the court judgments, are unacceptable. By the same token, we should not place overly much reliance on the undoubtedly sincere, but nonetheless unsubstantiated, pronouncements of polygraph examiners as to their success rates. These are invariably high. Aside from criterion problems, we undoubtedly have to bear in mind that most general of human propensities: while we can generally recount our successes with ease, we frequently experience difficulty remembering our failures! Only a rather small number of field studies are sufficiently free of such problems to warrant serious consideration.

In a study that is frequently cited by proponents of lie-detection Bersh (1969) had four experienced attorneys judge the guilt or innocence of suspects on the basis of their evidential files, minus of course any reference to polygraph examinations. The four attorneys were unanimous in 157 instances and managed a majority decision in a further 59 instances. The correspondence between their judgments and the original polygraph examiners' assessment is presented in *Table 3*.

Table 3   Bersh (1969): Summary of results of global evaluation

Study	Status of Suspects	Number of Suspects	% Accuracy	% Aggregate Accuracy	% Fale – ve	% False + ve
Panel Assessment						
Unanimous	Guilty	70	93	92.5	7	8
	Innocent	87	92			
Majority	Guilty	34	70.5	75.3	29.5	20
	Innocent	25	80.0			

Aggregate accuracy was an impressive 92.5 per cent where there was a unanimous panel decision, although it was only 75 per cent in instances of a majority decision. However, rather than clinch the matter in favour of polygraph lie-detection, the Bersh study merely reveals the limitations of relying on global accuracy rates. High accuracy rates cannot be attributed in any significant measure to the polygraph where there exists other salient clues to guilt or innocence. As with the laboratory research already considered, Bersh's examiners could make use of a range of verbal and non-verbal behaviour exhibited during polygraph examination. Further in contrast to laboratory practice, but in line with general field practice, Bersh's examiners also had access to the evidential files upon which the attorneys based their judgments. The accuracy rates reported by Bersh are, in fact, precisely what would be expected had a fifth assessor judged guilt or innocence on the same information as the original panel of four. Accordingly, it is possible that the original polygraph examiners relied decidedly more on the case files than on the polygraph charts. There is certainly nothing in the study to allay such suspicions. A compelling case for the polygraph could be made in this instance only if it could be demonstrated that an interrogator with no polygraph, but with access to the case files, reached decisions that were significantly less in accord with the panel's judgments than were the polygraph examiners' decisions.

A requirement such as this is given particular force when one considers the results of field studies using 'blind' chart evaluation. The outcome of these studies is presented in *Table 4*. The Barland and Raskin (1976) study employed a panel of five experienced attorneys to ascertain guilt or innocence on the basis of evidential files. While Barland conducted the polygraph examination, Raskin, 'blind' to the case files, analyzed the charts. Of the 92 original cases, sufficient panel agreement was reached on 64 of them. Of these, 13 were classified as inconclusive by Raskin; accordingly, the data presented deal only with the remaining 51 cases. Horvath (1977) approached the matter of assigning guilt or innocence in a different manner. Guilt was presumed where there was a confession of guilt, and innocence where there was a confession of guilt by another. Horvath located 28 examples of each from the police files and distributed the polygraph charts to 10 trained polygraph examiners for 'blind' evaluation. Five of the examiners had more than three years' experience; 5 had less. Thus the data presented are, in fact, derived from 560 judgments. Aside from the data presented in *Table 4*, one other result is worth mentioning: examiner experience did not significantly affect accuracy. The Kleinmuntz and Szucko (1984) study adopted a similar approach, selecting for evaluation the polygraph charts of 50 confessed thieves and 50 innocents, who although initially suspected of the same crimes, were subsequently cleared through the confessions of the actual thieves. The charts were distributed among six professional polygraph examiners for 'blind' evaluation of guilt or innocence. Aside from the data presented in *Table 4*, one other result is again worth mentioning. Overall aggregate accuracy of 69 per cent conceals a range of individual examiner accuracy that never exceeded 80 per cent (63–76 percent).

These data largely speak for themselves; overall aggregate accuracy is much lower than that reported by Bersh and the rate of false positive judgments extremely high. The overall detection rate for innocent individuals is at chance levels. Thus, polygraph data *per se* would seem to be remarkably insensitive, particularly to a suspect's innocence.

Given the discrepancy between these data and those reported by Bersh, it

Table 4 Summary of results of field studies that involved blind assessment of the polygraph records

Study	Status of Suspects	Number of Suspects	% Accuracy	% Aggregate Accuracy	% False −ve	% False +ve
Barland and Raskin (1976)	Guilty	40	97	71	3	55
	Innocent	11	45			
Horvath (1977)	Guilty	28	77	64	23	49
	Innocent	28	51			
Kleinmuntz and Szucko (1984)	Guilty	50	76	69	24	37
	Innocent	50	63			
Average Accuracy			83	68	17	47
			53			

would seem that accurate assessments, particularly of innocence, in the course of a usual polygraph evaluation have little to do with the pattern of a suspect's physiological reactions. On what, then, might the examiner be relying? The two most likely sources of information have already been mentioned: the data in the evidential files, and the suspect's general demeanour during interrogation. Having said a little about the former, let us briefly consider the latter. In order to assess the utility of this possible non-polygraphic source of information it is necessary to add to the usual procedure, as a control, either an interrogator or an observer with no access to the polygraph. Such a control was included by Ginton *et al.* (1982) in a CQT investigation of Israeli policemen known to have cheated or not on a mathematics test. Unfortunately, only 2 dishonest subjects were available for testing, and so attention will focus on the 13 innocent subjects. The data are presented in *Table 5*. There were three different assessors: the interrogator (access to polygraph data and subject's general demeanour during questioning); the observer (access only to demeanour); the 'blind' evaluator (access only to polygraph data). While the observer's accuracy matched that of the original interrogator, the 'blind' chart evaluator performed no better than chance. These data suggest that the subject's general demeanour offers more accurate grounds for attributing innocence than the polygraph chart, and that the polygraph, in fact, brings nothing of merit to interrogation as far as innocent suspects are concerned.

Table 5 Ginton et al. *(1982): Summary of results for innocent subjects*

	Original Examiner	Observer	Blind Evaluator
Classification			
Guilty	2	2	3
Innocent	11	11	7
Inconclusive	0	0	3

The field studies, then, would not appear to offer much of a case for the polygraph. The Bersh study offers no evidence that the impressive accuracy rates owed anything to the polygraph. Subsequent studies using 'blind' chart evaluation, strongly suggest that Bersh and other field examiners rely heavily on non-polygraphic sources of information, since 'blind' evaluation yields aggregate accuracy rates that are no greater than 70 per cent. Of particular concern, in this context, is the high level of false positives; 'blind' evaluation identifies the innocent at round about chance level. In addition, although few data exist, it would appear that an observer, regarding the suspect's general behaviour from another room, does just as well as an experienced polygraph examiner, and better than someone blindly evaluating the polygraph charts.

Floyd Fay's Revenge

It might be argued that in certain contexts (e.g. state security) detecting the guilt is of such importance that the price of possibly wrongly classifying many innocent people is worth paying. However, it would appear that there is at least anecdotal evidence that with proper training even the most deceptive of individuals can outwit the polygraph.

While Floyd Fay was serving this wrongful prison sentence, he decided to get his own back on the device that had put him there. The prison routinely used the polygraph to investigate charges against inmates of infringing prison regulations. Fay studied the relevant research reports, and taught his fellow prisoners how to increase their responses to neutral and control questions (by, for example, covertly biting their tongue) and thus mask any large reactions to accusatory questions. By the time of his release, Fay had schooled 27 inmates in such techniques. All, according to Fay, were unquestionably guilty. Only 4 failed to be pronounced innocent by the polygraph examiner.

Tutorial Discussion Questions

1 Might the likelihood of having to undertake a polygraph test encourage guilty persons to confess?
2 Could the polygraph act as a deterrent to crime and deceit?
3 Might it be possible by structuring the questions in a different manner to increase the accuracy of the test?
4 Should employers in this country include the polygraph as part of the selection process?
5 Should it be available to the police?
6 Can you conceive of any alternative ways of accurately determining honesty or dishonesty in employees or potential employees?
7 From your knowledge of what might affect physiological reactions, what strategies might you suggest to someone to enable them to pass a polygraph test?

References

BARLAND, G. H. (1981) 'A validity and reliability study of counter-intelligence screening test', Security-support Battalion, 902nd Military Intelligence Group, Fort George G. Meade, Maryland, USA.

BARLAND, G. H. and RASKIN, D. C. (1975) 'An evaluation of field techniques in detection and deception', *Psychophysiology*, **12**, pp. 321–30.

BARLAND, G. H. and RASKIN, D. C. (1976) *Validity and Reliability of Polygraph Examinations of Criminal Suspects*, US Department of Justice Report No. 76–1, Contract 75-NI-99-0001. (Department of Psychology, University of Utah, Salt Lake City).

BERSH, P. J. (1969) 'A validation study of polygraph examiner judgements', *Journal of Applied Psychology*, **53**, pp. 399–403.

GINTON, A., DAIE, N., ELAAD, E. and BEN-SHAKHAR, G. (1982) 'A method for evaluating the use of the polygraph in a real-life situation', *Journal of Applied Psychology*, **67**, pp. 131–7.

HAMMOND, D. L. (1980) 'The responding of normals, alcoholics, and psychopaths in a laboratory lie-detection experiment', unpublished doctoral dissertation, California School of Professional Psychology.

HORVATH, F. S. (1977) 'The effect of selected variables on interpretation of polygraph records', *Journal of Applied Psychology*, **62**, pp. 127–36.

Douglas Carroll

KLEINMUNTZ, B. and SZUCKO, J.J. (1984) 'A field study of the fallibility of polygraphic lie detection', *Nature*, **308**, pp. 449–50.
RASKIN, D.C. and HARE, R.D. (1978) 'Psychopathy and detection of deception in a prison population', *Psychophysiology*, **15**, pp. 126–36.
WAID, W.M., ORNE, E.C. and ORNE, M.T. (1981) 'Selective memory for social information, alertness, and physiological arousal in the detection of deception', *Journal of Applied Psychology*, **66**, pp. 224–32.

Further Reading

GALE, A. (Ed.) (1988) *The Polygraph Test: Lies, Truth and Science*, London, Sage.
LYKKEN, D.T. (1980) *A Tremor in the Blood: Uses and Abuses of the Lie-Detector*, New York, McGraw-Hill.

Chapter 17

Is Television Violence Harmful?

Guy Cumberbatch

Television violence has received more attention in public and research debates than any other issue in the field of mass communications. Concerns about crime and violence on television began in the earliest days of broadcasting and have remained persistent ones ever since. The continuing popularity of this topic can be seen by the attention it receives annually in our daily newspapers. For example, over a twelve-month period (from September 1989 to September 1990) we counted 135 articles on television violence in the quality British press alone. The majority of articles suggest that television violence is a social problem. In this recent analysis this was the message in 83 per cent of articles — a figure little different from that obtained in a similar exercise we carried out nearly two decades ago.

A wide variety of events makes television violence newsworthy, so that coverage varies a little from year to year. Most often it becomes newsworthy because some public figure (usually a politician) pronounces on the subject. Sometimes a particular crime is claimed to be linked to television. Occasionally a particular television programme is criticized for its 'gratuitous' violence. More rarely a new piece of research is published which is reported as 'proving' that television violence is harmful.

Newspaper coverage of social issues rarely explores topics in depth and can hardly be a reliable source of research evidence. However over the years we have noted some consistent claims made in the press about television violence:

1 That there is too much violence on television and that it is increasing.
2 That the public are concerned about television violence.
3 That television violence is harmful.

Each of these claims involves some research evidence which is controversial. The last claim about the potential effects of television violence provides the focus of this chapter. However the first two claims are also worthy of some attention.

Is There Too Much Violence on Television?

It is quite easy to be a scaremonger about crime and violence in the mass media. For example, Frederic Wertham, an American psychiatrist, claimed to have studied adolescents 'who in comic books, movies and TV have seen more than 10,000 homicides'. While others have made similar claims, none of these are based on any reliable evidence on the media exposure patterns of any individuals. Such figures are really guesstimates based on the average content of the various mass media. However just how much crime and violence there is on television depends considerably on how these terms are defined. Most researchers who have carried out content analyses of television follow the generous definitions given by George Gerbner at the Annenberg School of Communications in Philadelphia. His team has carried out annual analyses of 'prime time' television (8–11 p.m.), counting all acts of violence which included any 'overt expression of physical force'. Gerbner did not make any distinction according to motivation or context. Thus, not surprisingly, *Tom and Jerry* appears as one of the most violent programmes on television.

In the USA, violence on television has tended to fluctuate at a rate of between 5 and 6 violent acts per hour in dramatic fiction where roughly 80 per cent of programmes contain some violence. Very similar rates have been reported in various other countries such as the Netherlands and Australia with higher rates in Japan and West Germany. The lowest rate reported has been for the UK where in 1986 only 56 per cent of dramatic fiction programmes contained violence and the rate was one half that of any other country on which comparable data exists at only 2.5 violent acts per hour.

This very extensive British study based on over 2,000 programmes was also interesting in showing a decline in the amount of violence on television between 1970 and 1986. Moreover, programmes made in the 1960s had twice as much violence in them (4.5 acts per hour) compared with those made in the 1980s (2.3 acts per hour). This decline was most notable in police/crime drama where more recent productions involve community policing rather than the 'cops and robbers' so popular in the 1970s. Perhaps not surprisingly this study also found that American productions contained far more violence than did programmes made in the UK.

Whether this amount of violence on television is too much or too little is not a 'scientific' issue in that answering this would require a value judgement. However we can conclude that the UK has a relatively low rate compared with other countries and that it has declined in recent years. Whether this pattern will continue is a matter for speculation.

Are People Concerned About Television Violence?

Public opinion polls reliably show that when people are asked directly whether they think there is too much violence on television, most people (60 per cent) say that there is too much. However when asked to judge whether particular (named) television programmes are too violent only a minority agree that any particular programme is too violent. Further data clouding the picture even more comes from the broadcasting authorities who carry out regular surveys to discover what kind of things on television cause offence. In these surveys usually only around 1 in every 10 people mentions violence, while the numbers spontaneously complaining of violence in letters to the British Broadcasting Corporation (BBC) or the the Independent Broadcasting Authority (IBA) are quite tiny — one study reported only 3 letters on this out of the 1,500 received.

Thus, concerns about television violence, while they evidently exist, are rather difficult to quantify and there must be a suspicion that what viewers watch and what they say they disapprove of may not be quite the same thing. Indeed broadcasters tend to believe that violent programmes are likely to be popular ones. This is evidently true of spy films like the James Bond series, but the research evidence that violence *makes* a programme popular is rather weak.

Among the various concerns expressed about television violence is that it may lead to children imitating what they see. In a recent (1988) survey by the IBA nearly two thirds (64 per cent) of people surveyed agreed this might occur. Moreover nearly 8 out of 10 people agreed that 'people are justified in being concerned about the impact of TV violence on children today'. Identifying the particular programmes which people think might influence children results in less agreement. For example in one survey carried out by Channel 4 Television in 1988, nearly half of those questioned (49 per cent) said they had seen programmes which might encourage others to commit a violent act but only 4 per cent confessed to having seen a programme which had this effect on themselves. Additionally and perhaps surprisingly, the parents of young children seem less concerned about particular programmes than those without children. Indeed it is generally true that concerns about violence, both in television and in society, increase with age, being at their highest among the elderly.

To date research has not made much attempt to understand public attitudes about television violence. It would seem that while a certain degree of concern exists, the attitudes surrounding such concerns may not be very salient ones. Moreover it is possible that when invited to comment on television violence, people may indicate more general concerns about violence rather than their concerns about television as such. However very few people believe that violence on television can be therapeutic and in this they are in agreement with most research studies on the effects of mass-mediated aggression.

Is Television Violence Harmful?

Especially since the 1960s, there has been a considerable amount of research attention given to this issue. In many reviews, the conclusions to this research are presented as clear-cut: most studies conclude that television violence is a social problem encouraging aggression in the viewer. Introductory textbooks in psychology are especially prone to this conclusion. We examined 100 such texts and found that nearly one third (30 per cent) mentioned television violence. Of these, 7 out of 10 textbooks concluded that television violence was an important factor in contributing to the level of aggression in society. However a number of writers have expressed reservations about what the research evidence actually shows.

There are various ways in which the effects of television violence can be studied. Each methodology has its strengths and weaknesses. These will be examined in some detail.

Laboratory Studies of Filmed Aggression

The studies most often mentioned in psychology textbooks are laboratory studies. Here two names stand out both as pioneers in the early 1960s and as (later) theorists. These are Albert Bandura of Stanford University (famous for his social learning or imitation theory) and Leonard Berkowitz of Wisconsin (famous for various work, especially on impulsive aggression).

Albert Bandura started research in the field of television violence very obliquely. The experiment which led him on to television violence was concerned with whether the attractiveness of a teacher had an influence on children's learning. He found that it did: nice teachers were more effective. However one of the behaviours that the teacher expressed was an act of aggression. To Bandura's surprise, most children copied this regardless of the attractiveness of the teacher. Bandura then began a series of experiments to try and understand the conditions under which aggression was most likely to be imitated. One included looking at filmed models compared with live models. Filmed models were readily imitated. Following this finding, numerous laboratory studies have reported similar imitation of film-mediated aggression.

A few more details should be noted here about this style of research. The object of the aggression seen in the film and imitated by children was a 'Bobo' or 'Bozo' doll. This is a large inflated plastic clown which has a weighted base (usually filled with sand). When struck violently and knocked over it bounces back up again. Those who have experienced such toys may have appreciated this pleasure. My own Bobo doll was wrecked through the enthusiasm of an elderly psychology professor who seemed unable to resist the temptation to kick it whenever he came to my office.

In Bandura's research and that following it, the experiments on film-mediated aggression almost invariably involve some unusual conditions. One of these is that the subjects in the experiments (young children) are 'frustrated'. What this means is that after being shown a film of a model behaving aggressively towards a Bobo doll, the children are taken to a room where they are shown some attractive toys. The researcher then 'frustrates' the children by inviting their admiration of the toys and then telling them that they cannot play with them. The children are then led to a room where they have access to similar toys seen in the film and ostensibly left alone to play. In reality of course they are observed and their aggression monitored. Most children (up to 88 per cent) readily imitate the aggression they have seen in the film and reproduce up to 70 per cent of the responses shown by the model.

This research demonstrates a potentially important process — that of observational learning. However, before considering the value of this style of research for our understanding of media effects, it is worth summarizing the paradigm adopted by Leonard Berkowitz, whose work was centrally concerned with learning theory perspectives on aggression as pioneered by psychologists at Yale University. His use of film material was simply an extension of the techniques used to investigate the inhibition and catharsis of hostility. Earlier it had been argued that fantasy behaviour performed a drive-reducing (cathartic) function: those who saw an aggressive film were less aggressive than those who had not. Berkowitz was unconvinced by this evidence and demonstrated that any reduction in aggression from watching an aggressive film is more likely to be due to the film heightening a subject's anxiety about his own display of aggression rather than to the aggression becoming vicariously discharged owing to the film.

The general procedure adopted by Berkowitz involved six groups of university students who first of all received an intelligence test. Half of the groups were angered by an experimenter (who insulted the intellectual competence of the subjects) while the other half were treated in a neutral fashion. Following this, half of the groups saw the control film (about canal boats in England) while the other half saw a seven-minute film clip of the prize fight taken from *Champion* starring Kirk Douglas. One experimental group was informed that the aggression against Kirk Douglas in the film was 'justified' (in order to reduce subjects' aggression anxiety) while the other group was told that it was not (in order to increase their aggression anxiety). Finally a second experimenter invited subjects to complete a questionnaire on what they thought of the experimenter in order to send it to his boss.

The results showed that those angered by the experimenter made more adverse comments about him than those treated neutrally. In the angered groups those who had been instructed that the aggression in the film was 'justified' made significantly more aggressive responses than either the control film group or the 'unjustified aggression' film group. The films did not have any differential effects on the non-angered groups. Thus, Berkowitz concluded that 'media aggression depicted as being justified has the greatest probability of leading to aggression when the audience is already angry'.

Although studies from these two different styles of research remain distinctive, they have often been lumped together as showing that the 'conclusions from all this work must be that viewing violence increases the chances of aggression occuring' (Eysenck and Nias, 1978: 160–1).However such a conclusion glosses over some important distinctions and contradictions, as well as various methodological problems.

First of all, in the case of Bandura's research, there must be little doubt that children can learn by 'observational' or 'social' learning. This is clearly part and parcel of the way children become socialized. However, despite continuing research demonstrating such behaviour, children do not typically imitate all that they see or even attempt to do so. There is a quite fundamental discrepancy between the high incidence of imitation in Bandura's results and what children typically do after watching television (such as to play normally or have their tea). Undoubtedly the novelty of the Bobo doll was a crucial factor. For example, it has been found that children who were unfamiliar with the doll imitated *five times* more than did children with previous exposure to it.

Stanley Milgram reported a series of eight major field experiments on the effects of modelled behaviour in the mass media. Despite the fact that these studies involved sample sizes of, at times, millions, there was no evidence that television models were imitated. On the other hand, Eysenck and Nias cite many popular accounts of 'waves of violence' following media portrayals of particular acts. Bomb hoaxes, suicides and sundry other aggressive acts are attributed to television's power to encourage 'copycat' behaviour. However much of this evidence is anecdotal and ignores the role of news values in reporting such phenomena; for example, a wave of reports of dogs savaging children owes more to the newsworthiness of such stories increasing after the first report than on imitative behaviour in the canine species.

Returning to Bandura, as Ruth Hartley commenting on his work noted, he

> suggests that behaviour towards inanimate objects like toys, is equated with social behaviour, a suggestion which is not generally supported in the literature. In fact the bulk of the literature supports an opposite view, that children will express toward inanimate objects feelings that they will not dare to show openly toward other persons.

It would seem much closer to what many ethologists describe as 'rough and tumble play' than 'aggression' as usually understood.

A related issue is even more fundamental for experimental research. Even if Bandura's measures of aggression were shown to have a convincing validity, would this hold for *imitative* aggression? For example, intelligence tests are assumed to have some validity, but if, in an experiment, subjects are shown how to perform the test, a later intelligence test might not have much validity as a measure of intelligence. This unlikely experiment is in fact rather like that carried out by Bandura and highlights the serious weakness in the validity criteria.

Although there are numerous other methodological issues which could be raised about this research, perhaps the final points may be developed by noting the contradictions between the results of Bandura's research and those obtained by Berkowitz. While Berkowitz found only generalized aggression (subjects did not imitate the film), Bandura found only imitative aggression (subjects did not generalize). The idea of university students aggressing against Bobo dolls, acting out the film script with dramatic imitative renderings of 'whack him', 'sock it' and so on, may seem a trifle absurd but illustrates an important distinction Bandura himself made between learning and performance. We all may learn how to rape, rob or murder from what we see in films or on television but the barriers to our performing these acts in everyday life are more motivational than knowledge-based. Similarly the barriers to helping behaviour are more likely to be found in motivation or opportunity cost than in any absence of a behavioural repertoire of how to help. The contradictions between Bandura's results and those of Berkowitz might be due to the different subjects used in the experiments or to the different films used. However they may also be due to the different role subjects were expected to play. If this were true then the relevance of these studies to mass media effects in the real world must be seriously questioned.

The evidence that laboratory experiments on the effects of the mass media are flawed by demand characteristics is far from conclusive but sufficient to provide some grounds for reservation. First of all, the experiments are very contrived procedures, even for the nursery schoolchildren in Bandura's studies. However those of Berkowitz are remarkably so. Later experiments became yet more contrived, especially since students generally earned 'credits' for participating which counted toward their psychology degrees.

Quite apart from the problem of demand characteristics, many of the effects noted are probably more economically interpreted in terms of a state of *arousal* than a state of *aggression*. Direct evidence comes from experiments by Dolf Zillman who added an additional condition of no film to compare with the effects of seeing a violent film clip (from *The Wild Bunch*) with seeing a neutral film clip (*Marco Polo's Travels*). Physiological measures suggested that the neutral film depressed arousal relative to the no-film condition. This explained the results of the aggression measure (willingness of subjects to deliver electric shocks). Here there was no difference between the violent film and the no-film condition, both of which produced more aggression than the neutral film.

Within the mass communications literature there exists a very healthy scepticism about laboratory-based research. However close analysis of the problems such as given above is almost completely absent, thus leading to a suspicion that many reviewers simply dismiss methodologies with which they are not familiar. Greater ecological validity in experiments, and more thoughtful and thorough designs are all possible and certainly long overdue, in order to deal satisfactorily with the vexed issue of mass media effects.

By way of conclusion to this section, we may observe that laboratory experiments do not adequately address the problem of whether or not mass media violence actually causes real violence in society. The ecological aspects of crime and of media use have not been taken seriously in these laboratory studies. Broadcasters who are concerned about whether what they produce is harmful will find it impossible to use the experimental data to make policy decisions and for the most part may view such research with some incredulity.

Experimental Field Studies

At first sight field experiments attempting to manipulate the natural media diet of people in natural settings seem the most promising solution to the various criticisms of laboratory research. The first study and those that followed were a salutary reminder that field research generates its own very considerable problems and is a far from easy solution.

The first attempt in this area to apply experimental methods to a natural setting was carried out by Seymour Feshbach and Jerome Singer in 3 private schools and 4 boys' homes. The boys were subjected to either a diet of violent television or a diet of neutral television. Some immediate problems arose. The neutral group complained bitterly about their diet and by popular request the television series *Batman* (a 'violent' programme) had to be allowed. The experiment continued for six weeks, during which houseparents and teachers recorded the boys' behaviour. In the private schools little difference was observed between the violent television group and the neutral television group. However, in the boys' homes, aggression towards peers in the violent television group was almost half that in the neutral television group. Feshbach and Singer concluded that this was evidence for catharsis — an unpopular conclusion which stimulated some critical reviews. One of the more serious methodological problems reviewers pointed out was that the observers knew which television programmes the children had watched.

Historically the next study worthy of note was rather different, focusing on possible imitation of a popular television programme *Medical Center* which was edited to produce 2 antisocial versions and 1 prosocial version of the same basic story. In a large series of field experiments no evidence was found of imitative antisocial behaviour in the various audiences.

No study is perfect and, in reviewing studies which support a 'no effects' thesis of television, it is tempting to list each and every problem which researchers face in this field. However the methodological problems seem to produce bias in favour of effects being found.

In studies using experimental field techniques, the only important ones to conclude unreservedly that films mediate aggression have been associated with Leonard Berkowitz. In several studies, delinquent boys tended to become more aggressive during the week in which they were exposed to aggressive films, compared with groups exposed to neutral films. In common with many previous studies by Berkowitz the results seem very impressive at first sight. For example, the effects of one or more violent films was to increase aggression by more than fortyfold in some groups of subjects over the baseline measures. This is curious, especially since during the film experiment the delinquents were not allowed to watch television. Why should films be so dramatically more effective than television?

Experimental field studies seem at first sight a useful approach to understanding the impact that the mass media have on society. However to date, methodological problems undermine any confidence that we might have had in them.

Correlational Studies

Most people are aware that correlations do not necessarily show causal relationships. However correlational research showing that delinquents prefer aggressive television is all too easy to conduct. The bulk of the studies using this methodology claim a simple relationship between television violence and aggression in viewers, but one that becomes more and more elusive as the sophistication of the study increases.

The introduction of television in the 1950s stimulated a number of major studies on its potential impact. Happily the unique opportunity to carry out before and after studies was not missed either in North America or in the UK. Large-scale and fairly comprehensive evaluations were conducted by Himmelweit, Oppenheim and Vince (1958) in the UK and by Schramm, Lyle and Parker (1961) in both Canada and the USA. Both accounts make fascinating reading in that so few differences emerged between television viewers and non-viewers across the wide variety of measures taken. The measures of aggression were fairly perfunctory especially in the case of Himmelweit who asked teachers to complete check lists on children, only one item of which related to aggression. However, no effect due to television was found. Schramm, Lyle and Parker's results were a little different. In their first study young children (11–12 years old) in what was called 'radio town' were *more* aggressive than in the 'teletown', while no difference existed between older children. In their second study a weak trend was observed for heavy viewers of television to be more aggressive than light viewers.

For many people — including researchers — it is difficult to reconcile the marginal effects of television reported with the sheer ubiquity and richness of the medium. The belief that television *must* have antisocial effects has persisted. A flurry of studies followed. Only the most notable of these will be mentioned.

Other correlational data show a very curious pattern of inconsistencies. By and large where a link between television and aggression appears to exist, it is given by measures of violent programme preference rather than simply by exposure to violent programmes. It is worth noting that this in itself contradicts all of the experimental research where simply exposing subjects to violent films is claimed to increase aggressive responses — whether they like what they see or not is not recorded.

Quite apart from this, the problem that variables other than those investigated may explain apparent links between the mass media and aggression plagues the correlational studies. One study based on over 600 adolescents in Maryland and Wisconsin found exposure to violent television positively correlated with self-reported aggression. A number of other interesting findings were reported; one example is that total television viewing, violence viewing and self-reported aggression all declined from junior to senior high school and that boys watch considerably more violent television than girls. Unfortunately, the relationship between television and aggression seems due to a failure to control these variables of sex and age. When the various groups formed by subdividing the sample on the basis of sex and school placement are considered, only one correlation out of eight approached statistical significance (which is the kind of result that might be expected on a chance basis anyway).

Among studies which have focused on violence, arguably the most ambitious of correlational studies was carried out by Belson (1978). This study of 1,565 boys aged 13–16 in London set very high standards. It attempted to measure children's exposure to television violence in their earlier years and to link this to self-reported violent behaviour through a sophisticated system of matching those who were more exposed to television violence with those who were less exposed to television violence. This matching was done according to over 200 different measures and thus attempts — reasonably well in fact — to overcome the serious problem that any correlation between delinquency and exposure to television violence could be due to a third variable like social class causing both. It would be churlish to criticize Belson for not being thorough enough in this search for third variables, although his matching list is not exhaustive. Belson concludes that boys with high levels of exposure to television violence commit 49 per cent more acts of serious violence than those who see little. He then goes on to list policy recommendations and suggests that violence should be reduced on television especially in 'plays or films in which violence occurs in the context of close personal relations', 'programmes presenting fictional violence of a realistic kind', and so on.

This sounds like the kind of impressive data providing the specific recommendations needed to clean up television. Unfortunately closer examination of the vast array of data Belson presents suggests more caution. For example, the graphs for the full sample show that the results are far from as simple as his conclusions imply. In these graphs, where exposure to television violence is plotted against violent behaviour, it is clear that the relationship is curvilinear. Thus, very low viewers of television violence are slightly *more* aggressive than moderate viewers. More importantly very high viewers of television violence are *less* aggressive than the moderate to high exposure group (50 per cent lower in fact!). Moreover in Belson's data, exposure to non-violent television is also linked to aggressive behaviour, as indeed are comics/comic books and even newspaper readership.

Some other pitfalls in measuring media exposure are illustrated by a large survey carried out by Barlow and Hill (1985). This British study attempted to find out if children were exposing themselves to uncensored horror video films ('video nasties'). This was a reasonable concern since they found that 40 per cent of the 4,500 children surveyed claimed to have a video recorder at home. Barlow and Hill had been particularly worried that the lack of any regulating system for this new medium allowed films to be available which had even been refused certification for cinema distribution by the British Board of Film Censors. They presented children with a 5 page list of 113 film titles and asked them, if they had seen any of them on video, to rate them as 'great', 'just alright' or 'awful'. Their conclusions produced banner headlines in the press: 'Four children in ten watch video nasties' (*The Daily Express*, 24 November 1983) and 'The Rape of Young Minds' (*The Daily Mail*), 24 November 1983). I and my colleague were suspicious that children might have quickly forgotten the instructions and simply rated films they had heard of or liked the sound of. To investigate this we reproduced Barlow and Hill's questionnaire but made some slight changes to some of the film titles. We made up fictitious videonasty-type film titles ('Zombies from beyond space', 'Cannibal Fang and Claw', and so on). The results from 5 classes of 11-year-old children revealed that 58 per cent of children claimed to have seen films which do not exist in any film guide. Moreover, of the 72 per cent of children who claimed to have seen an adult film some 82 per cent also claimed to have seen a fictitious film.

Conclusion

The review has highlighted some of the methodological problems with research in this field. Doubtless better studies could be done and indeed should be done. Nevertheless the overriding weaknesses in this research are primarily conceptual.

First of all researchers and reviewers alike have difficulty in handling non-significant results. These are rarely part of any scientific debate and indeed are unlikely to be published at all. However, among the correlational studies, the vast majority show a preponderance of non-significant findings which should alert us to the danger of falsely concluding that there are genuine effects of mass media violence upon society. Few empirical studies are worth a second mention, but Belson for example finds no evidence that high exposure to television violence reduces boys' respect for authority, desensitizes them, makes them less considerate of others, produces sleep disturbance or was associated with stealing. Belson's findings contradict many previous studies. Thus, the convention of reviewers to consider only significant results is quite misleading.

A second conceptual problem in this field is the tendency to focus on the effects of television as an unidimensional process. This problem of unidimensional thinking is illustrated in the conclusions to a recent review by Berkowitz. He concluded:

> The chance that only one individual in 100,000 will exhibit overt aggression as a result of the depicted violence means 100 more violent acts will occur in an audience of 10,000,000. Whatever the exact numbers, our society has to decide whether the benefits of portrayed aggression outweigh the cost (Berkowitz, 1984: 424).

Even if it were accepted that research supported this probability of 1 individual in 10,000 being more likely to exhibit overt aggression, the aggressor is only part of the equation of violence as a social problem. It cannot be translated into more violent acts in this simple way. Are victims more or less vulnerable because of violence on television? Are witnesses more or less likely to report antisocial behaviour or even intervene because of violence on television? And what are the effects on the police, the judiciary or the legislature? Do governments become more or less active against crime and violence because of violence on television or the public concern over it? Since we have precious little evidence on these processes which 'cause' crime and alter the criminal statistics, society may well find it difficult to decide in the way that Berkowitz thinks it should. Moreover the use of the term 'violence' as if it were an easily defined homogeneous group of actions is a nonsense. 'Violence' on television can cover an enormous diversity of acts taking place in different contexts for different reasons and with quite different messages for different viewers. Violence has long played a vital role in the arts and is used with various dramatic effects by those who create our cultural forms. How successful a film producer is in conveying that violence is something to be condoned or condemned, to be appalled by or laughed at, is obviously an empirical question only answered ultimately by interrogating the audience. However the assumption made by so much research is that these distinctions do not exist for the viewer.

Whatever the role of the mass media in our lives it has become an important focus for research and has exposed a variety of methodological weaknesses in our research tools. Most importantly the research endeavours indicate that conceptual limitations provide a major barrier to understanding the media and a major rift between researchers and practitioners. Debates about the effects of television violence inevitably draw in other concerns — about rising crime, about broadcasting freedom, about the vulnerability of children, about parental rights, about media obligations and professional standards on television and sundry other issues. It is perhaps not surprising that the question about whether television violence influences violence in real life remains essentially unanswered.

Tutorial Discussion Questions

1 Is there too much violence on television?
2 What kinds of television violence might the public be concerned about, e.g. the news?
3 What different 'messages' might television give about violence?
4 How appropriate are laboratory experiments for helping to understand real-world problems?

References

BARLOW, G. and HILL, T. (1985) *Video Violence and Children*, London, Hodder and Stoughton.
BERKOWITZ, L. (1984) 'Some effects of thoughts on anti- and pro-social influences of media events', *Psychological Bulletin*, **95**, 3, pp. 410–27.
EYSENCK, H.J. and NIAS, D.K. (1978) *Sex, Violence and the Media*, London, Maurice Temple Smith.
HIMMELWEIT, H.J., OPPENHEIM, A.N. and VINCE, P. (1958) *Television and the Child*, London, Oxford University Press.
SCHRAMM, W., LYLE, L. and PARKER, E.B. (1961) *Television in the Lives of Our Children*, Stanford, CA, Stanford University Press.

Further Reading

CUMBERBATCH, G. and HOWITT, D. (1989) *A Measure of Uncertainty: The Effects of the Mass Media*, London, Libbey.
FRIEDMAN, J.L. (1984). 'Effects of television violence on aggression', *Psychological Bulletin*, **96** (2) pp. 227–46.
GUNTER, B. (Ed.) (1989) 'Violence on television: establishing the main issues', *Current Psychological Research and Reviews*, **7**, 1 (Special issue).
LIEBERT, R.M. and SPRAFKIN, J. (1988) *The Early Window*, New York, Pergamon.
OSKAMP, S. (Ed.) (1988) 'Television as a social issue', *Applied Social Psychology Annual*, **8** (Special issue).

Chapter 18

The Language of Television News

Howard Davis

Making News

The importance of 'news' in everyday life can hardly be overstated. Whether it is neighbourly gossip, information about local events, or the highly packaged forms of international television newscasts, it is one of the essential raw materials of social interaction. With personal experience, organizational cultures and local traditions, it constitutes the framework of social cognition.

According to one definition, news is what is 'new, true and interesting to the public' (BBC, 1976) but this begs a host of questions about the criteria for assessing novelty, truthfulness and interest and who chooses them. In practice, these questions are decided in complex modern organizations which have evolved highly elaborate methods for processing language and images. To understand how news language 'works', therefore, it is necessary to understand the routine procedures which journalists and editors use to construct their reports. This chapter concentrates on the language of television news rather than newspapers on the grounds that it is the most widely used medium for news and is exceptional in the way in which it contrives to create a powerful impression of 'naturalness' through techniques which are demonstrably rule-bound and artificial.

Several groups of people have an interest in news language. First, there are the journalists, editors and producers who shape it according to the 'rules' of their profession. Normally, these are not formal written rules. They are the value criteria, rules of thumb, traditions and customs which practitioners of journalism use almost instinctively in the daily process of news gathering, selection, writing and editing. Their interest in language is primarily in the production of texts which convey a sense of immediacy, accuracy and authority. This approach is strongly supported by the system of broadcasting regulation which requires BBC and ITN news to report with 'due accuracy and impartiality'. The second group is the audience for the news. Their interest in language is parallel to that of the journalists. The majority of viewers of television news see it as a factual record of the day's main events, a 'window on the world', and expect the language of news reports to be direct, unbiased and trustworthy. News is found to be interesting, not because the language is deliberately made exciting or entertaining, but because it is true. Survey evidence shows that since television news bulletins were first broadcast in the 1950s, viewers' confidence in the genre has been high, with only a slight decline from earlier levels in recent years. However, during this time there have been increasingly vigorous debates about news 'bias' involving politicians, journalists and pressure groups such as the Media Monitoring Unit. They base their criticisms on evidence of lapses of accuracy and impartiality using selected quotations and simplistic forms of content analysis to bolster their case. Interesting as it is to explore the views of professional journalists and their audiences, a full analysis has to go beyond the claims and counter-claims of 'bias' to consider how news language achieves its 'objectivity' and how this contributes to the wider processes of public communication. This is the point at which a third group of people with an interest in news language — social scientists — compete for attention. They reject the idea that news is (or can be) simply a pure representation of events and argue that language, including the language of news reports, is part of the social system and an integral part of the process of negotiation between social groups. 'News' is then interpreted as a form of social action by groups operating within a system of class, gender and ethnic inequalities; news media literally mediate (i.e. channel and modify) networks of the influence and power. An analysis of language should aim to show as convincingly as possible how this is done.

Some Views of News Language

In the relatively short history of media studies there have been two contrasting ways of thinking about news. They both illustrate the fact that theories of language are also social theories because there is no language apart from speech and writing, and these are forms of behaviour which invariably have a social purpose. One view of news language, which receives its inspiration from the Marxist theoretical tradition, begins with the observation that most news is produced within large and powerful institutions which have a definite affinity with the powers that be in the state, industry and culture. They tend to speak with the voices of the powerful, not to the exclusion of all others, but in such a way as to make them sound naturally authoritative. Analyzing news from this point of view is a process of ideology critique which explores the hidden assumptions of reporting, relates the news agenda to the priorities of the powerful, and shows how modes of speech are organized to dominate rather than liberate the audience. It emphasizes the lack of freedom which audiences have in the face of media institutions, and their power to shape what the audience accepts as 'commonsense'. It might be said to give theoretical substance to George Orwell's description of Newspeak in *Nineteen Eighty-Four* (Orwell, 1962).

The second view of news language emphasizes diversity rather than unity, communication rather than propaganda, the freedom of the audience rather than the domination exercised by the media. Such a 'liberal' interpretation of news stresses the autonomy of news organizations, the pluralistic values of journalism, and the independence and scepticism of the public. News is seen as the outcome of complex negotiations between news services, journalists and their audiences according to publicly acknowledged rules about honesty, confidentiality, balance, fair comment and so on. Questions of the limits to power do arise (e.g. the government's contested right to censor news at the time of the Falklands War, or the public's right to know the facts about the SAS killing of terrorist suspects in Gibraltar) but journalists in the quality press and television news are generally seen to be doing a fair job of reporting what is new, true and interesting to the public with an acceptable degree of skill and professional judgment. Liberal criticisms, if they are made, tend to focus more on the apparent limitations of media technologies and organizations (like the criticism that the need for 'good pictures' overrides the other important aspects of television news stories).

The key issues in the interpretation of news language revolve around the axis between these views. Who decides what is news? How is balance achieved? How flexibly can language be used? How deliberate is the process of writing and editing? Does the audience actually grasp the finer details of a news article or bulletin? There is a tendency (from which neither ideology critique nor liberalism is immune) to rely on preformed readings of news texts in which the language itself is taken for granted. However, these and other questions must be answered by empirical analysis. There are three aspects of the language process in news which need to be considered: the medium itself, its technical and organizational constraints; the story, the sources and content of the narrative; and finally the structural and stylistic features of news language itself.

Characteristics of Television News

A television news bulletin is a sequence of separate items, or 'stories' arranged according to a pattern which is usually described in terms of a hierarchy of *news values*, or the sense of what is important about a particular story. These values are rarely spelt out in any detail and most journalists would say that they are internalized in the course of doing the job. The alternative to asking journalists to explain their systems of news values is to infer them from the ranking of stories and topics over time (see, for example, Glasgow University Media Group, 1976, Chapter 4). There is ample evidence from both sources to show that the news values of British television journalism are more 'serious' than popular. Radio and television broadcasting in the UK developed historically as public service institutions and, to a far greater extent than in the USA, for example, they have news values which closely resemble those of the 'quality' press. Political and economic news receive high priority while crime and human interest stories appear lower down in the running order, if at all. Hard news rates more highly than soft news. From the point of view of language, this inheritance from the newspaper tradition sets the boundary of the *register*, the variety of language which is specific to television news. A register is often defined by a particular vocabulary, as in the case of technical occupations which have their own specialist terms, or what outsiders would call 'jargon'. The register of news does not have this kind of exclusive vocabulary because it covers such a wide range of topics and sources, but it is nevertheless distinctive in its level of formality, its 'neutral' tone and even pace. Most viewers appreciate this automatically; they are immediately aware of the fact when they have accidentally tuned into a news programme, even if they cannot explain precisely why they recognize it as such. Some of the formality comes from the requirements of balance and impartiality and some comes from the fact that most of a news script is written down, although in a form which is designed to be read aloud.

On the other hand, television as a medium differs fundamentally from print because it is a more highly condensed form and because it combines the spoken word with moving images, stills and graphics. The number of words in a relatively long television news item of about 4 minutes is likely to be between 700 and 725. This amounts to about two thirds of a single column on the front page of *The Guardian, The Independent* or *The Times*. The limited space for elaboration does not mean that context, comment and explanation are absent from television news bulletins, only that they tend to be more implicit.

The first clue to the interpretation of a particular story is the category into which it is placed. It is possible for a story of insider dealing in the City to be treated as an issue of crime, business, or personalities, but rarely all three. The compression of news normally requires one significant 'angle' to be selected. If the story is allocated to a correspondent specializing in financial affairs it will be treated as a business story and probably run alongside other business-related stories. It is likely to be taken up as a crime story only if it reaches the courts. These classifications (which have close parallel in the organization of news gathering) are the primary method of framing stories. They also shape the styles of coverage. 'Economic' stories are typically supported by independent experts and graphics while 'industrial' news stories are more likely to deal with events rather than facts, use film which symbolizes conflict, and hardly ever call upon independent experts for comment and analysis (Glasgow University Media Group, 1976: 19).

The term 'story' refers to the individual item within a bulletin or a sequence of items on the same subject appearing in a number of bulletins. It is the interface between the system of new categories and the 'real world', the point at which the complexities of social and political life are reduced to fit the format of a news item. Major stories can run almost indefinitely but this does not mean that greater depth of analysis can be achieved. For example, the miners' strike lasted for twelve months from March 1984 to March 1985 and received almost daily coverage, often at some length. This story fell naturally into the 'industrial news' category but its unusual length created the need for a variety of treatments. These included story angles on the economic impact of the strike, policing and picketing issues, the extent of the return to work, and the plight of miners' families. Therefore, news does not simply follow a narrative sequence given by the pattern of events as they happen; it actively searches for the appropriate 'angle' to create interest and register importance and novelty. The use of quotations is one of the preferred ways of achieving this. The words of an important figure in a story convey authority while the comments of lesser figures such as eye witnesses or 'vox pops' give freshness and immediacy. The selection of who speaks and what they say is the product of a constant negotiation between journalists and their sources, with varying degrees of power on each side. The government and large employers have powerful means at their disposal to control the flow of information, including public relations officers, information budgets and resources for independent media production. Having access to these, the Coal Board was able to exploit its significant advantage over the National Union of Mineworkers during the course of the strike, especially by using its monopoly of information about the precise number of miners returning to work in the later stages of the dispute. Television news frequently used the Coal Board sources without critical comment or balancing interpretations. The most obvious examples of collusion between journalists and their sources are to be found in the practice of delivering 'sound bites' — short, pithy, self-contained sentences and phrases deliberately embedded within public statements — which can be easily identified and incorporated into a short news report with the minimum of editing.

So far, I have described the large-scale features of television news language, namely its value assumptions and frameworks for interpreting news. The actual words and sentences used in news report are the products of experienced practitioners in the craft of journalism working to a further system of written and unwritten rules. These are twofold: first, there are the rules which govern the use of the language in general (in this case the rules of grammar and use of English) and second, the rules which are specific to the domain of news. These specific rules are most visible in the way vocabulary is selected in controversial subjects such as armed conflict, where the protagonists may be described as 'troops', 'freedom fighters', 'rebels' or 'guerrillas' depending on the story angle and interpretation. In some cases, these terms are the subject of precise editorial instruction to journalists, but most rules of selection are relatively slow to change and some hardly seem to vary at all. In industrial reporting, for example, the rules of vocabulary make it virtually certain that management will make 'offers' and labour will make 'demands'. The 'natural' assumptions which give rise to this asymmetrical vocabulary are so deeply embedded in the system of industrial relations that an 'offer' by labour in a negotiation would have a distinctly odd ring.

There are powerful images and *metaphors* at work here. In fact, it is hard to express any significant idea without the use of metaphor, or words which are used in a non-literal sense for emphasis, colour and comparison. In international relations, where the dominant themes are of war and peace, conflict and cooperation, it is not surprising to find words and phrases like 'threat to security', 'enemy', 'aggression' and so on. But it is interesting to find that words used in other domains can also become militarized through the frequent application of metaphor. Paul Chilton, for example, shows how clichés of the Falklands War carried over into peacetime talk, using the case of the Aslef train drivers' dispute with British Rail. The phrases in circulation included: BR had a *strategy* to *defeat* the train drivers strike . . . *tactical manoeuvring* on both sides . . . no alternative but to *stand and fight* . . . *pockets of resistance* to flexible rostering (Chilton, 1988: 69–77). As he points out, the logic of this arrangement of words is that industrial disputes are like war, that there is an enemy within and that withdrawing labour is an unpatriotic thing to do.

Such observations often provoke the question: how deliberate is this use of words? There is no simple answer but a detailed analysis of the writing and editorial process would probably reveal that much of the selection occurs instinctively; it feels right to the journalist and can be justified after the event as 'simply a metaphor' which enhances an otherwise dull description. Criticisms are dismissed as mere quibbles about semantics. However, these images and metaphors are not random phenomena but expressions of ideological themes which, in the case of industrial relations at least, have a permanent place in the political culture of the UK. There are numerous studies of news output which illustrate the importance of these ideological themes in the reporting of social welfare, crime and deviance, race, politics and other issues (e.g. Golding and Middleton, 1982; Chibnall, 1977; Braham, 1982).

A Worked Example

The disciplines of sociolinguistics, discourse analysis and conversation analysis —

which all have an interest in forms of language occurring in everyday situations — have developed rapidly in recent years to the point at which they can offer certain well-established techniques of analysis to the non-expert, although much of the academic literature is highly technical. In the following example a few basic principles of language analysis are applied through a number of simple steps, moving from the large-scale features of news construction, through the intermediate aspects of structure, to the finer details at the level of individual words. The aim is to illustrate some of the methods which can be used in relation to any standard form of news. It is not intended to be a fully comprehensive framework for analysis although it is designed to cover the main dimensions of new analysis.

Transcription

The first task in any analysis of news language is to obtain the raw materials, the data. In the case of print media this normally presents few problems except those to do with the selection of examples and classification of stories. Copies or cuttings can be used for analysis in the form in which they appear to the reader. Data from television involves an additional problem because it is necessary to obtain a transcript of the news broadcast or stories chosen for analysis. A videotape recording is a necessary starting point but the analysis cannot proceed without a written text or transcript. This may seem to present few problems but the procedure of writing down the spoken language of news has difficulties which reveal some interesting things about the genre (Philo, 1987). There is, for example, the problem of reconstructing the punctuation of the original and the fairly common incidence of ungrammatical usage. Interviews often involve interruptions and overlapping speech: should this be conveyed in the transcription? Outside the news studio there are frequently problems of audibility in noisy surroundings or intelligibility in the case of speakers with non-standard foreign accents. Researchers in all the branches of social science discover that there are basic methodological questions involved in the gathering and representation of data and this includes any who wish to make a systematic analysis of news language. For example, the transcript given below — like most other transcripts, including those which the news organizations use — is a highly selective representation of what was said. It conveys nothing about intonation, emphasis, hesitation and interruption, although these are features which may carry a significant weight of meaning. Any transcription therefore places some restrictions on the scope of the analysis.

Nine O'Clock News, BBC1, 20 January 1990

Item 5. Ambulance Dispute

Newsreader: Here, the Health Secretary Kenneth Clarke has denied today's newspaper reports that he is prepared to offer the ambulance crews more money if they will drop their demand for a formula to govern future pay rises. His Parliamentary Private Secretary, Philip Oppenheim, has admitted he spoke to journalists about the dispute last night, and the unions have accused Whitehall of trying to 'muddy the waters'. This from Sarah Barclay.

Reporter: The newspaper reports that more money could be on offer to the ambulance staff have again angered the unions and the opposition. It's the second time Mr Clarke has had to deny such reports. Two weeks ago, Sunday newspapers claimed he'd told them himself that more money was available. This morning he issued another statment saying: 'The situation has not changed . . . there is no more money on offer'. Labour's Health spokesman said the dispute had been plunged into a thick fog by Mr Clarke's own staff.

Robin Cook MP: Yesterday's story came from a lunch which both those journalists had with Philip Oppenheim. He happens to be Kenneth Clarke's Parliamentary Private Secretary; in that role he will have attended many meetings with Kenneth Clarke to discuss the aims of this dispute and one would have thought that he knew what was in Kenneth Clarke's mind yesterday.

Reporter: This afternoon Mr Oppenheim admitted he'd told two journalists last night negotiations were unlikely unless the unions dropped their demands for a pay mechanism. When asked by the BBC today if that meant more could be offered he said: 'you can draw any conclusions you want'. After a meeting with the other unions their chief negotiator said any offer of more money should be made properly.

Roger Poole: The government have got something to say to us and the government must realise that there's not going to be a settlement of this dispute at 6.5 per cent. If the government have got something to say to us then let them sit around a table with us and negotiate with us now to bring this dispute to an end.

Reporter: Even if more money was available, union leaders are unlikely to drop their demand for a pay formula for future years. They are coming under increasing pressure to bring the dispute to a head with a national strike ballot. Today's confusion leaves them wondering again what the government's position really is.

Bulletin Structure and Form

Once a transcription is available it is appropriate to begin with the large-scale structures of the news text which are marked by the boundaries between items, the use of headlines and hooking devices. The example above is defined as an item by the pause between it and the previous items, the word 'Here' at the beginning of the item and by the change of topic. Headlines, like those in a newspaper, have an important function in summarizing and highlighting stories but the cueing of stories is achieved by their place in the running order, the amount of time devoted to them, and the category in which they are treated, which is often signalled visually by a still photograph or logo behind the newsreader. The example from the coverage of the ambulance dispute is typical of a running story in that the viewer is assumed to have prior knowledge of the story and not to require background information. Boundary markers, such as 'here', 'and', 'and now', or the phrases which separate foreign and domestic news like 'in this country', are not part of the message of the news, they are functional in shaping the structure of the text. However, they can also be used in a way which prepares the viewer to read the story in a particular way: 'Good news today for . . . ' is a departure from neutral language but one which the journalists would justify in terms of lively and economical news style. It illustrates the way in which apparently simple connecting phrases can carry significant implications for viewers' understanding.

The example has a structure which consists of a newsreader's introduction to the item, commentary from a reporter, and two segments of interviews. These are predictable elements of television news organized in a predictable way according to aesthetic and editorial requirements. News items, in the press as well as television, have a patten which begins with a summary of the most important information followed by a series of elaborations on the theme. This allows an editor to reduce the length of an item rapidly without making fundamental changes to the remaining text. Thus, in the present example, the item could be closed after the newsreader's introduction and it would still be a coherent, if highly abbreviated, report. The requirement of balance is not always reflected in the sequence of interviews and film inserts but in a complex story such as the ambulance dispute it is usual to find several views juxtaposed as they are here. The aesthetic criteria are expressed in the use of filmed interviews, which give an impression of immediacy and authenticity, rather than reported statements. Although this piece of news about the ambulance dispute is like most of television news in being dominated by 'talking heads', the aim is to make the item as visually appealing as possible with rapid changes of image. There has been much debate about the extent to which the need for pictures constitutes an 'imperative' in the news selection and editorial process. The example of the ambulance dispute, and this particular item which is typical of the coverage, indicates that the visuals tend to play a supportive role; they do not tell a story in themselves. Thus, at the end of this item, the reporter speaks against the visul background of ambulance staff on a picket but the pictures are symbolic in that they do not have a direct relationship to the text.

The Mediation of Speech

The majority of news texts, surprisingly in view of their claim to impartiality, are not written from the point of view of the detached observer but include a large proportion of mediated speech: accounts of who spoke and what they said occur in wide range of permutations. Allowing the participants, witnesses and victims to 'tell the story' is seen as good journalistic practice because it encourages variety and gives the impression of seeing news in the making, as it happens. However, from the point of view of language analysis it raises some complex problems. The first step is to identify who is speaking. Looking at the above example we can see statements with the form 'he denied . . .', 'he admitted . . .', 'they claimed . . .' and 'he said . . .'. These are indirect references to words which were actually spoken but not represented here. The 'voice' here is the voice of the news. In another part of the item we hear a direct quotation prefaced by the verb 'saying' which runs: 'the situation has not changed . . .' but it is still the news reporter who is speaking these words. In the interviews, the speakers appear in vision, illustrating yet another form of direct speech. From a linguistic point of view there are two processes at work in the mediation of speech. First, there is the *referential* requirement of the language to report accurately what was said by whom, and second, the *relational* requirement to make it as interesing as possible to the listener. Journalists may decide to use a direct quotation because it is particularly apt, or contains a colourful image like the 'muddy waters' in the above example. Sources will collude with journalists to create such opportunities for quotable quotes so that the two requirements become closely intertwined, giving news language its distinctive texture.

A close examination of reported speech, which involves a process of transformation of language, leads to the question of whether this transformation is weighted in a particular direction and whether it is one of the ways in which the social hierarchies of power in society are expressed in the language of news. The Glasgow University Media Group, for example, in their study of the language of industrial reporting, advance the proposition that the higher the social and political status of the speaker, the less the mediation of their speech (Glasgow University Media Group, 1980: 163). The complexities of language prevent this from being a universal rule but the highly codified nature of news and the acute sense which journalists have about the relative authority, credibility and trustworthiness of their sources certainly means that there are consistencies in the process of transformation. Other authors (e.g. Kress and Hodge, 1979) have looked at similar 'ideological' transformations, like the change from the active form of a sentence to the passive, which has the effect of loosening the link between the actor and the process they are engaged in. One result is that causal processes ('pickets prevented coal deliveries') become more opaque ('coal deliveries were prevented . . . '). Nominalization is another type of transformation which can change a concrete description of participants ('pickets . . . ') into an abstract description of a process ('picketing . . . '). The outcome is a kind of mystification. So, in the above example, the phrase, 'there is no more money on offer' could be changed to read 'I will not offer more money', which would create a quite different and much more abrasive effect.

Vocabulary

The fact that words have meanings which change over time, and the fact that the same word can be used to different effect according to the context, shows that vocabulary, like other aspects of language plays an active part in the formation of social relationships. For this reason, a simple count of apparently significant words is not likely to be very revealing; it is the relationship between words, and between words and their referents, which is important. A proper analysis of vocabulary needs to be based on an extended sample of news texts if it is to be used as a basis for generalization, although a single item or story can be a useful starting-point. The conventionalized character of television news language extends to the use of vocabulary. It is restricted in the sense that television news more than than the other news media operates with a relatively small range of words used with high frequency and these words arranged in ways which reflect a strong underlying set of conventions. The asymmetry of the terms used in industrial negotiations ('offers' from one side, 'demands' from the other, but not the reverse) was mentioned earlier and is illustrated in the ambulance dispute item. Some of these relationships between words are part of a semantic structure which is more or less permanent because they relate to social institutions like the industrial relations system or the left-right spectrum in politics which are the outcome of such a long history that they appear almost immutable. Some have evolved slowly but significantly over time like the vocabulary and dominant metaphors which refer the 'the economy'. In the

1930s, phrases like 'the economic machine' or the 'general economy' were common currency. Then, as Keynesian economic theory replaced neoclassical theories and as the public came to accept that governments should manage the economic affairs of the nation, the term 'economy' acquired more active connotations and was used in conjunction with mechanical or biological metaphors (Emmison, 1983). Other relationships, such as the spillover of the Falklands War vocabulary into industrial news, have a shorter lifespan although they are still significant.

The analysis of the languge of news can therefore be applied at a number of levels ranging from the broad structures of the bulletin, through the organization of language within items, to the use of particular words and phrases. At each level, it can show how news maintains its natural, taken-for-granted appearance and supports its claim to impartiality in matters of social controversy. It is able to show that news output owes its remarkable homogeneity and consistency not so much to the selective recruitment of journalists or their shared political bias as to the organizational procedures which pass facts, events and personalities through a finely developed filter of news values and language. This demystifying task is of great importance because television news has the power to bring about an extraordinary reversal, which is to set a standard by which events in the 'real world' come to be judged. If events do not appear in the world of television news, they do not qualify as important. If the mass media have this power to detach the social frameworks of knowledge from social experience, how can we genuinely know the world we live in?

Tutorial Discussion Questions

Tutorial groups should have access to a video recording of at least one news bulletin so that the questions can be discussed with reference to concrete examples.

1 As a television viewer, how do you recognize 'news'?
2 Make a transcript of a television news item and discuss the problems involved. Does the form of the transcript affect the conclusions which you are able to draw from it?
3 Find examples of the following techniques which sources (e.g. government representatives, commercial organizations, pressure groups) use to get their message across in the news: press conferences and other 'media events'; 'sound bites'; publicity stunts; press releases and statements. How much reporting is initiated by sources rather than journalists?
4 How would you identify 'bias' in the language of a television news item?
5 Using examples from television news, examine the ways in which newsfilm relates to the spoken word. Is there evidence that the need for 'good pictures' has priority over the need for accuracy, impartiality and balance?
6 Does every word count in a news bulletin?

Howard Davis

References

BBC (1976) *The Task of Broadcasting News: A Study for the BBC General Advisory Counsil*, London, BBC.

BRAHAM, P. (1982) 'How the media report race', in GUREVITCH, M. BENNETT, T. CURRAN, J. and WOOLLACOTT, J. (Eds) *Culture, Society and the Media*, London, Methuen, pp. 268–86.

CHIBNALL, S. (1977) *Law-and-Order News*, London, Tavistock.

CHILTON, P. (1988) *Orwellian Language and the Media*, London, Pluto Press.

EMMISON, M. (1983) '"The economy": its emergence in media discourse', in DAVIS, H. and WALTON, P. (Eds) *Language, Image, Media*, Oxford, Blackwell, pp. 139–55.

GLASGOW UNIVERSITY MEDIA GROUP (1976) *Bad News*, London, Routledge and Kegan Paul.

GLASGOW UNIVERSITY MEDIA GROUP (1980) *More Bad News*, London, Routledge and Kegan Paul.

GOLDING, P. and MIDDLETON, S. (1982) *Images of Welfare*, Oxford, Martin Robertson.

KRESS, G. and HODGE, R. (1979) *Language as Ideology*, London, Routledge and Kegan Paul.

ORWELL, G. (1962) *Nineteen Eighty-Four*, Harmondsworth, Penguin.

PHILO, G. (1987) 'Whose news?', *Media, Culture and Society*, 9, 4, pp. 397–406.

Further Reading

FAIRCLOUGH, N. (1990) *Language and Power*, London, Longman. A well-illustrated, state of the art account of the Critical Language Study approach to the problems of linguistic analysis.

GLASGOW UNIVERSITY MEDIA GROUP (1976) *Bad News*, London, Routledge and Kegan Paul.

GLASGOW UNIVERSITY MEDIA GROUP (1980) *More Bad News*, London, Routledge and Kegan Paul.

GLASGOW UNIVERSITY MEDIA GROUP (1985) *War and Peace News*, Milton Keynes, Open University Press.

While the work of the Group carried out in the 1970s is still a valuable source of information, the more recent *War and Peace News* is more accessible.

SCHLESINGER, P. (1978) *Putting 'Reality' Together: BBC News*, London, Constable.

The most informative account of the professional organization of a television newsroom.

Chapter 19

Advertisements: Are We Seeing Through Them?

Michael Green

The triumph of advertising in the culture industry is that consumers feel compelled to buy and use its products even though they see through them (Horkheimer and Adorno, 1972).

In Western societies we day and night see them, hear them, walk by them. We get their punch lines, hum their tunes, recognize their stories, mock their absurdities, talk of them with friends. Advertisements in their tens of thousands surround us, call to us, decorate our rooms and cities, make sense of the world for us, invite us to a better future. Their illusions, assumptions, aspirations help form our mental landscape. Their messages about the future are commentaries on the present. Advertisements are part of media are part of us.

This chapter will look at some changes in advertising practice and at the historical developments of which they form part. It will ask some questions about how advertisements operate, and how we are part of how they operate. Last, it will look at academic and public debates about advertising practice.

Advertisements and the Advertising Process

Adverts themselves are but one highly visible moment in a more complex invisible process. In modern conditions, both nationally and globally, a product is not made, and then afterwards sold. Instead the planning of possible products for manufacture is at the same time the consideration of possible markets, and of the most efficient ways of appealing to them. Production, distribution, advertisement, sales are to the highest extent feasible, planned as an integrated operation, seeking to reach particular target audiences.

Considered most generally, advertising is the means used by industry (and increasingly by other groups you might think of) to try and organize our behaviour as consumers, and to make that (so far as possible) organized behaviour both enjoyable, part of our desires, and also spontaneous, unforced, a set of acts of choice. Consumers, said Herbert Marcuse in his *One Dimensional Man* (1964), 'bind themselves more or less pleasantly to the producers'.

In more detail, advertising is perhaps the most highly planned, most extensively researched and most costly form of communication in the world today. Some of the dearest, most highly skilled television now made is found in those 30-second segments, just as on some estimates advertising can cost an average 10 per cent of purchase price. While advertisers and their campaigns can certainly be fallible (with famous flops), and advertising theory make inflated claims for its own precision, it is to be remembered that companies, political parties, public relations agencies have their own strong evidence of big money well spent in the changing of images or the moving of products. Behind this process is an extremely elaborate and largely confidential research effort involving various skills from statistics, market research, sociology and many other disciplines including psychology.

Then in close-up, advertisements themselves offer us a dazzling and bewildering series of images, stories and messages. As they frame, surround, question the printed text, or as they lead in, segment, interrupt the programming in broadcast media, they require of us ever more sophisticated forms of attention. We struggle to come to our own terms with the quantities and types of communication before us. Adverts are both pitched increasingly at our moods, and yet offer us more simultaneous messages then ever before. These messages, themselves ambiguous, connect with other messages and images, inside and outside advertisements proper, both inter-textually (through and across a huge variety of texts) and in who we are, what we pick up on, even what we 'see' at all. A discussion group may soon find that particular advertisements are being looked at, made sense of, enjoyed, internally understood, perhaps loathed, in ways that vary by gender and in other ways around the group. Indeed, advertisements appeal directly to our reader-power and viewer-power (since consumption must be volunteered); we activate the texts in different directions and bring them to life, to our own life, in our own way. Even a 'mass' market is made up of constructed, and self-constructing, 'individuals'.

From Monochrome to Glossy Colour

For an instance of advertising complexity, consider the difference between the first commercial advert on British 'independent' television, and a well-known recent advertisement for jeans. In the first case, in black-and white television, a text about freshness was spoken over a shot of a toothpaste tube, diagonally frozen in ice. It seems now quite impossibly static, 'obvious' and old-fashioned, as the logic of advertising must always be to secure 'newness' by rendering previous styles archaic.

This archaism is itself one of many themes in the recent jeans film, a brief but complicated narrative in its own right. Filmed in a now self-conscious aesthetic monochrome, a grainy pastiche of *film noir* style, we follow a gaunt and haunted-looking young man home through a world of concrete housing blocks, empty roads, fluttering messages on wall-posters. With music to accentuate the visual and character tension he has smuggled a suitcase's contents past border guards themselves distracted by salutes to a passing general or commissar. Alone in his sparse flat he undoes his case and we see on the trouser label one small glow of red colour, the promise of forbidden consumer fruits in an alienated landscape. Subtitles suggest this is a foreign film, perhaps on Channel 4.

So much happens in the minute of this advert that comments must be limited.

We can pull out various themes from where we start as viewers. Since I am arguing that this is in general the case with much current advertising, what I myself see in, take from the text will not of itself represent the activities of other viewers. For me the issues touched on here include attitudes to youth and to authority; an association between black and white, the past, foreign and 'obscure' or underground movies, Eastern Europe contrasted with full colour and liberation in the West; public provision (those grim blocks — filmed in England, presumably) as dead, lifeless space compared with private space as a cherished refuge for enjoyment; and much more.

Above all, I would want to pull out two 'arguments' in the advert. That choosing to wear these jeans is an act of individual freedom, choice and even protest or defiance — although jeans are worn by millions of people across the surface of the earth! That there are connections between the West and consumer goods and freedom as between the East and oppression and poverty: a reading of freedom which arguably helped sustain the Cold War and what has followed from it, just as now with walls tumbling down (and a banner from Saatchi and Saatchi in the middle of Berlin reading 'first over the wall'), it is possible to see not the complexities and diversities of Eastern European countries and traditions, but only the apparently pitiable, and 'dated', lack of Western possessions. We have come a long way, historically, from toothpaste on ice. We have been drawn into a compact density of themes, as you will see thinking of issues in other examples, including how you think you have come to see and respond to those themes.

These all too intriguing particulars should not obscure larger movements over time. Changes in what advertisements do must be connected with social developments which are the preconditions of contemporary advertising practice.

Some mutations in advertising practice may be quickly illustrated from back covers of *Picture Post*, the British photo-weekly carrying photo-essays on current affairs from the late 1930s into the 1950s, when competition from women's magazines, in their record period of 3.5 million an issue, and from ITV itself, killed it off.

Thus a 1946 copy ends with several pages of small boxed monochrome ads, of which one is a drawing of a steaming gravy boat by a text asking us to add Brooke Bond cubes for a 'richer beefy flavour'. We have the product, a brand name and a minimal specification. A year later, back covers are using one colour on a full page, with line drawings. Two ads for Birds Custard using the caption 'That's the idea' show us respectively a girl, prettily in motion as a ballet dancer, and a boy, sturdily bashing a cricket ball with a cap at a rakish angle. There is now less of a linkage, directly, between the product and the offered social types and the establishment of gender differences.

By 1950, more colours are in use (still 'rudimentary' in terms of our own contemporary paper, print and photographic quality) for a series of short stories abut a wife, decorously serving her besuited husband with Batchelors food: soup, fruit or in one memorable case tinned baked beans on a silver serving dish. A 1950 text reads in part:

> 'Guest Husband'. Geoff is away on business most of the week. The first time he arrived home unexpectedly there were only meat left-overs... what a crisis! I ran for help to my neighbour. She overwhelmed me with good things from her shelf... Geoff awarded me nylons after my latest Batchelors meal. He thinks *I'm* the wonderful one.

Here the product becomes part of an elaborate commentary, felt to be socially plausible at the time, about a wife's duties and the relations between men and women, including the responsibilities of women to solve problems both gastronomic and sexual. By 1951:

> As a bride I'd spend hours preparing meals, then be exhausted . . . With Geoff silent too our marriage seemed doomed . . . Geoff, well-fed and full of praises, is silent no longer. No iron curtain any more!

The brief history repeats what had already happened in the USA, where in 1938 the trade journal *Printer's Ink* noted that 'with each step the advertisement moved farther away from the factory viewpoint and edged itself closer into the mental processes of the consumer'.

From the product to mental processes; from general claims to detailed instruction in social roles: these changes in the appeal and emphases of advertisements are established by the post-war expansion into a full consumer economy during the 1950s. We have travelled much further still, into 'target identities', 'nicheing' and 'lifestyling' by the 1970s.

Such progressions are not 'internal' to advertisements or to the strategies of advertising agencies. They reflect, as they also help form and stimulate, much larger social processes over a century of industrial, political and cultural history. Three sets of historical conditions seem to make possible the nature of contemporary advertising practice.

'You can get it if you really want'

First, industrial capitalist societies have in their distinctive and uneven ways come to periods in which their production capabilities are immensely enhanced, by means including new machinery, new investment and new forms of labour discipline. Primary manufacture in heavy industry can develop into new kinds of manufacture and goods from light industries, often with a higher female and white-collar workforce. Model T Ford cars rolling off the new production lines (and how immensely Henry Ford misjudged the potential of advertising and the future shape of consumerism in declaring customers could have 'any colour that they want so long as it's black') inaugurated both greater mobility by 'private' individuals and an era of other production lines, producing other goods: chocolates, vacuum cleaners, radios. At this stage the problem, economically, is to stimulate demand sufficient to meet the greater capacities of production (although other tactics include the often-observed introduction of 'planned obsolescence'). At the same time the possibility 'socially' is to organize the labouring classes as consumers — as purchasers of their own production. The stake of these groups in society may now not be work itself (or the questioning of a society organized into owners and owned) but the promise of consumption: of leisure, of pleasure, enjoyed in 'their own' time. Higher pay for lower hours can then be offered by employers in return for a converging interest by employees in the prospect and promises of domestic goods. 'Consumption', said Mrs C. Frederick in her *Selling Mrs Consumer* (1939; cited by Ewen, 1976) is:

> the greatest idea America has to give to the world; the idea that workmen

and masses be looked upon not simply as workers and producers but as consumers . . . Pay them more, sell them more, prosper more is the equation.

Second, the organization of local markets into vast national markets for mass production needs to be facilitated not just in production methods, or through distribution and transport facilities, but by the construction and then the proliferation of 'mass' media. This term has however had the damaging and entirely misleading implication that readers and listeners are then, like the products themselves, only homogeneous 'masses' who think and act in standardized ways. To say that most forms of media are heavily dependent on advertising revenue, though true (to the extent of anywhere between 60 and 80 per cent of all revenue in the case of most print media), rather misses the point. Many media indeed come to exist at all only because of products, needing advertising, seeking channels of communication with potential buyers. The Canadian media analyst Dallas Smythe (1981) has remarked that media do not so much bring programmes to audiences as deliver markets to advertisers.

Such was the case with the establishment of women's magazines as women took part-time jobs in industry, returning with wages to help in the purchase of domestic items for home and family for which they were deemed largely responsible. It was the case too with the foundation of ITV just as later Channel 4, and now Channel 5. It is the case now, when men and male bodies are sought as new sites of consumption, that new kinds of men's magazines are uncertainly seeking a hold. The volume of potential advertising-seeking outlets prompts the release of new radio and television channels. The further prospect of global media for a global market drives satellite and other technologies, the hardware and software for which has in any case to be purchased.

Third, consumption above all requires (although the requirement can never be more than imperfectly and partially met) that we 'find ourselves', our pleasures, even our identities, as free individuals in our private lives and our own homes. As workers, our identity is bound up with what we do and with the forms of social organization of which we are part and may help to change. As citizens, we have rights and duties of participation in how our society works and how it might develop. But as consumers we are invited not to think of wider affiliations and loyalties but to live 'for ourselves'.

In this dimension of our lives, advertising appeal is enhanced by other social changes: the dispersal from neighbourhoods with common work patterns into suburbia, the intricate and shifting landscapes of social class, a widespread sense that 'community' has been lost or needs to be found, and that its representation in more and more soap operas offsets, compensates for, tendencies towards private living and private pleasures. It could be argued, without necessarily pessimism or nostalgia, that forms of public leisure activity, of public participation (e.g. in political meetings) decline as reading, listening and above all viewing figures (already an average 25–30 hours a week for adults) rise and rise. The 'box in the corner', soon to become in any case a high quality picture with stereo sound projected on a full living room wall, 'brings home' stories from an outside world: especially the intricately varied yet entirely consistent set of messages that we can possess more than we have, become more than we are, and do what we want.

Simultaneously, advertisements convey pleasure, 'good feelings', but that there is further to go, more to achieve. In women's magazines it often seems that the whole issue, not just the ads, presents being female as itself constituting a set of problems to which the magazine and its advertisers suggest solutions, in an endless cycle of lack and wants, of frustrations and desires: cook better, dress better, make love better, care better . . . In his book Ewen (1976) quotes O'Dea, an advertising analyst writing in the USA in 1937:

> We've a better world with a bit of the proper kind of fear in advertising . . . fear in women of being frumps, fear in men of being duds.

Yet this appeal has at the same time to be made plausible to us (connect with who we think we are), and also enjoyable to us.

Advertising must contend with other ideas about out identities and our future; but it contends now with powerful forces at its disposal, including its own 'knowledges' of who we are, and its control of social and media spaces in which to engage us through intricately crafted images and narratives. When, and only when, these conditions are present can advertising start to 'take off' from a world of goods to one of meanings and fantasies, or rather to a systematic rendering of the one through the other. This takes us into two difficult areas of advertising: the relations between the worlds advertising depicts and those we inhabit; and the relation between goods and the meaning set in process around them. The relation between representations and what is represented becomes more elusive: we are often not sure what is being said, unsure what is being represented at all.

It's the Real Thing?

Two writers, one Welsh and one French, tried thirty years ago to illuminate this process in different ways. For Raymond Williams (1980), in his 'Advertising: The Magic System', the starting-point was the realization that in modern advertising

> the material object being sold is never enough . . . we have a cultural pattern in which the objects are not enough but must be validated, if only in fantasy, by association with social and personal meanings.

This he suggested was

> very similar to magical systems in simpler societies, but rather strangely coexistent with a highly developed scientific technology.

For Roland Barthes (1972, 1979), language in advertising was an example of a general process in language (including the language of fashion) which he then thought should be analyzed by semiology, the proposed (and 'scientific') study of signs. For if signs serve to denote objects in the world, they more extensively connote other meanings, and can be used, inflected, in other directions: a rose is a rose is passion is a new model Labour Party; a cigarette is a drug is a clear mountain stream. He wrote that beauty advertising plays on the combined properties of water and grease, presenting water as

> volatile, aerial, fugitive, ephemeral, precious

and oil as

> holding fast, weighing down, slowly forcing its way into surfaces,
> impregnating, sliding along the 'pores' . . . Every campaign declares a
> miraculous conjunction of these enemy liquids . . .

Similar studies of current beauty advertising are well worth carrying out.
Taking another example, he wrote that in the advertising of soap powders and
detergents 'foam' acquires a set of desirable, almost mystical and spiritual
characteristics:

> what matters is the art of having disguised the abrasive function of the
> detergent under the delicious image of a substance at once deep and
> airy . . . A euphoria which must not make us forget that there is one plane
> on which Persil and Omo are one and the same: the plane of the Anglo-
> Dutch trust, Unilever.

Such arguments help us go beyond the historical circumstances of advertising
and its general kinds of appeal to us into some details of advertising practice. In
particular they suggest that advertisements (for all the charges of excessive
materialism) pull us away from the material into values, ideals, fantasies which
speak to us in highly condensed and charged ways about our perceptions of
ourselves and other people. There is and can be no manual to advertising's
mechanisms (which involve risks, ingenuities and what agencies themselves call
'creativity') but we should approach adverts thinking that they seek to set up
certain kinds of response, and not others; but that the responses should also be
those which we voluntarily and imaginatively bring into play, and may lead in
various directions. Here there is a distinction between propaganda, with its more
overt, specific messages and its tighter, more didactic and unifying appeal to an
immediate and common response, and advertising's more 'open' ways of working
within limits.

For instance, the meanings set in motion by adverts must point us in directions
which close off others. Cigarettes and alcohol possess potentially antisocial, harmful
and even destructive properties. Fast cars may involve danger. Menstruation may be
a source of discomfort and difficulties. In these similar cases advertising puts other
areas of meaning in play before us, which then constitute their own maps (or
playgrounds) of alternative images: the 'freedom' of the 'natural' world, modes of
humour and good humour, such 'safe' and 'appealing' groups as animals or
children, the 'exotic' pleasures of 'abroad'.

Ads need us also to recognize, make sense in, enjoy, information presented
briefly and at speed. By repetition we become used to selected settings and
lifestyles, selected backgrounds and landscapes, selected versions of 'working
people', selected social types. Since adverts give us shorthand signals, they are a rich
minefield for the analysis of stereotypes: of national character, of parts of the
country, of experts and scientists, of women. Through photography, some
misperceptions, or generalized partial perceptions, are grounded as natural because
repeatedly 'there': men as taller and stronger, families as universally happy and
joyous. As always with stereotypes we might ask which aspects of people or places
have been selected out for emphasis (or attributed to them); what kinds of people
have been chosen to be shown and why, and who we never see; how stereotypes are

verbally and visually established. In this plethora of material for thought, on any channel on any evening, we might look briefly here at just two, though related, issues: the dominance in adverts of the nuclear family form, and the relentless exclusion of black British faces.

Of course advertising's rendering of social life neither is nor claims to be documentary! Yet it might seem remarkable that at a time when of all household forms the nuclear family in its 'classic' type (waged father, part-waged or unwaged mother, two or so children) is shrinking to a very small percentage, and other forms (such as people living alone or people without children sharing a dwelling) rising, there should still be so much attention to nuclearity. Perhaps this is because wide-scale advertising seeking to draw in an extensive market to a shared reference might lose audiences' interest in showing a real diversity of types of life. Perhaps also because so much ideological labour over the decades has gone into the construction of 'family values' at Christmas and as a social norm, and so little positive validation made of other types of living. Perhaps advertising is not so forward-looking after all. Even elderly people seem to figure mainly as grandparents to the young: will there be changes here with the growth in the elderly population into the next century, or is that not, in advertising, the point?

At the same time, a multiracial Britain views television adverts from which (unlike stories of problems in the news) black faces are virtually absent. An American agency director has said that 'in the States, Crest finds no problem in featuring a black woman barrister in a toothpaste ad, yet such a strategy would be unthinkable here'. How should we explain this?

If then we see, in the adworld, milieux designed to give us pleasant associations; if we see a range of types and characters in particular, repeated, recognizable ways while others are never there at all; so we are also led, by various means including the latest techniques of lighting, direction and storytelling, into a world which needs us, our wit, our experiences, our dissatisfactions, to fill out and complete. Narratives need our completion, allusions invite our recognition, melodies seek our participation, enigmas require our speculative interpretation. Some advertising now offers a density, a lack of resolution which requires us to solve its puzzles for our pleasure. In David Lodge's novel *Nice Work*, a feminist lecturer argues that Silk Cut advertisements appeal to 'sensual and sadistic impulses, the desire to mutilate as well as penetrate', but her manufacturer (and male) friend comments that she 'must have a twisted mind to see all that in a perfectly harmless bit of cloth'.

Questionable and Questioned: Advertising Studies and Debates

If advertising has grown more various and complex in its strands and directions, so too has the study of advertising, and debates about it which are far from academic. In looking at the process, academic studies try increasingly to keep open two paradoxes. One of these is that while advertisements need attention in themselves, singly or in clusters, it can be a constraint to focus down too narrowly on instances while attitudes and themes — many of which are not mentioned here, for example versions of 'primitive' or third world peoples — flow between and across so many examples. There are advertisements, but there is a larger map of all advertising (although real individuals will only see parts of it) and this in turn relates to modes of organization and ways of life in the societies which adverts address. The agenda is a wide one: to start on examples is to enter an historical and interpretative labyrinth with many routes and paths.

At the same time, since some of the same adverts may now be seen from Bangkok to Bradford, the worldwide process becomes a paradigm for the broader study of media processes. Told one way, the story presents advertisers as powerfully in charge of parts of our lives and our psyches: captains indeed of our consciousness. It was the German Frankfurt School of the 1930s, dreading the conjunction of mass media and mass Fascism, which first attributed to media (as cultural, or even consciousness industries) that awesome power. Told another way, it is we, in different social groups in various circumstances in particular times and places, who select out, make sense of, engage with, reject, that advertising. It is we, or some of us, who at times can change the consumption agenda, as the green movements suggest. Advertising offers to make sense of the world, but we make our own sense of advertising. The process is a negotiation, taking different forms for different people at different times. Little is known about this in detail, not least because more is involved than our 'conscious' responses.

Yet, finally, the debates around advertising have been both conscious and vehement. In view of the force attributed to all media including advertising in public common sense, the industry has itself conceded codes of practice (decent, honest, legal, truthful) while the Independent Broadcasting Authority issues guidelines for commercials on television. The force of some of these you may judge by just a few of the current regulations in practice from the IBA *Code* of 1985. Advertisements for alcohol may not imply that drinking is essential to social success or acceptance or that refusal is a sign of weakness . . . must neither claim nor suggest that any drink can contribute towards sexual success . . . treatments featuring special daring or toughness must not be used in any way which is likely to associate the act of drinking with masculinity.

This has by no means satisfied campaign groups deploring both the expenditure on and mystification of (for instance) tobacco ads, or groups deploring racism and sexism in mainstream advertising, including (as an example) such attitudes to women as 'underneath they're all lovable'. The uses of the spray-can and the sticker show the resistance to some of the advertising in public places. It is now less common to hear in the West, in public discussion (though not in some third world countries) arguments that advertising dangerously exaggerates the promise of commodities over other human interests, values and achievements.

At present, indeed, Western advertising has rarely seemed more confident of its social importance. While advertising seeks to break up some of its older mass markets into smaller and more specialized (though always quite well-off) 'lifestyle' groupings (part real, part imagined), and as large department stores break up their space into smaller particular units so, so advertising also extends its reach into new commodities (water), new social spaces (public transport, symphony concerts, the shopping malls planned to supersede the High Street shops) as part of the total environment of 'enterprise culture'. Commentators on the left, previously sceptical of consumer commodities as a human goal, now talk more positively in some cases of the centrality of consumerism and a 'politics of style'. As Eastern Europe changes, are we joined or divided by market forces?

Tutorial Discussion Questions

1   Do advertisements still play on fears of inadequacy? If so how can that be pleasurable to us?
2   Do advertisements effectively represent the variety of household arrangements in Britian, *or* that we are a multiracial society? If not, why not — and what do they do instead? Why?
3   What do people in this discussion group do with advertising, what do we take from advertisements? Do we 'just treat them as a joke', and if so what do we mean in saying that?
4   What, if anything, should not be advertised at all?
5   Could our society do without advertising?
6   What could or should psychology as a discipline contribute to the understanding of advertising?

References

BARTHES, R. (1972) *Mythologies*, London, Jonathan Cape.
BARTHES, R. (1979) *The Eiffel Tower*, New York, Hill and Wang.
EWEN, S. (1976) *Captains of Consciousness*, New York, McGraw-Hill.
HORKHEIMER, M. and ADORNO, T. (1972) *Dialectic of Enlightenment*, New York, Herder and Herder.
MARCUSE, H. (1964) *One Dimensional Man*, London, Routledge and Kegan Paul.
SMYTHE, D. (1981) *Dependency Road*, Norwood, NJ, Ablex.
WILLIAMS, R. (1980) *Problems in Materialism and Culture*, London, Verso.

Further Reading

EWEN, S. (1976) *Captains of Consciousness*, New York, McGraw-Hill.
    Absorbing history of American advertising.
GOFFMAN, E. (1979) *Gender Advertising*, London, Macmillan.
    Detailed and amusing account of visual representations of gender relations.
MYERS, K. (1986) *Understains*, London, Comedia.
    Lively and polemical study of issues and campaigns.

Chapter 20

Psychology and the Nuclear Threat

Chris Leach

On 18 November 1987, a fire at King's Cross underground station in London caused 31 deaths and 51 injuries. Several thousand people had to be evacuated from the station. The fire was probably caused by a discarded match igniting muck and grease under one of the Piccadilly line escalators. Two factors made the evacuation extremely hazardous. The fire sprinklers were out of action, so no water was available for fifteen minutes until the fire brigade hoses could be set up. The station itself is a very complex structure, catering for 100,000 people a day, and many people were directed up the Northern line escalator to supposed safety in the ticket office. Unfortunately, there was a flashover into the ticket office from the fire, since the Piccadilly line escalators fed into the same ticket office. Psychological help was made available to the most severely burned. Everyone who rang a public helpline was offered counselling, as were members of the transport staff, police and emergency services. They were also asked to give an account of their experiences and to complete a number of questionnaires, including the General Health Questionnaire (GHQ), commonly used for screening people thought to be suffering from psychological disorders, and Horowitz's Impact of Events Scale. The same questionnaires were later posted to 800 people who made witness statements to the official inquiry. Of those interviewed, 40 per cent were showing clear signs of psychological disorder. This was more common among passengers than police, with the most prominent symptoms being anxiety and insomnia. There was not much evidence of depression.

On 11 May 1985, 56 people died in a fire at the Bradford City football ground. The 399 police officers involved with the fire were later contacted by Douglas Duckworth's team from Leeds. Two hundred and thirty-four completed the GHQ, with 55 showing clear evidence of psychological distress. Thirty-four attended a series of confidential counselling sessions, with problems such as performance guilt, reconstruction anxiety, generalized irritability, focused resentment and motivational changes. Among the experiences that caused them particular trouble were the following. Several officers described how their advice was not followed by the crowd, who then later blamed them for not acting. One at the back of the stand that caught fire tried to stop people running to the exit doors at the back, which he knew to be locked — nobody paid any attention to him, with disastrous consequences. Others described personal life-threatening experiences, thinking they were not going to get out alive, which sometimes put them out of action. The memory of such thoughts would keep returning. Life-threat to relatives or children was also difficult to cope with. One officer later attended the funeral of a child, thinking it was his own. Another saw a badly burnt child with no skin running away. On seeing his own child later, all he could see was a skull. Their uncertainty about attempting to rescue people at the time, when such rescue attempts would have been life-threatening, later returned as guilt ('Could I have gone in?'). Some officers were particularly disorientated by seeing people die while caring for others — they were used to seeing their job as dealing with the 'toe-rags' of society. Many also saw it as being particularly unfair that it was *their* home football pitch that was violated, with relatives or people known to them among the victims.

On 26 February 1972, a dam gave way in Buffalo Creek in southern West Virginia. Thousands of tons of water and black mud were unleashed, killing 125 people and leaving 4,000 homeless. Interviews 2 years later revealed traumatic neurotic reactions in 80 percent of the survivors. Common symptoms were unresolved grief, shame at having survived, impotent rage and hopelessness. People became apathetic and seemed to have forgotten how to care for one another. The close-knit mining community was destroyed.

What have such disasters to do with the nuclear threat? Until recently, there have been few detailed studies of the psychological aspects of disasters, whether of people's reactions to them or of psychological factors that might help bring about a disaster. An understanding of such factors may throw light on the nuclear debate. Nuclear accidents, such as those at Chernobyl or Three Mile Island, are potentially far more hazardous than those described above. In the event of a nuclear war, an attack on the UK of the sort considered likely by military planners will create damage so extensive as to destroy any functioning civilization. There will be large numbers of dead and injured. Industries, ports and communications will be destroyed. This makes it difficult to calculate with any precision likely psychological reactions. Even a few bombs on urban centres will produce a worse catastrophe than any since the Black Death in the fourteenth century, when bubonic plague is estimated to have killed about one third of the population between India and Iceland. Since we fortunately have few case studies of the results of nuclear attack, studies of other disasters give us some idea of people's likely reactions in nuclear disasters.

This chapter takes up two main themes. We first look in more detail at people's reactions to disaster. We then turn to the danger of nuclear accidents, looking in particular at human fallibility when designing and operating complex systems.

Reactions to Disaster

One of the most common reactions in the early stages of a disaster or any life-threatening event is denial. For example, hostages interviewed after the Kuwait Airways hijack in April 1988 said they took a long time to realize it was a hijack. They gave a benign interpretation of the events going on around them, choosing to view a hijacker threatening a steward as 'just a passenger arguing with a steward' or as a practice drill by Kuwaiti staff. When eleven hijackers took turns to go to the toilet to collect arms, one interpretation was that they were probably going to change into Western clothes. In 1957, when the Rio Grande flooded, crowds gathered to cheer the rising floodwaters, and in 1960, there was minimal evacuation during the Hawaiian tidal wave. Denial is a common psychological protection that helps everyday life along — without it we might never cross the road. It is related to the myth of personal invulnerability — it won't happen to me. This mechanism also explains why there has been so little research on people's reactions to disasters. It took seventeen years before any study was carried out of the psychological consequences of the bombings on Hiroshima and Nagasaki.

Before looking at specific studies, a general account of typical reactions at different phases of disaster will be given. The five phases used here (threat, warning, impact, recoil and post-impact) have been found useful when studying all sorts of disasters.

Phases of Disaster

Threat. In general, people are not accurate at assessing risks. There is some evidence that the risk of nuclear war is underestimated, although it is very difficult to evaluate such research, as 'objective' estimates of risk are difficult if not impossible to obtain. Nevertheless, we currently live under conditions of threat. Reactions to this vary. Although the most common reaction is one of denial, there is evidence of an increase in anxiety about nuclear war, particularly among children. One study found that 52 per cent of British teenagers felt that nuclear war would occur in their lifetime and 70 per cent felt that it was inevitable one day.

Warning. Even when a warning has been given, denial may still be a common reaction, as shown by the reactions to the Hawaiian tidal wave and the Rio Grande flood. Once the danger is acknowledged, there is likely to be over-reliance on official announcements, although it typically happens that conflicting advice is given, leading to confusion and an inability to decide what to do. In the case of a nuclear attack, it is unlikely that a warning will be given until very late, if at all, as this is most likely to be seen by governments as politically risky.

Impact. With sudden and severe disasters, most people feel that they are at the very centre. In tornados, people often believe that only their house has been hit. This illusion of centrality helps call into question the myth of personal invulnerability. Mood and beliefs oscillate wildly, with feelings fluctuating between terror and elation, invulnerability and helplessness. After a short time, these oscillations give way to the 'disaster syndrome', with people being apathetic, indecisive, unemotional and behaving mechanically. Contrary to popular belief, there is no evidence of panic at this stage. Like denial, the disaster syndrome is a protective reaction or, in some cases, an acknowledgment of helplessness in the face of massive damage.

Recoil. Once an all-clear has been announced, most people show a return of awareness and recall. They become highly dependent, talkative and childlike. There is an obsession with communicating their experiences, as a way of working them through to give them meaning. Monitoring the news is one way of giving meaning to uncontrollable events. For example, American adults spent an average of 8 hours a day listening to the radio or watching television in the 4 days following the assassination of President Kennedy. There may be a need to find scapegoats. The most likely initial targets may well be those bringing relief. Some may respond with totally psychopathic behaviour. When rescue work can begin, it is typically people without family ties who coordinate the work. Others may find conflict between family and civic duties.

Post-impact. Individual rescue work gradually gets coordinated into a more organized approach. The scale of the disaster and cultural norms may determine how successful this will be. Many people will be suffering from loss and bereavement and will need to express their feelings. Some cultural norms may prevent this and will reduce their ability to cope. Eleven months after the King's Cross fire, there was an increase in depression among the survivors. Those who had been able to talk in detail about their experiences in the fire were those most protected from later illness. There will be fear of recurrence of the disaster, and later bad occurrences will further reduce people's ability to cope. One survivor of the Kuwait Airways hijack lost a sister-in-law in the Clapham train crash in December 1988.

Hiroshima and Nagasaki

The bombs used on Hiroshima and Nagasaki were very small by present standards. They were used without warning and with no general knowledge of the effects of radiation. They provide the closest examples of what might occur in a nuclear war. In these cases, though, as in the other disasters looked at here, there was an intact outside world able to give support. In a nuclear war, outside support is likely not to be available.

Robert J. Lifton (1967) asked survivors to recall their experiences and to say how they were currently affected. The bomb on Hiroshima was dropped at 8.15 a.m. on 6 August 1945 just after an all-clear had sounded. Everyone thought that a bomb had fallen out of a clear sky directly on them. They were shocked out of normal life into an overwhelming encounter with death, a memory that stayed for ever with each survivor. After that, survivors saw profound scenes of horror, often describing images of hell:

> Perhaps the most impressive thing I saw were girls, very young girls, not only with their clothes torn off but their skin peeled off as well . . . My immediate thought was that this was like the hell I had always read about.

After such experiences, survivors were numb, incapable of emotion, behaving mechanically — the disaster syndrome.

Seventeen years later, the survivors felt that all aspects of their lives had been affected. Trying to make sense of why they had survived while others had not caused intense guilt and shame. Quite apart from their own extreme reactions, they became stigmatized by others, who did not wish to be reminded of the horrible experience. For example, those with skin burns were asked not to use public swimming pools. It is noteworthy that there have been no proper follow-up studies, although there is some evidence of long-term depression and anxiety about cancer, fear of death and difficulty in coping. Psychotic disorders appear to be uncommon.

Three Mile Island

On 28 March 1979, there was a loss of coolant at the nuclear reactor at Three Mile Island, initiating an accident which resulted in the evacuation of 40 per cent of the population. The core of the reactor was partially uncovered and considerable damage to the plant occurred. No deaths were caused and there was no damage to property. There was, however, a major threat of explosion and radioactive contamination, made worse by conflicting reports over the few days during which the emergency developed. There was a distrust of officials, both over evacuation arrangements and over the accuracy of information about the dangers they were exposed to. The evacuation was not well coordinated, with distress caused to parents and children who had been separated when schools were evacuated. Hospitals and prisons could not be evacuated, placing many workers in role conflict. Even among the well-informed, such role conflict was evident. In one hospital, half the nuclear medicine radiological staff evacuated themselves.

Psychological distress increased in the community, particularly among those close to the reactor. There was an increase in demoralization, helplessness and depression. Some of the symptoms eventually decreased again, but a small percentage were still affected when contacted four months later. The most commonly expressed fear was that they were exposed to a danger they could not see, hear or feel. It was quite outside ordinary experience.

Dangers of Nuclear Accidents

Complex Industries and Tightly Coupled Systems

Many high technology industries pay a lot of attention to safety. However, their very complexity makes it difficult to predict when things are going wrong. Anyone who has tried writing a long computer program will tell you that seemingly simple routines in one part of the program can go wrong in totally unforeseen ways when added to the rest of the program. These are known as 'tightly coupled' systems. Failures of individual components may be quite unimportant on their own, but when several happen together quite complex interactions can occur which may be incomprehensible for a critical period. When accidents occur, it is easy to blame human error or equipment failure, but those who have studied accidents in high technology settings see the complexity of the system as the major culprit.

The Presidential Commission reporting on the Three Mile Island accident blamed it on a combination of human, institutional and mechanical failures. The failure of the water pumps initiated the accident, but poor training, bad decisions and the operators' failure to understand what was happening made things worse. Commenting on this, Perrow (1984) argues that each failure was trivial by itself, but the system was tightly coupled and the interactions set up could not be seen by the operators and were therefore not believed. Instrument readings are often rejected because they are not believed, and this can make matters worse. In fact, such behaviour is necessary to the effective running of high technology industries. If every warning signal were attended to, the plant would not operate. In addition to this, there was bad equipment design in the Three Mile Island plant. For example, the control room had 1,900 displays, 26 per cent of which could not be seen by the operators standing at the front panel, a clear case of information overload.

Other Factors Affecting Decision-Making

Stress and boredom. Nuclear plant operators and nuclear weapons personnel have very responsible jobs, but many of their duties involve monitoring complex equipment. A lot of them will feel they have little control over what they do and the job can be very boring. Low perceived control in a highly responsible job can be very stressful, which in turn can affect the ability to make rational decisions.

One reaction to such stress is to take drugs. Thanks to the US Freedom of Information Act, the high incidence of drug abuse among nuclear weapons personnel is now acknowledged. Other nuclear countries are likely to have similar problems, but this sort of information is not willingly revealed by governments. In the USA, about 5,000 of the 120,000 nuclear weapons personnel are removed from duty each year. Of these, between 1,300 and 2,000 are removed because of drug abuse.Many of these will have been high while on duty, as suggested in Table 1, taken from a survey sampling all military personnel (not just nuclear) reported in the *Congressional Record*: 1981.

In this survey, 1 in 5 of the service personnel reported lower performance on duty resulting from drug abuse. Some indication of what this might mean is given by the results of an autopsy performed on fourteen marines and sailors killed when a marine aircraft crashed on the deck of the USS *Nimitz* in June 1981. Six of the 14 had recently taken drugs.

Other means of reducing boredom can be equally dangerous, as exemplified by the Minuteman crew who, as a practical joke, recorded a launch message and played it when the next crew came to relieve them.

Table 1   Percentages answering yes to the question, 'During the last month, have you used any of the following while on duty (during working hours)?'

	Navy	Army	Marines	Air Force
Marijuana/Hashish	42	38	24	5
Alcohol	21	28	19	16
Uppers	27	10	14	0
Downers	10	5	5	0
LSD and other drugs	9	3	2	0
Cocaine	4	3	4	0
Heroin	1	2	1	0

Simplifying strategies. People respond well to familiar problems. They do this partly by using simplifying strategies (or heuristics) to cope with the complexities of even the familiar world. In some cases these heuristics can seriously mislead us. One such heuristic is attention narrowing, which allows us to focus all our attention in one direction. It is responsible for a lot of accidents. For example, Dixon (1976) cites the case of a flight crew continuing to search for reasons why the light confirming lowering of the undercarriage did not come on. They failed to notice that they had accidentally disengaged the autopilot and were losing height. The plane hit the ground.

Another fatal example is the Moorgate train crash of 28 February 1975, when an underground train was driven through the station and into the end wall of an overrun tunnel, killing 42 passengers and the driver, and injuring 72. There was no evidence of equipment failure, or of drugs, illness or suicidal intent by the driver. It was the driver's third journey of the day and he appeared to be his usual self. Studying all the evidence, James Reason (1982) came to the conclusion that the most likely explanation was in what he called 'imperfect rationality' — the driver had a mental lapse and 'lost his place' in the sequence of stations, imagining there to be still one station left before the end of the line. In support of this explanation, the lights in the approach tunnel to Moorgate were lit on the first two journeys but had been switched off on the third, making it appear like the earlier tunnels. Despite many safety systems and a long history free of accidents, such accidents caused by human error can still occur.

Dangers of Accidental Nuclear War

Accidents involving nuclear weapons are rarely admitted, but the US Department of Defense acknowledged 32 major accidents in US forces by 1981. Information is less easily available for other countries, but 6 accidents and 16 incidents are known to have occurred to Warsaw Pact forces, while 4 incidents have occurred to French forces and 8 to British forces. One example occurred in 1961, when a B-52 bomber broke up in flight and released two 24-megaton bombs. On 1 of the bombs, 5 of the 6 safety devices had been set off by the fall, leaving only 1 to prevent an explosion. Another occurred in 1980 in a missile silo, when a technician dropped a wrench onto a fuel tank. The tank later exploded, blasting open the silo's 740-ton door and shooting a 9-megaton warhead into the air. A different type of example is the low level nuclear war alert set off in 1979, when a war game training tape was accidentally fed into a computer and accepted as real.

These and other examples show that it is unrealistic to expect any system to be error-free. Even the safest systems can sometimes go badly wrong through a combination of human error, bad equipment design and unanticipated errors due to sheer complexity. Add to this the enormous psychological burden placed on operators and military personnel and it is not surprising that accidents occasionally happen. In the case of nuclear power plants and nuclear weapons, information on the number and gravity of accidents is nearly always withheld from the public.

Acknowledgments:

I am grateful to James Thompson and Douglas Duckworth for permission to use their unpublished information on the King's Cross and Bradford fires and for their comments on a draft of this chapter. Much of the information in the chapter comes from James Thompson's (1985) book.

Tutorial Discussion Questions

1 Why has there been a recent upsurge of research and public interest in disasters?
2 To what extent can a knowledge of reactions to disasters help us in understanding the likely impact of nuclear war?
3 Does the research on likely reactions during different phases of a disaster help us understand the disasters at Chernobyl, Lockerbie or Hillsborough?
4 What is known about reactions of others to survivors of nuclear attacks or accidents?
5 Given the likely human reactions, how should local and national governments make preparations for possible nuclear attacks? Should any preparations be made?
6 Can safety of nuclear plants and nuclear weapons be made acceptable?
7 What are the likely reactions to stress among nuclear weapons personnel?
8 To what extent can human error be blamed for nuclear accidents?
9 How can the dangers of nuclear war be communicated to people whose main way of coping with threat is denial?

References

DIXON, N. (1976) *On the Psychology of Military Incompetence*, London, Jonathan Cape.
LIFTON, R. J. (1967) *Death in Life: Survivors of Hiroshima*, New York, Random House.
PERROW, C. (1984) *Normal Accidents: Living with High-Risk Technologies*, New York, Basic Books.
REASON, J. (1982) *Absent-minded?*, Englewood Cliffs, NJ, Prentice-Hall

Further Reading

KAHNEMAN, D., SLOVIC, P. and TVERSKY, A. (1982) *Judgment under Uncertainty: Heuristics and Biases*. Cambridge, MA, Harvard University Press.
THOMPSON, J. (1985) *Psychological Aspects of Nuclear War*, Leicester, The British Psychological Society and Chichester, John Wiley.

Notes on Contributors

Alan Blair is an Honorary Research Fellow at the University of Birmingham, where he undertook post-doctoral research into the interpersonal and intrapersonal dynamics underlying individuals' eating behaviour. Previously, he completed a D.Phil. at the University of Sussex (1986) on 'Locating distress: Social class and the contextualisation of illness experience'. He is most interested in social psychological theories that are informed by a reading of Marxist, feminist, social anthropological and sociological critiques.

Douglas Carroll is Professor of Psychology at Glasgow Polytechnic. He has published widely in the area of psychophysiology. Recently, he was actively involved in discussions surrounding initiatives in the UK regarding polygraph lie-detectors. On invitation, he presented evidence to the Employment Select Committee of the House of Commons and was part of the working party that prepared the British Psychological Society statement on lie-detection.

Raymond Cochrane is a Professor and Head of School of Psychology at the University of Birmingham. He has worked previously at the University College Cardiff, Michigan State University and the University of Edinburgh. His main research interests are in the processes of immigrant adjustment and social factors in mental illness.

Guy Cumberbatch is Director of the Communications Research Group at Aston University where he teaches applied social psychology. He is currently carrying out research on the role of television in fantasy for the Broadcasting Standards Council and a study of minorities on television for the BBC. His most recent book is on pornography.

Howard Davis is a Senior Lecturer in Sociology at the University of Kent at Canterbury. He began his research career with the Glasgow University Media Group and is one of the co-authors of their well-known studies of television news. He is also the editor (with Paul Walton) of *Language, Image, Media*, a collection of essays on media discourse. His current research is on changes in media organizations and systems of media regulation in Western Europe.

Barbara Dodd graduated in psychology and sociology in 1975 and obtained an M.Sc. in clinical psychology in 1977. She was a Lecturer in the Departments of Psychiatry and Psychology at the University of Birmingham from 1978 to 1988.

Clive Eastman completed his doctoral research into alcoholism before receiving his master's degree in clinical psychology. He is a Lecturer in Psychology at Birmingham University, devoting most of his teaching time to the clinical course. His current research interests are in the fields of stress management and service evaluation.

Hugh Foot graduated from the University of Durham in 1962 and obtained his Ph.D. from St Andrews University in 1967. He is currently Reader in Psychology at the University of Wales College of Cardiff. His main teaching interests lie in social and developmental psychology, and he has researched children's social development for over fifteen years. He has published widely and co-edited a number of books in the fields of children's friendship and social relations, children's humour, children's pedestrian accidents and, more recently, in peer tutoring and cooperative learning.

Michael Green is a Senior Lecturer in the Department of Cultural Studies (previously Centre for Contemporary Cultural Studies) at the University of Birmingham, and has published on education, media issues and popular fiction. He is currently working on questions of cultural policy in relation to changes in the culture and visual design of cities.

Christine Griffin teaches social psychology at Birmingham University. She has worked at the Centre for Contemporary Cultural Studies, Birmingham University, on a study of young women's entry to the job market, and at Leicester University's Centre for Mass Communication Research, conducting a survey of young adults' experiences of racial discrimination in the local job market. Her research interests include sex/gender relations, young people and the transition to adulthood, power relations and everyday experience, and qualitative research methods.

Moira Hamlin is a chartered clinical psychologist who is Director of HealthSkills Consultants and Honorary Research Fellow at the University of Exeter. Previous posts include head of a community addiction centre in the NHS and Lecturer in Clinical Psychology at Leicester University. In 1986 she was awarded a Winston Churchill Fellowship in drug abuse and in 1990 a Council of Europe Medical Fellowship to study alcohol policies in the workplace in Scandinavia.

Gill Harris is a developmental psychologist who specializes in work with infants. For the past ten years she has studied both verbal and non-verbal aspects of interactions between infants and their caregivers. More recently, she has carried out work on infant taste perception and psychophysiological development. She now specializes in infant feeding behaviour and feeding problems. Some of her findings are put into practice at the Children's Hospital, Birmingham, where she is an Honorary Associate Psychologist.

Chris Leach is a clinical psychologist with Dewsbury Health Authority in West Yorkshire, with a research interest in psychological aspects of disasters. Formerly a Lecturer in Psychology at Newcastle University, he is a Fellow of the British Psychological Society and a former Editor of the *British Journal of Mathematical and Statistical Psychology*.

Vivien J. Lewis is a clinical psychologist with Shropshire Health Authority and an Honorary Research Fellow at the University of Birmingham. She works extensively, both clinically and in research, in the area of disorders associated with food and body image, and also has a special interest in wider gender issues.

Patti Mazelan has been actively engaged in social psychological research since 1978. Her areas of interest include: rape victimization, arbitration, the social context of anger, and subjective perceptions of quality.

Allan Norris is Head of Psychology Services to a Midlands health authority and is an Honorary Lecturer in Psychology at the University of Birmingham. He has run a health service smoking withdrawal clinic for ten years and has lectured locally and internationally on smoking topics. He has also personally trained over 2,000 British GPs in smoking cessation methods.

Keith Phillips is Head of the Department of Psychology at the Polytechnic of East London. His current research interests include human psychophysiology and health psychology. He is a member of the Polytechnic's AIDS Research Unit.

Susan Phillips is a Research Fellow in the School of Psychology at Birmingham University. She has conducted a number of studies in policing, both nationally and locally, which have been in the areas of community relations, training and crime prevention. Currently she is working on a contract with the West Midlands Police where she is engaged in action research, developing strategies to overcome organizational problems.

Graham Stokes is Consultant Clinical Psychologist at Gulson Hospital, Coventry with responsibility for psychology services to elderly mentally ill and infirm people. He graduated from the University of Leeds in 1976 and obtained both his Ph.D. and M.Sc. in clinical psychology at the University of Birmingham. His postgraduate research investigated the psychological health effects of redundancy and unemployment. He has published widely in the areas of unemployment and health and the psychology of abnormal ageing.

Glyn Thomas is a Senior Lecturer in Psychology at the University of Birmingham. He has published numerous articles on animal learning and on the use of learning theory in clinical psychology. His recent research interests include the development of writing skills and emotional expression in children's drawing. He is currently carrying out a study of drawings made by sexually abused children and has recently co-authored (with Angele Silk) *An Introduction to the Psychology of Children's Drawings*.

David White lectures in developmental psychology at the Polytechnic of East London. His recent research activities have centred on the broad area of health psychology. He is Head of the AIDS Research Unit, which is an active group of eight researchers.

Index